IN THE SAME SERIES BY STANLEY SCHULER
THE GARDENER'S BASIC BOOK OF TREES AND SHRUBS

THE GARDENER'S

BASIC BOOK
OF FLOWERS

STANLEY SCHULER

SIMON AND SCHUSTER · NEW YORK

DESIGNED BY EVE METZ
MANUFACTURED IN THE UNITED STATES OF AMERICA

1   2   3   4   5   6   7   8   9   10

Library of Congress Cataloging in Publication Data

Schuler, Stanley.
    The gardener's basic book of flowers.
    1. Flower gardening. 2. Flowers. I. Title.
SB405.S38   635.9′0973   74-10629
ISBN 0-671-21819-0

CONTENTS

·1·

SELECTING FLOWERS
FOR THE GARDEN

It is interesting that anything as fragile and fleeting as a flower can mean so much to people engrossed in worldly pursuits and staying alive.

I can remember the pink cosmos my grandparents grew at their little summer home in Mattapoisett, Massachusetts. I don't know what magic there was in those flowers which makes them so vivid to me today, almost fifty-five years later. I don't recall any especially pleasant incident connected with them. Nor do I recall picking them or smelling them or helping my grandmother stick them into a vase. But there they are—a bright spot in the distant past.

I can remember picking a bunch of violets for my mother on the May morning Tessie, our maid, announced my baby brother was born. The violets grew just down the road in a vacant lot. I could show you the exact spot right now—if it is still there. The day was bright and warm; and the dew still lay on the blossoms as I gathered them.

I can remember taking a flat box filled with tuberous begonias to the Berkeley post office to airmail to my wife-to-be in Kentucky. I had given her flowers on occasion before—but never anything like these exquisite blossoms. They were to be her introduction to California, where we expected to live after our wedding.

One of the most brilliant perennial gardens I have ever seen. It is located in northern Vermont in Zone 3! This picture taken in late August shows monkshood, phlox, lythrum and lilies at their height.

I can remember . . . but you can, too. I have my memories of flowers; you, yours. It would be a mistake to say that flowers have shaped mankind. But surely they have lifted us, soothed us, gentled us.

The Gardener's Basic Book of Trees and Shrubs, the book I wrote just preceding this one, dealt with trees and shrubs because these are the most important plants in every garden and should theoretically be the first the gardener considers when he buys a new home. But I am not at all sure that flowers aren't the first he actually plants. Not a lot of flowers—perhaps only a handful of spring bulbs or a brilliant yellow chrysanthemum or a flat of pansies to work their magic on property and mind.

Home is where the heart is. Is heart where the flower is?

To get down to mundane matters, and properly speaking, a flower is a blossom—any blossom, whether it be on a tree, shrub, vine, vegetable or slender stem of a daffodil or daisy. But the plants we refer to as flowers are, with one exception (roses), rather small, herbaceous* species grown strictly for ornament. They include annuals, perennials, biennials, bulbs and certain roses.

Annuals are flowers usually grown from seeds which bloom and die within a few months of planting.

Perennials are flowers propagated by several methods which produce flowers year after year. Most die down in the fall and come up again in the spring, but a few are evergreen.

Biennials are flowers which make their initial growth in one year and then bloom and die the next year. They are grown from seeds.

Bulbs are flowers which come up year after year from rather large, fleshy, underground parts. Botanists classify these parts as bulbs, corms, rhizomes or tubers. The last three, in other words, are not true bulbs and should not properly be known as such. But in the layman's world, they are.

Roses, finally, are roses. They are actually shrubs with woody stems; but to the average gardener, the types of rose usually grown in gardens are flowers.

As noted above, all these different kinds of flowers are grown strictly for ornament—to bring beauty to the property and, in many cases, to

* With succulent—not woody—stems.

the house. They are used outdoors in many ways:

 —in flower beds and borders (the two words have come to mean the
  same thing)
 —in shrubbery borders and foundation plantings
 —in hedges
 —in edgings (not only in beds but along walks, etc.)
 —in rock gardens
 —in wall gardens
 —in naturalized areas
 —in ground covers
 —as screens
 —in pots, hanging baskets and other containers
 —in window boxes and planters

The fact that no one flower is suitable for all purposes adds an extra
dimension to the always happy but not always easy job of selecting the
flowers you want to grow. It's not enough to know what the height,
color and general appearance of flowers are. It's not enough to know
that you like the looks of this flower but not the looks of that. You must
also determine whether flowers can be used effectively in the place you
want to use them—or, vice versa, whether you have a place to use them
effectively. And you must consider the flowers' planting and cultural
requirements and their adaptability to the area in which you live.

CLIMATE ZONES

One of the best and most popular ways to select flowers for the garden is
to look at the catalogs put out every year by the outstanding nurseries
that sell seeds and plants by mail. To me, these make as happy and
exciting reading as the world affords. I go through them as soon as they
arrive in January; and I go through most of them at least once again
before I finally decide what to order. Garden catalogs are both inspiring
and informative. But some of them are not as clear about the climatic
requirements of plants as they might be; and this can lead to disappoint-
ment for the gardener.

Some years ago one of my publishers asked me to write a book about
the effect of climate and geology on gardening in the United States.
Because I had always enjoyed geography and geology and had lived in

A garden of gentle curves bright with tulips and doronicum in early spring. The brick wall serves not only as a backdrop for the flower beds but, more important, screens the entire area from the road.

several parts of the country and traveled in almost all parts, I was well aware that the effect was enormous. But as I traveled back and forth across the country photographing gardens and talking to gardeners, I was amazed to find that a great many people had never given the matter the slightest thought. They assumed that whatever they grew in one part of the country they could grow equally well in another part; and when they were transferred from, say, Boston to Houston and tried to grow some of the plants they had once had in Boston, they finally discovered the sorry truth: most plants have definite climate preferences. That is why it is common practice today in garden books to indicate the climate zones in which different plants grow best.

The United States and Canada are divided into ten of these zones. They range from Zone No. 1, with minimum winter temperatures averaging $-50°$ F., to Zone No. 10, with minimum winter temperatures averaging from $30°$ to $40°$ F.

The temperature differential within each climate zone shown on the map on page 12 is 10 degrees. On a more detailed map developed by the U.S. Department of Agriculture,* each zone is divided into two subzones—"a" and "b"—with a temperature differential of 5 degrees. Subzone "a" is colder than subzone "b." For example, one of my daughters and I both live in Zone 6; but she is outside Boston in Zone 6a whereas I am in southeastern Connecticut in Zone 6b. As a general rule, most plants that grow at all in Zone 6 grow in both 6a and 6b, and this rule applies to any other zone. But there are a few plants that grow in one subzone but not in the other.

The purpose of dividing the country into climate zones and making a climate zone map is to help gardeners in all parts of the country determine which plants they should be able to grow. For example, daylilies grow in Zones 3 to 10—meaning that you can raise them successfully everywhere in the United States except the most frigid areas in Alaska. Other bulbs and perennials called lilies, however, have a more restricted range, as the following list† indicates.

* The map is available from the Superintendent of Documents, U.S. Government Printing Office, Washington, D.C. 20402. Send for Miscellaneous Publication No. 814 titled "Plant Hardiness Zone Map." It costs 25 cents.
† This list includes only those plants which can be left outdoors the year round. A few bulbous plants called lilies can be grown in all parts of the United States but only if the bulbs are dug up and brought indoors in cold climates in winter.

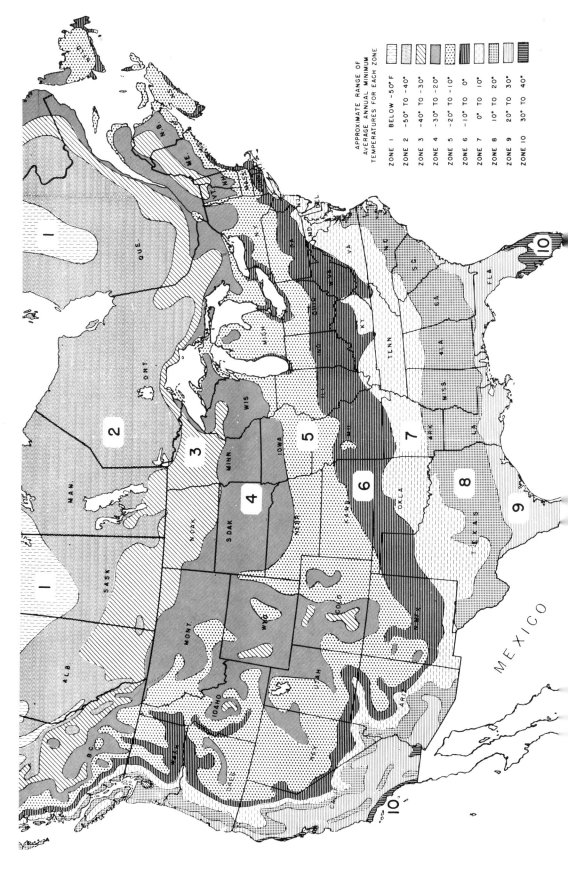

APPROXIMATE RANGE OF
AVERAGE ANNUAL MINIMUM
TEMPERATURES FOR EACH ZONE

ZONE 1   BELOW -50° F
ZONE 2   -50° TO -40°
ZONE 3   -40° TO -30°
ZONE 4   -30° TO -20°
ZONE 5   -20° TO -10°
ZONE 6   -10° TO 0°
ZONE 7   0° TO 10°
ZONE 8   10° TO 20°
ZONE 9   20° TO 30°
ZONE 10   30° TO 40°

Amazon lilies	Zones	9b–10
Belladonna lilies	ʺ	5–10
Blood lilies	ʺ	9–10
Calla lilies	ʺ	7–10
Foxtail lilies	ʺ	6–8
Ginger lilies	ʺ	9–10
Kaffir lilies	ʺ	8–10
Lilies (true lilies)	ʺ	4–10
Lilies of the valley	ʺ	3–7
Mariposa lilies	ʺ	6–10
Peruvian lilies	ʺ	8–10
Scarborough lilies	ʺ	9b–10

THE SITE FOR THE GARDEN

Determining which climate zone you live in is just one thing you should do in order to select flowers that will do well for you and to avoid those that won't. The other thing you should do is to decide where you are going to grow your flowers. Here are the questions you must answer.

Will the flower bed be in sun or shade? Most flowers need sunlight to grow and bloom their best. Just a couple of hours of sunlight is not enough; flowers need about 6 hours at the very least, and if they can have 12 or 15, so much the better. This means that if you want to raise a fairly wide range of the best flowers—roses, zinnias, delphiniums, tulips, for example—you must locate your flower beds in an open area well away from houses, trees and hills, which cut off the sun for a good part of every day. If this can't be done, you must choose from the somewhat less distinguished list of flowers that grow in shade. These are listed below. Note that very, very few of them tolerate deep shade, such as you find under a Norway maple. The great majority do well only in light or partial shade; and among these are many which actually prefer sun.

Plant Hardiness Zone Map developed by the Agricultural Research Service of the U.S. Department of Agriculture. On a more detailed version of the map, each zone is divided more or less in half into two subzones: "a" and "b." The former is farther north and somewhat colder than the latter.

Sunny corner of a large garden which in the spring is filled with daffodils and tulips. These are followed by perennials and flowering shrubs.

FLOWERS FOR SHADY PLACES

	Type of flower
Acanthus mollis	Perennial
Achimenes	Bulb
Air plant	Annual
Alyssum, sweet	Perennial
Anchusa	Perennial
Anemone, Japanese	Perennial
Arabis	Perennial
Astilbe	Perennial
Aubrieta	Perennial
Balloon flower	Perennial
Balsam	Annual
Beebalm	Perennial
Begonia, tuberous	Bulb
Begonia, wax	Annual
Bergenia	Perennial
Bird of paradise	Perennial
Bleeding heart	Perennial
Bletilla	Bulb
Blood lily	Bulb
Bugbane	Perennial
Caladium	Bulb
Camassia	Bulb
Campanula	Perennial
Candytuft, perennial	Perennial
Canterbury bell	Biennial
Cardinal flower	Perennial
Cardinal's guard	Perennial
Chinese lanterns	Perennial
Cineraria	Annual
Clarkia	Annual
Clivia	Bulb
Coleus	Annual
Columbine	Perennial
Coneflower, purple	Perennial
Cosmos	Annual
Cuphea	Annual
Cyclamen	Bulb
Cynoglossum	Annual
Daisy, English	Biennial

FLOWERS FOR SHADY PLACES (*cont.*)

	Type of Flower
Daisy, Swan River	Annual
Daylily	Perennial
Dogtooth violet	Bulb
Doronicum	Perennial
Elephant ear	Bulb
Erigeron	Perennial
Eupatorium	Perennial
Forget-me-not	Biennial
Foxglove	Biennial
Fritillaria	Bulb
Gayfeather	Perennial
Geum	Perennial
Ginger lily	Bulb
Ginger, shell	Bulb
Ginger, spiral	Bulb
Ginger, torch	Bulb
Globeflower	Perennial
Goatsbeard	Perennial
Godetia	Annual
Heliotrope	Annual
Hibiscus	Perennial
Honesty	Annual
Hosta	Perennial
Lamb's ears	Perennial
Layia	Annual
Lily	Bulb
Lily of the valley	Perennial
Lobelia	Annual
Lobster-claw	Perennial
Lythrum	Perennial
Maiden's wreath	Perennial
Mariposa lily	Bulb
Meadow rue	Perennial
Mignonette	Annual
Monkeyflower	Annual
Monkshood	Perennial
Morea	Bulb
Nemophila	Annual
Nicotiana	Annual
Nierembergia	Perennial
Oxalis	Bulb
Pansy	Biennial

On a lightly shaded terrace, white alyssum and pink begonias tie the planting beds in with a red, white and blue mural on the end wall.

FLOWERS FOR SHADY PLACES *(cont.)*

	Type of Flower
Patience	Annual
Pearly everlasting	Perennial
Penstemon	Perennial
Peruvian lily	Bulb
Petunia	Annual
Polemonium	Perennial
Poppy, Himalayan	Perennial
Poppy, plume	Perennial
Primrose	Perennial
Pulmonaria	Perennial
Puschkinia	Bulb
Queen's tears	Perennial
Ranunculus	Bulb
Rehmannia	Perennial
Scabiosa	Annual
Scarborough lily	Bulb
Scilla	Bulb
Shasta daisy	Perennial
Snowdrop	Bulb
Snowflake	Bulb
Snow-in-summer	Perennial
Torenia	Annual
Valerian	Perennial
Vinca rosea	Annual
Viola	Perennial
Virginia bluebells	Perennial
Wallflower	Biennial

Will the flower bed be exposed to strong winds? Except for roses, flowers are not constructed to withstand very much wind. So if you live in a windswept location, you must either (1) stick to the low-growing, compact flowers that resist toppling; (2) do an unusually extensive job of staking tall flowers—a rather tiresome chore which does nothing to improve the appearance of a garden; or (3) protect the flowers with a windbreak.

Will the flower bed be in a frost pocket? If your property lies at the bottom of a valley or if you make a flower bed in a depression or in an area surrounded by high walls or a solid fence, your flowers will succumb to frost before those planted on higher ground. It is therefore obvious that the best way to protect them is to plant them not in a low

Flowers are here planted in the foreground of a curving shrubbery border partly because it's the best place for them on this property and partly to protect them from winds sweeping through the river marsh behind the property.

spot where frost settles first, but at an elevation. If this is impossible, you can prolong bloom in your garden later in the fall and have bloom earlier in the spring by putting in species that have above-average resistance to freezing temperatures. In the list that follows, those marked with an asterisk bloom in the summer and/or fall; the others bloom in winter and spring.

FLOWERS WITH UNUSUAL RESISTANCE TO FREEZING COLD

	Type of flower
Adonis	Perennial
Anemone	Bulb
Aster*	Perennial
Bergenia	Perennial
Bulbocodium	Bulb
Christmas rose	Perennial
Chrysanthemum*	Perennial
Cornflower*	Annual
Crocus	Bulb
Cyclamen (some)	Bulb
Daffodil (some)	Bulb
Glory-of-the-snow	Bulb
Grape hyacinth	Bulb
Iris (some)	Bulb
Larkspur*	Annual
Lenten rose	Perennial
Poppy, Shirley*	Annual
Primrose	Perennial
Pulmonaria	Perennial
Puschkinia	Bulb
Salvia*	Annual
Scilla	Bulb
Snapdragon*	Annual
Snowdrop	Bulb
Snowflake	Bulb
Sternbergia*	Bulb
Tulip (some)	Bulb
Winter aconite	Bulb

A FINAL WORD ABOUT SELECTING FLOWERS

The first flowers that beginning gardeners plant are almost always annuals and bulbs. I have never sought an explanation for this, but I think there are two reasons: These flowers appear to be the easiest and the cheapest to grow. Actually, this is not necessarily so, but that does not make the choice wrong. I am sure there are gardeners who raise nothing but annuals and bulbs and have lovely gardens, just as I am sure there

Late spring frosts and early fall frosts are the nemesis of this garden, but the big informal border of mixed perennials, annuals and bulbs escapes some of the onslaught because it is on a slope a little above the low ground in which the frosts first settle.

are other gardeners who raise nothing but roses or nothing but perennials and have lovely gardens. The point is that each major category (not including biennials, which are limited in number) is a rich mine of beautiful bloom.

Using a broader combination of flowers, however, yields even greater beauty for the obvious reason that you have that many more species— and that many more superlative species—to choose from.

In addition, you get a longer period of bloom and more profuse bloom at all times. This is because perennials, biennials and roses are at their peak in the spring and fall whereas annuals are at their peak in the summer. (Bulbs give bountiful bloom in all seasons.)

So I urge you not to restrict yourself to one or two categories of flowers. Pick from all.

·2·

PREPARING
THE SOIL

One of the benefits gained from naturalizing bulbs is that you don't have to prepare the soil for them. You just open a hole in the ground, drop in a bulb, close the hole and hope that the bulb will thrive. But for all other flowers, careful soil preparation is essential to the most luxuriant possible bloom.

MAKING A SOIL TEST

No one, not even the world's most successful farmer, can look at soil and describe it perfectly. To be sure, you can tell whether it is sandy, gravelly or full of clay. If you know the definition of "loam"—a soil containing fairly even amounts of sand, silt* and clay—you probably can also tell whether a soil is loamy. But you may not be able to tell whether a soil contains humus; and you certainly cannot tell what minerals it contains. That's why it is a good idea before making a flower bed of any description to have the soil tested.

Unfortunately, most people ignore this suggestion. I warn you of this because if you should ask your neighbors, "Did you ever test your soil?" some of them would undoubtedly look at you in a supercilious way and answer, "Why should I?" as if testing were a silly waste of time. And

---

* According to the U.S. Department of Agriculture, silt is soil made up of particles ranging from 0.05 to 0.005 millimeters in size. By contrast, clay particles are smaller than 0.005 mm., while particles of "very fine sand" range from 0.10 to 0.05 mm.

indeed I have to admit that many gorgeous gardens have been created without benefit of soil testing. But testing takes the guesswork out of gardening. It tells you precisely what your soil is like and precisely what must be done to make it fully productive. Thus it enables you to have a successful garden from the outset. In addition, it keeps you from devoting time, energy and money to soil improvements that may be unnecessary.

Soil testing is one of the easiest and cheapest of all gardening chores because the hardest part of the work—the actual analyzing of the soil—is done for you by your state agricultural extension service. A list of these agencies is given on pages 275–76. The price they ask for making a test ranges from no charge to about $2.

The best time to test soil is in early spring or late fall, but it can be done at any time. All you have to do is dig up about ten small samples of soil from different parts of the area in which you plan to grow flowers. Take the samples from the upper 8 inches of soil. They should be of about equal size. Toss them all together in a pail and mix them thoroughly. If they are wet, let them dry before mixing. Then pour six or eight ounces of the mixture into a plastic kitchen bag or any other clean container and send it to your extension service with a request that they analyze it and give you a report on it along with recommendations for treating it.

Your letter to the service should also contain the following information: (1) The size of the area from which the samples are taken. (2) The plants you intend to grow. You need not be specific; simply indicate annuals, perennials, bulbs or roses, as the case may be. (3) Plants which have been growing in the area up to this time. Again it is necessary to indicate only the general category of plants. (4) How well drained the soil is. (5) What, if anything, you have previously done to the soil to improve it.

DIGGING THE FLOWER BED

The chances are that the area in which you are establishing your flower bed, border, edging or whatever already has something growing in it. This may be grass or weeds or a tangle of perennials and bulbs left over from a previous garden. In any case, it is going to complicate preparation of the flower bed to some extent; but in the end it may reward your efforts by contributing to the vigor and beauty of your flowers.

Partly because of the existing vegetation, the new bed should be dug by hand with a spading fork or sharp spade. If the bed is enormous, use of a rotary tiller is permissible because it saves work; but I do not recommend it because it does not dig much deeper than 6 to 8 inches. This is not really enough for a brand-new flower bed, although it is adequate in an established bed. Forks and spades have blades about 12 inches long, so you can turn the soil over to this depth with one thrust of the blade; and if you must dig deeper, as in a rose bed, you can.

There are five reasons for digging a flower bed—some obvious and some not.

The first is to define the bed—set it off visually and physically from the surrounding area.

The second is to loosen and pulverize the soil so that the plant roots can work their way through it easily and so that water, air and fertilizer nutrients will penetrate readily.

The third is to permit you to mix in whatever additives are needed for maximum flower growth.

The fourth is to expose undesirable foreign matter in the soil—large stones, plaster rubble, beer cans, broken glass, woody roots, etc. All stuff of this nature should be removed.

The fifth is to reverse the positions of the topsoil (the upper layer) and the subsoil so that the valuable organic matter* in the topsoil will be closer to the roots of your flower plants. But here you can run into problems if the vegetation presently carpeting the area includes plants that simply refuse to die when buried alive. An experience I had several years ago serves as illustration.

Along the west side of my carport was a flower bed which the previous owner of the property had planted with orange daylilies. When I bought the place, the bed had developed into a miniature jungle; so I dug it up and planted it anew with annuals. But despite the fact that I took pains to remove all the daylily roots I encountered, the bed was soon taken over by daylilies again. Explanation: Daylily roots have

---

* Organic matter is material resulting from the decomposition of vegetation and animal wastes. All soil which has been covered with vegetation contains organic matter; and all living vegetation will in time turn into organic matter. Another name for organic matter is humus.

extraordinary vitality and recuperative powers. Even a small thread of root buried 12 to 18 inches deep is likely to survive and develop into a sturdy plant.

Other plants have the same ability, but since it's impossible to list them all here, I can only offer a bit of general advice: Although it is almost sinful to throw away potential organic matter, you should, when digging a flower bed, remove from the soil all plants with large root systems, all with fleshy roots and all with threadlike roots that snake outward for considerable distances in all directions.

Grass and other small plants, whether weeds or not, should be left in the soil. Turn them upside down in the bottom of the bed to rot and provide extra nourishment for your flowers.

FUMIGATING THE SOIL

If soil is infested with weeds and weed seeds, microscopic insects called nematodes and soil-borne diseases, the quickest way to make it suitable for planting is to treat it with a fumigant such as Vapam, Chloropicrin, Nemagon or Dowfume. (For general application directions, see page 55.) But how can you be sure such treatment is necessary?

Frankly, you can't, until you have raised flowers long enough to discover what, if any, problems arise from the soil. To me, a wait-and-see approach makes good sense because fumigants are hazardous not only to humans and animals but also to trees, shrubs and vines growing nearby. Furthermore, I see no point in borrowing trouble.

On the other hand, if you live in California or another warm climate, it is a pretty safe bet that your soil contains nematodes, which are likely to do considerable damage to various flowers. Similarly, if the area you dig up is full of daylilies, Mexican bamboo (a very tall reed with big bamboolike stems and sprays of tiny white flowers), chrysanthemum weed (a pest that exactly resembles chrysanthemums without flowers) and quackgrass (a coarse weedy grass with slender white roots running every which way), it is a certainty that no matter how often you pull them up, they will come back and threaten to choke out your flowers. In these cases, therefore, fumigating the soil prior to planting flowers is advisable.

DRAINING SOGGY SOIL

There is a limit to the amount of moisture that flowers need. If they get too much, the great majority drown, just like humans. Only a few can survive in a wet location. Consequently good soil drainage is essential in your flower bed.

If the bed is in a low spot with standing water or in a low spot that becomes sodden after heavy rains, you must either build a raised bed (see Chapter 5) or install some sort of drainage system to carry the water away to a sewer, a stream, or a low spot where it will do no harm. Frequently all you need to do is dig a ditch through the flower bed and use the soil dug out to raise the elevation of the planting areas on either side. A more attractive, more efficient solution is to install 4-inch-diameter, perforated composition drainpipes under the bed. If the bed is to be planted with annuals, perennials and bulbs, the pipes should be installed, perforations down, with the bottoms no less than 12 inches, and preferably 15 inches, below the soil surface. In a rose bed, they should be 24 inches deep. The pipes must, of course, be pitched slightly away from the bed toward the disposal point.

If the low spot is small, a single straight run of pipe is usually enough to carry away water. In a larger area, however, you may need several straight runs; or you can arrange the pipes in a Y or fishbone pattern.

Clay soil presents another kind of problem even when it is on a hillside. After a storm, it turns into a spongy mire and stays that way for days. In extreme situations, the only solution is to install drainage pipes. But, as a rule, you can correct matters by digging the flower bed to a depth of 18 to 24 inches and pouring into the bottom a 4- to 6-inch layer of crushed rock. The soil above this should then be mixed with massive quantities of pea gravel and coarse humus.

LIGHTENING SOIL

The process described in the preceding sentence is called "lightening" soil. It is used not only when you are dealing with heavy clay but also when soil contains moderate amounts of clay but not enough to make it very sticky and cold when wet. The adobe that abounds in California and other western states is an example of such soil.

Soil needs to be lightened to make it drain better and also to allow oxygen to penetrate to plant roots.* Any material that will separate the clay particles can be used for this purpose. Humus is the most popular because most soils need more of this material than they contain (see below). But crushed rock, gravel, sand and vermiculite are also good because, unlike humus, they remain permanently in the soil. That is why I prefer a mixture of humus and coarse mineral material. The amount you should add depends on how much you can afford and on how heavy your soil is to start with. If you mix 1 to 1½ parts humus and 1 to ½ part mineral material (a total of 2 parts) with each 4 parts soil, you will accomplish wonders. But even if you add just a little, it will be better than none at all.

INCREASING A SOIL'S WATER-HOLDING CAPACITY

The opposite of lightening soil is to make it heavier, but for some reason, gardeners never use such a phrase. Instead they speak of increasing the water-holding capacity of soil, which is the aim of the process.

Some soils are so very sandy or gravelly that water leaches through them rapidly and they dry out before plants can absorb enough moisture. To correct this condition, add clay or humus or—preferably—both.

IMPROVING SOIL WITH HUMUS

As noted earlier, almost all soils are improved by the addition of humus (the exceptions are peat soils, which are already almost pure humus). Humus makes heavy soil lighter; it makes porous soil more moisture-retentive; and it adds essential nutrients to all soils.

Because it is widely available at moderate cost, dry, clean, odorless peat moss is the most popular source of humus used by flower growers. The type derived from sphagnum peat is particularly desirable because of its coarse texture and exceptional ability to absorb and retain mois-

---

* Without oxygen at the roots, plants suffocate and die. This explains why trees planted along city streets are always surrounded by open soil, loose-laid bricks or steel grilles. If solid paving were laid close up against the tree trunks, air could not reach the roots.

ture. But all types fulfill the three primary purposes of humus and are pleasant to handle.

Two even better sources of humus are manure and leaf mold. The former is especially rich in the nutrients essential to plant growth, but it is a bountiful supplier of humus only if it is mixed with straw or hay. Leaf mold contains fewer nutrients than manure but more than peat moss. Its principal advantage is that it costs nothing.

Leaf mold consists of decayed leaves, grass clippings, hay and other green plant parts. To make it, just toss the leaves, clippings, etc., into a pile in an out-of-sight corner of your yard and let them rot. In about a year, what was once a mountain will be reduced to a couple of inches of brown, crumbly, semidry material looking exactly like peat moss. (Decomposition can be hastened somewhat by shredding the leaves into small particles before you pile them and/or by mixing in a special chemical such as Adco.)

Whatever type of humus you use to improve the soil in a flower bed, you can hardly use too much. In a brand-new bed I try to add 1 inch of humus for every 4 inches of soil. Thus, if a bed is dug to a depth of 12 inches, I add roughly 3 inches of humus. But it is not essential that you follow suit. An excellent way to add copious amounts of humus to soil—but at a slower, less costly rate—is to mix the two together initially in proportions of 1 inch of humus to 12 inches of soil and to keep the flower bed covered thereafter with an organic mulch (see Chapter 3).

CHANGING THE pH OF SOIL

Like water, soil can be acid, alkaline or neutral. pH is the symbol used to indicate its exact condition. Soil with a pH of 7 is neutral. As the pH drops below 7, soil becomes increasingly acid; and as the pH rises above 7, it becomes increasingly alkaline.

Some plants have a definite preference for either acid or alkaline soils; but in the cultivated-flower kingdom, almost all genera* do best in

---

* Genera is the plural of genus, which is a closely related group of plants including one or more species, which, in turn, may include one or more varieties. In botany, plant names are in Latin. The first name stands for the genus, the second for the species and the third for the variety. For example, *Narcissus bulbocodium conspicuus* is a miniature daffodil popularly known as the Yellow Hoop Petticoat daffodil.

essentially neutral soils—those with a pH ranging from approximately 6.5 to 7.2. The most notable exception is the calla lily, which requires a pH of about 5.

The soil test you have had made will reveal the pH of your soil. If it is nearly neutral, there is nothing you need to do to it unless you plant calla lilies. If it is definitely acid or definitely alkaline, however, you should correct it by mixing in the appropriate chemical.

Lime is used to raise the pH of acid soil—or, as old-time gardeners say, "to sweeten the soil." It is applied in the form of either ground limestone or hydrated lime. One is as good as the other: ground limestone lasts longer, whereas hydrated lime works faster. Another difference is that hydrated lime must be applied at least a week before or a week after you fertilize soil; but ground limestone and fertilizer can be used together.

Liming is best done in early winter or late fall but it is not absolutely necessary to hold to this schedule. Repeat applications are usually needed only every three or four years. Apply the amount called for on your soil-test report. Light sandy soils need less than half as much lime as heavy clay soils.* The maximum amount of lime which should be applied at one time to 100 square feet of soil is 5 pounds. If more than this is required, apply it in two or more 5-pound doses at six-week intervals.

To lower the pH of alkaline soil in most parts of the country, use finely ground sulfur. Apply this at the rate of 1 pound per 100 square feet of soil of average quality. Two pounds per 100 square feet are required on clay soil; about ¾ pound, on sandy soil.

In arid sections of our 17 western states, however, lowering the pH of soil is a more difficult task because both the soil and the water used for irrigation are exceptionally alkaline. As a result, once you have reduced the pH of the soil to the desired level, the water you give plants by hose soon raises it again. One way you can control this exasperating cycle to some extent is to water your garden very, very heavily in the early spring in order to wash the excess salt out of the soil. In addition, you should mix sulfur or gypsum into the soil according to the recommendation of your state agricultural extension service.

* Lime is doubly beneficial to clay soils because, in addition to changing the pH, it in effect cements the tiny particles of clay together into larger particles, and thus improves porosity.

FINAL STEPS IN PREPARING A FLOWER BED

Whatever additives your soil requires—humus, sand, gravel, clay, lime or sulfur—should be mixed into it after you have turned over the flower bed (and fumigated it and installed drainage pipe, if such steps are necessary). The first application of fertilizer is also mixed into the bed at this time (see Chapter 3).

Spread the materials on the bed in even layers, and then work them in thoroughly, to the full depth of the bed, with a fork or hoe. The soil should be dry enough so that it breaks up readily; if it is wet and sticky, wait until it dries out somewhat. When you have finished mixing and pulverizing the soil, level the bed with a rake. You will undoubtedly find that the surface is higher than the surrounding ground. This is partly because of the materials you have added and partly because you have aerated the soil. Do not plant anything at this time and don't let people walk through the soil. Allow it to settle for a couple of weeks. If the surface is still much too high, skin an inch or two off the top and use it elsewhere around the yard. I don't mind a flower bed that is up to 2 inches higher than the adjacent lawn or other area, because it is easy to keep the soil from drifting out by cutting a shallow ditch around the edges of the bed. But a bed that is higher than this looks peculiar. (More on this subject in Chapter 5.)

Planting can start any time after the soil is reasonably firm, will support plants properly and will not settle drastically when you run water on it with a hose or watering can. (For the actual techniques of planting, see Chapter 5.)

·3·

GENERAL CARE
OF FLOWERS

Once planted, all flowers are cared for in roughly the same way during the growing season. But there are some things you do for one that you don't do for another; and in the winter and early spring, there are things you must do with, say, perennials that you don't do with annuals. In other words, if you are one of those who sometimes complain that life is a rut, you will find ample variation in flower growing to put zest into living. Yet you won't feel you have turned into a jumping jack.

In this respect, the flower gardener is like a carpenter. He does a number of basic tasks over and over again, but because each species of plant he works with (like each building) is different, his work is always different. I won't go so far as to say this makes the carpenter's life fun, but for the flower gardener it does.

WATERING

One of the questions all gardeners—even experienced gardeners—ask about a plant they do not know is: "How much water does it need?" A precise answer is rarely possible. If they chose to figure it out, lettuce farmers in the Imperial Valley of California could tell you within a quart how much water is required to raise a head of lettuce to marketable size. But they would be able to do this only because they have been coping with a climate that varies little from year to year. Gardeners—and farmers—in other areas are in no position to be accurate about plant needs and resulting plant performance.

The moisture requirements of flowers vary with the species of flower, with the season of the year, with the area in which the flower is grown, with climatic conditions, and so forth. But despite these variations, there is an old rule-of-thumb which holds that if a plant receives the equivalent of 1 inch of rainfall every week during the growing season, this will keep it thriving.

Even though I can find no authority for this rule, I don't doubt that it is sound. Most parts of the country receive less than 1 inch of rainfall per week during the growing season; yet almost all plants grow well without further assistance. So given a full inch, they should, by and large, do *very* well.

Nevertheless, the rule presents two problems: First, if you have to make up for a deficiency of precipitation, how do you measure the depth of water issuing from a hose on porous soil? (It can be done, but it's a nuisance.) Second, since the rule is applied across the board to all plants, the 1-inch figure is obviously a desirable average; and that being so, what is the effect of 1 inch of moisture on flowers that really need less or really need more?

It's clear that the rule is not meant to be a rule at all. It is simply a guideline—a way of emphasizing that plants need a rather considerable amount of moisture to grow.

Here are some less specific but more practical rules for watering flowers:

1. Give them water as soon as the surface of the soil in which they are growing starts looking dry but before it is bone dry.

2. Water the soil around each plant individually with a slow-running hose. Thus you keep the foliage dry and give diseases less chance to take hold and spread. The water sinks in where it is most needed—right around the roots—and little, if any, is wasted. In addition, you can pretty well tell how much water you are applying and whether it is enough or too much.

The best alternative to hand-watering individual plants is to use a canvas or plastic soil-soaker to serve a number of plants at one time. Laid on the ground around plants, soakers emit water slowly enough to allow it to sink in almost exactly where it comes out of the soakers. Like a slow-running hose, they keep the foliage dry and put the water where it is needed; and they do this automatically, while you are busy elsewhere around your garden. But until you have had experience with them, you have only a hazy idea whether they are giving your plants enough water. Probably the worst drawback of soil-soakers is that they emit much less water at the end farthest from the faucet than at the near end; but this is not always apparent from the puddle on the ground.

The third way to water flowers is with a sprinkler. But besides wetting the foliage, this usually gives poor results since, within the area reached by the sprinkler, some spots get more moisture than others because of wind and unevenness of the spray. The very thick foliage of some plants keeps the soil under these almost dry. And the amount of water is, in a flower border at least, impossible to measure.

3. When you get out the hose to water flowers, give each plant enough water to wet the soil to a depth of at least 1 foot. This assures that most of the roots on each plant have access to moisture. True, the roots that extend down deeper than a foot may receive an uneven, insufficient supply of moisture and may ultimately die; but since there are relatively few of these, plant growth is usually not seriously affected.

How can you tell whether and when you have wet the soil to the desired depth?

Some gardeners use a device called a tensiometer. Buried in the ground, this measures the amount of moisture in the surrounding soil and automatically records the information on a gauge. But despite the desirability of this system, it is not widely used, and I doubt that it ever will be except in arid regions.

Most gardeners use two less accurate ways of judging how much water they must apply to satisfy plant requirements. Both come under the heading of "learning by experience."

One method is to run water onto the garden for a few minutes; then let it sink in for a few more minutes; and then dig down with a spade to see how deep it has percolated. After you have done this a few times, you have a reasonably good idea of how much water it takes to wet your garden soil to a given depth.

The other method is to time how long it takes for a slow-running hose to fill a kitchen kettle 9 or 10 inches in diameter to a depth of 1 inch. You should then take a close look at your garden soil to determine whether it is sandy and very porous; clayey and very dense; or about halfway between. What you might call good average soil. You can then put to use the following bit of time-tested garden lore:

One inch of water applied to dry sandy soil wets the soil to a depth of 16 inches.

One inch of water applied to dry clay soil wets the soil to a depth of slightly less than 5 inches.

One inch of water applied to dry average soil wets the soil to a depth of 8 inches.

4. As long as you are reasonably careful not to splatter the foliage, it doesn't make any difference at what time of day you water flowers. But if you use a sprinkler or are not careful to avoid splattering the foliage with a hose, you should do your watering only in the morning. The reason: this gives the plants plenty of time to dry off before nightfall and thus helps to keep down fungus diseases, which spread most rapidly during darkness.

5. If you live in an arid Western state, you must supersaturate the soil with water every now and then to drive out salts which may injure and even kill flowers. The best time for this treatment is in the early spring just before you plant your garden. To remove most of the salts from the upper 2 feet of soil, apply at least 12 inches of water (put a kettle under the sprinkler to measure the depth of the water). Then, in order to get rid of the salts as they gradually build up again, give the plants a double dose of water every other time you water them during the summer.

USING MULCHES

A mulch is a covering, or blanket, which is spread on garden soil primarily to retard evaporation and thus keep the soil moist, and to prevent growth of weeds and thus eliminate the need for cultivation during the summer. In addition, mulches made of organic materials add humus and valuable nutrients to the soil as they decompose, retard water run-off and consequent erosion, and keep the soil cool so that plant roots will not be cooked by the heat of the sun.

Mulches are made out of a variety of inorganic as well as organic materials; but except in rock gardens, where stone chips and pebbles are sometimes used to give the visual effect of a glacial moraine, the inorganics are almost never used around flowers, mainly because they are

These petunia seedlings are mulched with grass clippings to give them extra nourishment and to prevent loss of moisture from the soil. The white flowers at left are perennial candytuft.

not very pretty. Organic materials of many types are in widespread use, however.

Undoubtedly the most popular is peat moss—the same material that is mixed into new flower beds to provide humus (see Chapter 2). As a mulch, its main advantage is that it is reasonably attractive and does an excellent job of holding in moisture and keeping down weeds. But it washes away in storms and has the odd characteristic of actually repelling water when it is dry (but as soon as it becomes damp—which it soon does—it turns into a sponge).

For most flower beds, and especially for rose gardens, I prefer chopped tree bark because it is more attractive, stays in place and decomposes slowly—which means that you don't have to replenish it every year, as with peat moss. On the other hand, slow decomposition also means that it does not enrich the soil so rapidly as peat moss. And because of the bark's coarse texture, it is not quite so effective in controlling weeds and preventing loss of moisture.

Several other attractive organic mulching materials are buckwheat hulls, cocoa beans, pecan shells and sawdust. But judging by recent experiments at the Connecticut Agricultural Experiment Station in New Haven, the best mulch of all is made of grass clippings.

I must admit that in some of my earlier books I downgraded grass clippings because I felt—and still do—that they are never very good-looking and may be downright unsightly if they become matted and moldy. (This last can be prevented, however, if you keep them stirred up a little so they dry out more evenly.) But this now seems like a minor objection.

Used for mulching, grass clippings do everything that other organic materials do. But their main advantage is that, because they are still fresh and green when they are spread on a garden, they contain more nutrients than other mulches. As a result, the plants they surround grow bigger and better.

To be precise, the Connecticut tests disclosed that petunias mulched with grass clippings grew twice as large and produced three times as many flowers as petunias which were not mulched at all. And in comparison with petunias mulched with other materials, those in grass clippings were roughly 50 percent larger and produced almost twice as many flowers.

In short, here is the perfect way of getting rid of a mountain of garden debris and at the same time producing masses of extra-beautiful flowers.

Whatever the organic material you use for mulching, it should be applied just as soon as your flower beds are planted. The thickness of the covering should be maintained at from 2 inches to 4 or 5 inches. On the sound theory that soil exposed to the sun dries out faster than that in the shade, some gardeners use a 2-inch layer of mulch directly under plants and a 4-inch layer in the open spaces between plants. In spreading the mulch, be careful not to cover the bases of small plants or the shoots of perennials which are spearing up through the ground, otherwise it may smother them like weeds.

Once the mulch is down, you should not have to disturb it for the rest of the summer. Cultivation of the soil underneath is unnecessary unless you foolishly tramp around in the garden and pack the soil down in a hard, concretelike layer. When you put the garden to bed in the fall, leave the mulch as is. After the soil is finally frozen, the mulch will keep it from thawing and refreezing repeatedly and disturbing the roots of perennials. However, if you mound up soil around roses to protect them from winter cold, you must rake the mulch to one side.

What you do with the mulch the following spring depends on a number of things. For instance, if the mulch is a small-particled material such as grass clippings, peat moss or buckwheat hulls, it probably will have decomposed to such an extent that it has little remaining value as a blanket. In that case, the best thing to do is to work it into the soil and spread a new mulch on the surface after planting has been completed.

On the other hand, if the mulch is a coarse material such as ground tree bark, it probably will not have decomposed very much; therefore it has less value as humus in the soil. Furthermore, it isn't as easy to dig in and mix with the soil as, say, peat moss—especially if the garden is full of perennials, biennials, bulbs or roses which have spread their roots far and wide. So you may leave it undisturbed and use it as a mulch for another year. (But you will have to add some fresh material to provide the recommended thickness.)

If the soil in the garden has become compressed, however, it definitely should be turned over and broken up, regardless of the condition of the mulch. In this case, you may want to rake some of the old mulch aside to save it. Or you can work it into the soil and apply a new mulch.

CULTIVATING THE FLOWER GARDEN

The verb "to cultivate" has several meanings; but to the gardener its principal meaning is to stir up the soil—much as you stir a colander full of steaming rice. The purpose is to kill or remove weeds and to keep the soil broken into fairly small particles so that air, water and fertilizer nutrients can percolate down to the plant roots and so that the roots

This clump of ageratum is getting a lot of competition from weeds and in time will suffer if the weeds are not pulled out.

themselves can spread and nourish the plants and anchor them securely against winds and heavy rains.

Flower gardens are cultivated initially when they are first established. Thereafter, the kind and amount of cultivation you do depends on whether you use a mulch and on the condition of the soil.

If the garden is not mulched, it should be turned over with a spade or spading fork every spring to loosen the soil and so that you can add whatever humus and fertilizer are needed for plant growth. The process is like that outlined in Chapter 2, except that you must take care not to damage perennials, roses or bulbs already in the garden.

During the summer, you should cultivate the unmulched garden every week or two just to eliminate weeds, and you may also have to cultivate it occasionally to keep the soil broken up.

To a new gardener, weeding may seem like an unnecessary lot of work. "What's really so wrong with weeds?" I was once asked. "I know they make the garden look messy. But I can't see that they do much harm otherwise."

But the sad truth is that weeds are a serious threat to the garden. That's why experienced gardeners and farmers worry so much about them. Unlike grass clippings, which promote more vigorous growth of flowers when used as a mulch, weeds slow the growth of flowers (as well as other desirable plants) and may actually cause their death. They do this by stealing moisture and nutrients away from the flowers. They surround and literally choke them out. And they attract and nurture diseases and insects which attack the flowers.

Weeds, in other words, cannot be tolerated in the garden. They must be destroyed regularly. And if you don't cover the garden with a mulch which smothers those that try to come up, you must dig them out by hand. To do this easily, you need either a cultivator, a hoe or a trowel. Of the three, the cultivator is the best tool in the flower garden provided you use it often enough to keep weeds from becoming established. If you don't, you will need a trowel, a hoe or perhaps even a spading fork to do the job efficiently.

Cultivators for use around flowers are shaped like steel rakes but have only three or four very sharp tines. They are made with long handles for stand-up, two-hand operation, and with short handles for on-your-knees, one-hand operation. I use both: the long-handled tool for plants that are spaced fairly far apart; the short-handled tool for work close in around plants. In either case, all you do is press the teeth into the ground and pull the cultivator toward you. This simultaneously rips out weeds and pulverizes the soil. The only thing to be careful about is that you don't dig too deep and injure flower roots. If they have not gone to seed, weeds you remove should be thrown on the leaf pile to decompose. They can be used the following year for humus. Weeds which have set seeds, however, should be carted off to the town dump, since the seeds would germinate and spring up in your garden if the dead plants were used for humus.

Cultivating an unmulched garden in the summer in order to keep the soil broken up and loose—expert gardeners use the word "friable" to describe such soil—is necessitated by the fact that, unless the soil contains a lot of sand and gravel, sun and rain soon give it a rock-hard consistency that stymies plant growth.

Generally, cultivating to remove weeds also pulverizes the soil sufficiently to make it friable again. But if your garden soil is heavy, you may also have to cultivate it with a spading fork several times during the growing season to break it up around the deep-down roots. This can be ticklish work—especially if the garden is closely planted. The trick is not to go at it too vigorously. Above all, don't attempt to turn the soil over—as you do in an empty garden in early spring—because that will loosen plants and rip out roots. Just drive your fork straight down into the soil about as far as it will go and wiggle it back and forth slightly. Do this over every few inches of the soil's surface so that it is thoroughly peppered with holes.

In a flower garden which is covered with a mulch, cultivation can be reduced substantially. In early spring, follow the recommendations on page 37. In summer, cultivation to keep the soil friable should be unnecessary unless it becomes too hard. If that happens, poking holes deep into the soil with a spading fork will correct matters.

Weeding, unfortunately, is not completely eliminated by mulching because there are always a few tough customers that manage to poke up through even the densest blanket. But at least you don't need a cultivator to dispose of these. As a rule you can tug them out by hand without disturbing either the mulch or the soil beneath.

FEEDING FLOWERS

At the risk of sounding like a rusty wheel, I must again mention one of the values of mulching the flower garden with an organic material: As the mulch decomposes into humus, it gives forth nutrients and microorganisms which are washed down into the soil where they are taken up by the plant roots. Just how valuable these nutritive elements are can be seen in our vast forests and prairies, where plants flourish even though they never receive an ounce of fertilizer. All their strength and beauty are derived from the leaves and grass that fall to the ground in autumn and winter, decay and gradually mix with the soil.

Today's organic gardeners have demonstrated that you can achieve the same growth in flower and vegetable gardens if you make a habit of mixing plenty of humus into the soil and maintaining a mulch on top. For maximum results, however, you should also use fertilizer.

The organic enthusiasts, of course, use nothing but organic fertilizers; and of these the best is manure. Whether this be manure from cows, horses, sheep, pigs or poultry doesn't make much difference. All contain the three major elements needed for plant growth: nitrogen, phosphorus and potash. In addition, if they are mixed with straw, all break down into a splendid humus.

But manure has drawbacks. For one thing, even though it is available in such superabundant supply on some farms that it is becoming a serious pollutant of springs, streams, rivers and lakes, it is difficult for the average home gardener to come by. For another thing, it must be allowed to rot for several months before it is spread on the garden, for in its raw state it is so hot that it kills small plants. Finally, of course, manure—even when well rotted—has a pervasive aroma.

If you use barnyard manure, spread it on the garden in the late fall, after growth has stopped, or during the winter. Apply a layer 1 to 3 inches thick. It is not necessary at this time to work it into the soil, although this is a good way to reduce the odor. In early spring, however, mix it in as deeply as you can. You should then have a bountiful supply of flowers until frost cuts them down.

If you cannot use barnyard manure, there are several good organic fertilizers to replace it. Dehydrated manure is one. It has most of the values of the real article; and though it is odoriferous when applied and watered in, it loses this characteristic shortly. Two of the material's advantages are that it does not contain weed seeds, which are present in barnyard manure, and it does not burn plants even when they are thoroughly coated with it. Nevertheless, the best way to use dehydrated manure is to mix it into the soil when you prepare the garden in the spring. Later applications should also be mixed in.

Bone meal is a whitish powder containing nitrogen and phosphorus. Known as a slow-acting fertilizer, it gives off nutrients at snail's pace, which means that it feeds plants over a considerable period of time. It does not burn.

Cottonseed meal, fish meal and dried blood are other slow-acting organics in powder form. They are reasonably rich in nitrogen but have only a little phosphorus and potash. Cottonseed meal is especially recommended for plants that do well in acid soils. All these fertilizers are applied in early spring and once more in late spring or early summer. In early spring, use about 3 to 5 pounds per 100 square feet and mix it thoroughly into the soil like dehydrated manure (which is used at the same rate). Later in the year, simply sprinkle about a half handful around each plant and scratch it into the soil with a cultivator. This is called side-dressing.

Inorganic fertilizers are pulverized materials derived from minerals. They are used much more widely than organic fertilizers. Without them, in fact, American farmers would probably be unable to feed the nation, and the United States certainly would not be the world's principal food source.

Inorganic fertilizers are more plentiful than organics and therefore less expensive. They generally contain a higher percentage of nitrogen, phosphorus and potash. And contrary to some dyed-in-the-wool organic gardeners, they produce flowers, vegetables and other plants which are every bit as sturdy, healthy, nourishing and beautiful as those produced by organic fertilizers.

One of the disadvantages of inorganic fertilizers is that they have no humus content and consequently do not contribute this valuable material to soil. It follows that if you mixed nothing into a flower bed except inorganic fertilizer, the soil would ultimately lose most of its natural humus and its productive value would decline. This problem, however, is easily avoided by mulching the bed and digging in the humus the mulch yields or simply by adding humus to an unmulched bed in the early spring. The resulting soil is then no different from that which is enriched with organic fertilizer.

A second disadvantage of inorganic fertilizers is that, if they remain long in contact with plant leaves, stems or roots, they may cause bad burns and perhaps kill the plants. For this reason, you should try not to get any more on your flowers than you can help; and you should then wash them off with a hose.

The final disadvantage of most inorganic fertilizers is that, unlike organics, they are very fast-acting. They are therefore quickly dissolved in water, and the nutrients they release become immediately available to plants. Although, in one way, this produces desirable results because the plants make a prompt surge of growth, the effect is short-lived. If you want to sustain vigorous growth, you should soon make another application of fertilizer. Another difficulty stemming from this fast-acting characteristic is that, if you happen to give a plant too big a shot of fertilizer at one time, you're likely to burn it from inside out.

Inorganic fertilizers that contain only a single element—nitrogen or phosphorus or potassium—are widely used on farms and are also used in gardens when the soil shows a pronounced deficiency in one element. But most home gardeners use so-called balanced, or complete, fertilizers containing all three elements.* These mixtures are identified by three hyphenated numbers on the package label—for example, 5–10–5. The first number indicates the percentage of nitrogen in the fertilizer; the second, the percentage of phosphorus; the third, the percentage of potash. The total of the three figures indicates the total percentage— which can be translated into poundage—of the nutrients in the package. For example, a 100-pound bag of 5–10–5 contains 20 percent, or 20 pounds, of nutrients: 5 pounds of nitrogen, 10 pounds of phosphorus and 5 pounds of potash. Inert matter makes up the remaining 80 pounds.

Balanced fertilizers are formulated in innumerable ways to supply the needs of specific plants or to make up for the deficiencies of specific soils. When buying a balanced fertilizer, therefore, you would do well to ask your agricultural extension service or a reliable garden-supplies store what it recommends for *your* garden. However, if there is no great difference in formulations—that is, if the proportions of the three major elements are about the same—one is about as good as the other. Generally, throughout the United States, the favorite mixtures for flower gardens are 5–10–5, 10–6–4 and 10–10–10. These are used interchangeably without ill effects.

The first application of a balanced fertilizer is made in early spring when the garden is readied for planting. Scatter 2 to 3 pounds over each 100 square feet of soil surface and work in well. Subsequent applications are made by side-dressing individual plants with 1 to 3 teaspoons of fertilizer. Use the smallest amount on young plants, and the maximum amount on big, established plants such as roses. Generally these individual applications are made at 30- to 60-day intervals.

OTHER WAYS OF FEEDING FLOWERS

The fertilizing materials and methods described above have been in use for many years. They are tried and true. But fertilizer manufacturers

---

* In a few cases, some of the elements are supplied by organic materials and some by inorganic materials.

continue constantly to develop new fertilizers which are used in new ways. Here are two you should know about:

Foliar feeding is the name given to the system of feeding plants through their leaves rather than through their roots. Research has proved that it produces fast and very effective results—especially on small plants, such as flowers, and on those growing in a porous soil, which loses moisture and ordinary fertilizer quickly through leaching.

Fertilizers used for foliar feeding are concentrates of inorganic materials. Put up in liquid or crystalline form, they contain high percentages of the three major elements and usually a number of minor elements such as magnesium and zinc. To use them, simply mix in water and apply to the tops of plants with a sprayer or watering can until the leaves are dripping wet. (These fertilizers may also be fed to the plant roots by pouring them on ground which has first been soaked with water.)

Foliar feeding is not a complete substitute for other feeding methods. You must still see that the soil in the garden is enriched with humus and/or mulched; and it is also advisable to mix a powdered fertilizer into the soil in the early spring. But once your flowers are up and growing, you can satisfy all their nutritional needs with foliar sprays applied every ten days to two weeks. Or you can use foliar sprays simply to give your flowers a shot in the arm whenever they seem to need it.

An even newer method of feeding flowers is to use a slow-release, or controlled-release, fertilizer consisting of a balanced formulation of inorganic nitrogen, phosphorus and potash. The fertilizer is manufactured in the form of small granules or pellets coated with varying thicknesses of a plastic which breaks down slowly upon exposure to moisture. Thus, by making one application of fertilizer in the spring, you can feed your flowers for the entire growing season.

Like ordinary balanced fertilizers, slow-release mixtures are formulated in various ways. For instance, one designed for use on the general run of flowers is a 14–14–14 mixture which will feed the plants for about four months. Another is an 18–6–12 formula for roses which lasts about eight months. In all cases, application should be made according to the manufacturer's directions.

Easy-to-read plant label.

LABELING FLOWERS

You don't have to label your flowers to enjoy them; but if you fail to label them, the odds are that you will soon forget the names of some of them and then you won't know what to reorder when you want more. You may also be embarrassed when some one asks, "What's that pretty flower?" and you can answer only, "Well, I did know. Now let me see—Oh, I can't remember."

Labels are needed for all seeds and cuttings and for all individual plants or plant groups in the garden. Most of all, they are needed for bulbs and perennials that die down completely in the winter, because if you don't mark their locations, you will at some time dig them up when you don't want to or cut them into shreds with a spade.

For seedlings, cuttings and annuals the best labels—because they are the least expensive—are small, flat, pointed strips of white-painted wood or white plastic, which are stuck into the ground.

For established perennials and bulbs, use T-shaped plastic labels. These are more durable than wood and easy to read because the plant name is parallel with the ground. A good alternative, though not quite so neat, is a metal strip embossed with the name of the plant and attached by a slender wire to a sturdy wire stake thrust into the ground.

Roses should also be labeled with plastic Ts or embossed metal strips. The practice of tying labels to the plant stems is unsatisfactory because, if the labels do not eventually fall off, the stems eventually are pruned off. Furthermore, fishing a tied-on label far enough out of a rosebush so you can read it is a rather hazardous undertaking.

DISBUDDING FLOWERS

Disbudding is a minor but essential flower-growing task that many gardeners misunderstand. My wife, for instance, has done plenty of gardening, but when she brings home a box of seedling marigolds and then watches me pinch off the bud or perhaps the little flower on the top of each plant, she protests because I seem to be holding back the plants and depriving her of immediate bloom. She may protest similarly when she sees me removing the side buds on chrysanthemums because her instant reaction is that I am reducing the amount of bloom the plants will put out in the fall.

In both cases, the actual effect of my actions is quite the reverse of what she is expecting.

Disbudding—removing the buds of flowers with your fingernails, shears or knife—forces small annuals (and certain perennials which are handled in the same way) to grow into bigger, bushier plants that will reward you with more blooms than you would get if they were not disbudded. This happens because, after the first flower bud is removed, the little plant transfers its energies from producing a flower to putting out side branches, each of which will have flowers.

Disbudding of established perennials is done in the same way; but instead of removing the terminal bud at the end of each stem, you remove the smaller side buds growing out from the stems. This forces the plant to concentrate on making the terminal bud produce a larger flower. If you remove all the side buds, the central flower should be of exceptional size—big enough to win a prize in the local flower show. My usual practice is to leave one or two of the side buds. This reduces the size of the central flower a little, but as soon as it fades, I cut it off in

Pinching off the terminal buds on this small petunia will make the plant put out more stems with more flowers.

If the side buds on this peony are removed, the terminal bud will produce a larger flower. But if some of the side buds are kept, there will be more flowers over a longer period.

order to encourage the remaining side buds to bloom and extend the flowering season a week or two.

THINNING OUT

Thinning out produces results similar to disbudding of established perennials; but instead of pinching off side buds, you cut out entire stems at the base of the plant.

Phlox and coreopsis are examples of perennials that respond well to thinning. Normally both put up a veritable thicket of stems with numerous small flowers. But if you remove all but about six of the stems while they are still small, those left will grow bigger and bear bigger flowers.

CUTTING FLOWERS

Much of the pleasure of growing flowers is in cutting and bringing some of them indoors to decorate and perfume the house. The pleasure is diluted considerably, however, if the flowers don't keep. Some flowers are naturally better keepers than others. For example, perennial phlox lasts only three or four days whereas some lilies may go on for three or four weeks. These are differences you come to recognize with experience.

But much of the keeping ability of cut flowers depends on how carefully you cut and handle them in the first place. There are no tricks, such as dropping pennies or aspirin tablets in water, you can count on.

The best time to cut flowers of all types is in the late afternoon or early evening. The second-best time is in the morning. They should never be picked during the heat of the day because they are likely to wilt rapidly. Picking flowers from mildewed plants that are damp should also be avoided since it is very easy to spread the disease at such times.

Cutting flowers with a razor-sharp knife rather than with shears is generally preferred on the theory that shears compress the stem tissues and interfere with the intake of moisture. This has not been proved. But however a flower is cut, the cut should be made on a slant so more tissue will be exposed to the water in the vase.

Carry a pail of tepid water with you while cutting flowers and plunge the stems deep into this at once. Always keep the cut flowers out of direct sunlight. Just before you arrange such flowers as poppies, dahlias and heliotropes, dip their stems in boiling water for one minute to prevent loss of fluid from them later on.

The vases in which you arrange flowers should be spotlessly clean. After every use, wash them in a solution of household ammonia to remove dirt, scum and bacteria.

Fill the vases almost full with room-temperature water. Remove all leaves that would otherwise be under water, since they would soon decay. For longest life of the flowers, set the arrangements out of the sun and well away from radiators, registers and other heat sources. Moving the flowers into a cool room at night also helps to extend their life.

Adding aspirins or copper pennies to the water in a vase has no effect on the beauty or keeping quality of flowers. If you want to try anything like this, use 1 teaspoon of sugar per pint of water or one of the carbohydrate-containing preservatives sold in garden-supplies stores and florist shops. The best treatment for cut flowers is to give them a change of water every day or every two days (but don't let them go longer than this). Before changing the water, it's advisable to cut the ends off the flower stems while they are still underwater. This is awkward to do, but in effect opens up the pores of the flowers so they will take in more moisture.

REMOVING FADED BLOOMS

Regardless of the size or multiplicity of blossoms which annuals, perennials and roses produce, all blossoms which are allowed to bloom in the garden should be removed as soon as they fade. This improves the appearance of plants and garden; but there are other more important reasons for the practice.

In the first place, if the flowers are not removed, they will start to set seed, and this saps the strength of the plants. Annuals and roses will stop blooming earlier than they should; perennials will develop less sturdy root systems.

In the second place, if a flower is allowed to go to seed and the seeds then scatter, your garden may become overgrown with seedling plants which will interfere with the growth of established plants. Furthermore, if the plant producing the seeds was a hybrid variety, most of its offspring will bear no resemblance to it. On the contrary, they will revert to the appearance of earlier ancestors.

The final reason for removing spent flowers from some perennials is to encourage the plants to produce a second crop of flowers. After spring flowers of delphiniums die and are cut off, for instance, they will bloom a second time in the late summer. This is also true of phlox and lupines and several other genera. (The way in which the flowers should be removed is described in Chapter 7.)

STAKING PLANTS

I dislike staking flowers because the stakes detract from the appearance of the garden; and whenever someone is picking flowers, I fear that in leaning down to cut a stem he may spear himself on a stake that is partially hidden in foliage. But unfortunately, staking is a must to keep the garden neat.

A number of medium-size plants, such as gaillardia and smaller varieties of sweet pea, should be staked because they have slender stems which are unable to bear the weight of the flower heads and tend to flop. And almost all tall plants must be staked to hold them upright against wind and heavy rain. True, some of the latter appear sturdy enough to be ignored. One of the best flower borders I ever had contained several cosmos plants and a tithonia which grew to such proportions—with stems as big as broomsticks—that I never thought to worry about their toppling over. But then one day in early September we had a deluge which left the plants broken and sprawling over the lesser lights below. Ever since then, I have taken no chances.

Somewhat surprisingly, huge branching plants such as cosmos, tithonia and large dahlias are easier to stake than many smaller flowers. All you need to do is drive long, stout (at least 1 inch in diameter) stakes deep into the soil a few inches away from the central stem, and tie the stem to them at 1-foot intervals as the plants increase in height. One stake is enough when plants are small. Two are almost essential when they are fully grown. Set the stakes on opposite sides of the stem. To tie these large plants, I like folded strips of cotton cloth because they don't cut through the stem when the wind blows. Knot each strip tightly around a stake, and then tie it loosely around the stem. The stakes should project aboveground to about 75 or 80 percent of the ultimate height of the plant.

Lower flowers that branch (for example, zinnias) or those which have a single straight stem (such as gladiolus) are staked in the same way except that the stakes are much more slender and you need only one per plant. Use soft jute, cotton twine or raffia (fiber from a palm

How to stake a delphinium: use four stakes and a crisscross arrangement of twine. I painted the stakes white and used white string for picture purposes only; ordinarily these would be green.

tree) for ties. Paper or plastic strips reinforced with wire can also be used; but when you clean up the garden in the fall, these are a nuisance because you must untwist each one from the plant and the stake before you dispose of it. Twine and raffia are easily cut with a knife.

Flowers which put up a multitude of stems—delphiniums and balloonflowers, for example—are more difficult to handle because one or two stakes are not enough. The best practice is to set about four stakes around each plant (if the plants are in a large clump, the number of stakes can be reduced because one will serve two or three plants); tie a string around them to form a square; and then tie the string diagonally across the square in both directions. This job should be started when the plant has made about a foot of growth. Place the stakes fairly close in around the plant so they will be concealed by the foliage. Guide the

Peonies are best staked with heavy wire loops supported on three wire stakes. Garden stores sell this gadget with either one or two loops.

stems up through the strings, and add a new set of strings each time the plant grows another 9 to 12 inches. As is true with stakes used for other plants, these should extend aboveground roughly three-quarters of the maximum height of the plant.

Peonies can be staked in the same way; but a more attractive solution is to use the circular wire supports sold for them in garden-supplies stores. These have four upright wire stakes to which horizontal wire loops are welded at 12-inch intervals.

For small and medium-size flowers with wiry stems, use twiggy branches as stakes. Stick these into the ground close around each plant when it is small. As the stems elongate, most of them will be trapped and held in the branches without further attention on your part.

Another way to support sprawling plants is to surround them with collars of steel mesh made with large square openings and covered with green plastic. These must be set in place while the plants are young—not more than 10 inches high—so that the stems and branches will grow through them; otherwise, the effect is rather like that of a flower arrangement in a narrow vase.

CONTROLLING INSECT PESTS AND DISEASES

The only sensible approach to the problem of insects and diseases in the flower garden is to recognize that you are going to have trouble with them from time to time but not to get excited about them. This is not to say that I minimize the harm they can do if they take hold. Twice in recent years I have suddenly discovered that aphids were on the verge of destroying my spring roses and delphiniums. But on both occasions I disposed of them quickly with malathion. This is the usual pattern. If you keep a close eye on your flowers (I don't mean inspect them with a magnifying glass; just take a look at them every day), you will notice when something is awry; and then all you have to do is pin down the cause of trouble and take steps to bring it under control. Major problems arise, as a rule, only when you let down your guard.

Preventive measures (as opposed to control measures) are necessary in the case of a few pests which are so ubiquitous and persistent that it is almost a foregone conclusion that they will give you trouble every year.

But once again I caution against alarm and the desperate measures which often follow. The best way to prevent insect and disease problems is not with an arsenal of chemicals or beneficial insects, but with common sense.

1. Grow your flowers well. If you give them good soil, ample moisture and just enough fertilizer, their strength and vigor will ward off many pests.

2. Follow good sanitary practices in maintaining your entire property (and any woods and fields surrounding it). Rip out and destroy sick and dead plants. Keep trash picked up. Remove weeds and wild plants, which often harbor pests. In the fall, after your flowers are killed by frost, send the remains of those which were infested with insects or disease during the summer to the town dump.

Having done these two things, you should not have to devote very much time to other pest-fighting measures. But, organic gardeners to the contrary, there will be times when a certain amount of chemical warfare must be undertaken.

The appropriate chemicals to use will be indicated as the various pests and diseases and methods for fighting these are discussed later on. Most are applied in two ways—by dusting and by spraying.

Dusting is the less popular method although it is a little faster. To be effective, it must be done on an almost windless day after a rain. The foliage should be dry; if not, the whitish powder will stick to it. Your clothes and nose will also be white with powder.

The secret of good dusting is to apply a thin, even coat of the powdered chemical, not a thick one. To do this you need an efficient duster. The choice (short of expensive motor-driven equipment) lies between a Flit-gun-type device and a crank type. The former is cheaper but is tiresome and awkward to use. The latter is better because all you do is turn a crank and out comes a steady, even cloud of dust. But if you don't clean this duster carefully after every use, it will "freeze up" and give you endless trouble.

Spraying gives better coverage with less waste; is less dependent on the weather; and is neater and cleaner (although some chemicals may leave white blotches on dark foliage). The best time to spray is after a rain, when plant diseases are rampant; however, after a spray has dried on a plant, it will often retain its killing powers through a succeeding storm. Use a chemical that is put up either in liquid or wettable-powder form.

Aerosol sprays are handy and effective but too expensive for outdoor use and too difficult to use on large plants, especially roses. You should also avoid Flit-gun-type sprayers, larvacide-bottle-type sprayers and hose-end sprayers: in the flower garden they have more drawbacks than advantages.

The compressed-air sprayer is preferred. It consists of a tank which is partially filled with diluted chemical and an air pump which compresses the air above the chemical. The chemical is discharged through a flexible hose and a rigid metal tube at the end of which is a nozzle for adjusting the spray from a fine mist to a solid stream. I recommend the 2½-gallon size for the average gardener. It is not too heavy to carry when filled, yet holds enough to spray a big garden.

When using a compressed-air sprayer, mix the chemical with water in a bucket; then pour it into the sprayer through a piece of screen wire in order to strain out hairs, lumps, specks, etc. (This is important because the nozzle is easily clogged.) During spraying, shake the tank occasionally to keep the chemical in suspension. When the job is done, empty the chemical out on the ground; it should not be saved and reused. Then rinse the tank thoroughly with water and force water through the spray tube under pressure. Leave the tank open and hang it upside down to drain and dry.

Caution: A sprayer used for insecticides and fungicides should not be used for applying weed-killers on lawns, poison ivy, etc. Weed-killers are very difficult to clean out; and if not cleaned out perfectly, the trace remaining will kill your flowers.

Three other common ways to cope with certain garden pests are by systemic poisoning, fumigating and soaking.

Systemic poisoning is a method used to control aphids, mites, thrips and other pests that suck the juices of plants.* The chemicals used come in liquid or granular form. The liquid is sprayed on plants and absorbed by the tissues, and then kills the insects when they feed. The granules, which will protect plants for six to eight weeks, are sprinkled on the ground around the plants and watered in. They are then absorbed

---

* These are known, obviously, as sucking insects.

through the roots and carried throughout the plants. A new systemic poison named Benomyl is used to control black spot and mildew on roses and other plants. It is put up in the form of a wettable powder and is applied by spraying the foliage, but I have had no experience with it up to this writing.

Fumigating is done in the flower garden to control nematodes and other insects which live in the soil and feed on plant roots. The application method varies, but generally consists of mixing the chemical thoroughly into the soil, watering heavily, and then covering the ground with plastic film to prevent evaporation. The entire treatment usually takes several weeks, and must be done with care because the chemicals are poisonous. Furthermore they are injurious to plants, which means that they cannot be used close to trees, shrubs and vines; and after the soil is treated, flowers should not, as a rule, be planted for several weeks.

Soaking simply involves immersing or drenching parts of plants with a chemical solution.

The following insects are common pests in flower gardens. If you encounter an insect you cannot identify, send one and/or a sample of the evil work they have done to your state agricultural extension service for identification and recommended controls.

Ants. These familiar insects generally cause no trouble unless present in large colonies, in which case you should destroy them because they corral and store up aphids and aphid eggs and kill beneficial insects called aphid lions. Sprinkle the anthills with chlordane dust or set out ant traps. Note that although ants are often seen running all over peony buds and flowers, they themselves do no damage.

Aphids. Aphids are tiny sucking insects which cluster on the stems of roses, delphiniums and numerous other flowers. You may not at first see them, but you can tell they are at work when you notice that buds, flowers and leaves are distorted. If you don't do anything about them, entire plants will become stunted. Spraying with malathion, nicotine, rotenone or pyrethrum will kill them quickly. You can also protect plants with a systemic poison.

Asiatic garden beetles. These oval, ½-inch brown beetles are found east of the Mississippi River. They feed at night on leaves of a variety of flowers. Most of their damage is done near the ground. Spray with Sevin. Dusting your lawn in the spring with chlordane will kill the grubs.

Blister beetles.   These are slender ½-inch beetles colored black, brown, gray, yellow or striped. Their name derives from the fact that if you crush them in your fingers, they will blister your skin—so use Sevin to control them. They are widespread and attack many different flowers.

Colorado potato beetles.   A menace to potatoes, these also feed on the leaves of petunias, nicotiana and other flowers—not just in Colorado but almost everywhere. They are yellow beetles with wide, black-striped bodies and black-spotted heads. You may see their orange egg clusters on the undersides of leaves in the spring. Spray with Sevin.

European corn borers.   Found east of the Rockies, these pests do most damage when they are 1-inch whitish caterpillars with dark spots; but the time to get them is in late July and August when you may see the egg clusters on the undersides of dahlia, chrysanthemum and hollyhock leaves. Then spray several times with Sevin or rotenone.

Gladiolus thrips.   These tiny black insects with white on the wings may be a problem everywhere gladiolus are grown. They are hard to see but you'll know they're up to no good if gladiolus leaves develop silver streaks and then turn brown. Flowers of infected plants are deformed, if they open at all; and the bulbs are corky and worthless. The best way to prevent thrips is with a granular systemic poison scattered on the ground where the bulbs are planted. Thrips may also sometimes attack iris and a few other flowers but they don't turn up often.

Iris borers.   These pinkish, fat caterpillars up to 2 inches long make a nasty mess of iris once they get into the rhizomes in the summer. The rhizomes become riddled with holes and rotten; the leaves above turn slimy. Normally you can keep borers under control by cutting them out with a knife when you divide the rhizomes after blooming is finished. Rhizomes which are partially rotted should also be soaked in bichloride of mercury. If you have a particularly bad infestation of borers, however, spray the iris plants with malathion about once a week from the time they are 6 inches high until they start to bloom.

Japanese beetles. Japanese beetles are found here and there east of the Mississippi. They often appear in great numbers for a few years after they first get started; then they migrate elsewhere leaving a small rear guard behind. But even one beetle can do a lot of damage chewing on leaves and blossoms of big, bright-colored summer flowers such as zinnias and marigolds, and especially roses. Happily the beetles are as easy to spot as the damage they do. They are handsome, ½-inch oval fellows with coppery wings and metallic green bodies. You can crush them between your fingers or easily pick or brush them off into a can of kerosene. But for fastest results, spray with Sevin.

Leafhoppers. These are ⅛-inch wedge-shaped green insects which hop around and suck the juices of dahlias, marigolds and a few other flowers. Spray with malathion when you see them; or treat plants with a systemic poison.

Leaf miners. Leaf miners are tiny, white maggots which feed inside the leaves of columbines, asters, chrysanthemums, cinerarias, delphiniums and primroses. They leave whitish blotches or serpentine lines on the undersides of the leaves. Spray with malathion when you first notice this damage.

Leaf rollers. Leaf rollers are small, greenish caterpillars which roll leaves around themselves and then eat away happily. They attack hollyhocks, carnations and other flowers. Spray with Sevin.

Mites. These microscopic insects are a nuisance everywhere. They favor delphiniums, cyclamens and many bulbs, including tulips, daffodils, hyacinths and Easter lilies. Since you can barely see them, they are hard to cope with; but they give themselves away by causing leaves to turn brown and then drop. Leaves may also be distorted and plants stunted. To protect plants, treat with a systemic poison. Soaking bulbs in a systemic poison before planting will prevent damage at least during the year following.

Nematodes. Nematodes are also microscopic insects which live in soil everywhere. They feed on roots of numerous flowers, causing the plants to lose vigor, turn yellow and stop growing. The worst are called "root-knot" nematodes because they cause swellings on the roots. These are prevalent in California and the South; and the only sure way to control them is to treat the soil with a fumigant such as Nemafume, Dowfume, Chloropicrin or Nemagon. However, research has shown that soil which contains a goodly supply of humus has relatively few nematodes. And in cool-climate areas, where meadow nematodes are the main cause of trouble, growing marigolds for a summer will drive the pests out of the soil for as long as three years. (If marigolds are interspersed with other plants in a flower bed, change their location every year.)

Rose chafers. A pest in the Northeast, these are light-tan, ⅓-inch beetles with long legs which attack roses particularly but also go after peonies. They skeletonize leaves, feed on flower petals (especially of white flowers), and leave excrement on the flowers. Control by spraying with Sevin.

Rose sawflies. These wasp-like insects with transparent wings feed on rose leaves. Spray with malathion.

Tarnished plant bugs. These are flat, oval, ¼-inch bronze-colored bugs with a yellow mark on both sides of the body. They cause spots on leaves, which may also become deformed. Buds may wilt and not open. Spray with methoxychlor.

Thrips. These insects are similar to gladiolus thrips and cause similar damage to a number of other flowers. Control like gladiolus thrips.

Whiteflies. Whiteflies are tiny white moths which fly up in clouds when you brush against plants they are feeding on. They cause general weakening of plants such as ageratums and geraniums by sucking on leaves and stems. Control with malathion or a systemic poison.

BENEFICIAL INSECTS

Interest in friendly insects that prey on insect pests is growing by leaps and bounds. Those which have gained the most attention and are now widely available for sale to gardeners who want to establish colonies are the following:

Ladybugs. Also called ladybird beetles, these are pretty orange-red flying beetles with black spots. They feed voraciously on aphids and mealybugs.

Praying Mantises. Huge skeletal insects that feed on a wide variety of bugs, large and small. Fortunately they are said to leave ladybugs alone.

Aphid lions. The proper name of this beneficial insect is "green lacewing fly." The adult fly is up to ¾ inch long, green, and has transparent wings. The larvae are the real lions. They forage far and wide for aphids, mites, thrips, whiteflies and other pests. If you import aphid lions into your garden, you must kill the ants in the garden because they feed on the lions.

Trichogramma wasps. These are tiny wasps which do not harm humans but are the natural enemies of many moths and caterpillars. They kill these pests by laying their own eggs inside the moth eggs.

By themselves, beneficial insects cannot control all pests that attack flowers. They are useless against diseases and animal pests and are helpful only against certain insect pests. You must therefore use some of the other control methods discussed to protect your garden completely.

CONTROLLING DISEASES

For a general discussion of how to control diseases, see the preceding section, pages 52–55. The following are common diseases of flowers:

Anthracnose. On rose leaves anthracnose causes dark spots which develop whitish centers. On snapdragons, stems are girdled by dirty white spots. Spray with zineb. Destroy infected plant parts.

Aster yellows. This is a serious, widespread virus disease attacking annual asters. Leaves turn yellow and plants are stunted. Destroy diseased plants promptly. To control the spread of the disease, look for leafhoppers, which carry the disease, and spray with malathion, or use a systemic poison.

Black spot. This is the most troublesome disease affecting roses. You may run up against it anywhere, but it is most prevalent in humid climates. It causes distinct, roughly circular black spots with fringed edges on leaves. Control by spraying plants with phaltan every week to ten days from the time leaves first develop until frost. You can also use the systemic poison called Benomyl.

Botrytis blight. This is characterized by brown, rotten spots and a gray mold on leaves and petals of peonies, gladiolus, lilies, tulips and other flowers. The disease spreads fastest in cool, damp weather. Destroy infected plant parts. Spray with zineb or ferbam.

Bud blast. A disease of peonies, this prevents flower buds from opening; they then turn black. Flowers and leaves may turn brown. Pick off and destroy infected parts; and when the plant dies down in the fall, remove all remnants of stems and foliage and destroy them. Then, the following spring, you should spray the new shoots when they first appear and then twice more at ten-day intervals with zineb or ferbam.

Crown rot. Common in colder climates, crown rot attacks delphiniums and iris especially. You may notice it first during humid weather when white threads form at the base of the stems, and the stems then fall. The only possible way to stop the disease is to catch it promptly. Make a solution of 1 tablet of bichloride of mercury (a deadly poison) in 1 pint of water and drench the crown of the plant and surrounding soil. If the plant doesn't soon revive, or if it is already in hopeless shape, rip it out and destroy it. Then, before planting anything in the same area, disinfect the soil with more bichloride of mercury or fumigate with Chloropicrin.

Damping-off. This is an extremely common disease of all flowers grown from seeds. If the seeds germinate at all, the seedlings topple over and die. Fortunately, prevention is easy. Either sow the seeds in a sterile medium (see Chapter 5) or dust them with a seed disinfectant such as Thiram or captan.

Fusarium wilt. This disease is most often associated with annual asters but also affects carnations, gladiolus, lilies and narcissus, plus other plants. Plants become discolored and wilt without warning. Nothing will bring them back. And there is no real control. Plant wilt-resistant varieties, especially of asters. Destroy infected plants and sterilize the soil in which they were growing with formaldehyde.

Mildew. There are two common kinds of mildew. Downy mildew causes downy patches of white, gray or purple on foliage. Powdery mildew makes white, powdery blotches. As far as you are concerned, however, it doesn't make much difference which is which. Both occur in damp weather, spoil the appearance of plants and make them sickly. Garden phlox, zinnias, roses and calendulas are particularly affected; but other plants may also be attacked. Regular spraying for black spot and similar fungus diseases takes care of the problem on roses; and I use the same spray on the same schedule—but only during the summer months—on phlox, zinnias and calendulas. If mildew appears on other flowers, spray them with Karathane or zineb.

Rust. This is an aptly named disease because the brown or reddish spots that appear on leaves—usually in fairly cool weather—resemble rust on iron. Many plants are affected, most especially hollyhocks, snapdragons, asters and chrysanthemums. Spray with zineb or ferbam at the first sign of trouble and every ten days thereafter.

Soft rot. Mainly a disease of iris, soft rot also attacks calla lilies. It is characterized by discolored, slimy leaves and mushy rhizomes. The disease is spread by iris borers, so the best way to prevent it is to control them. If you fail to do this, seriously infected plants should be ripped out and destroyed. In the case of mild infections, cut the rotten areas out of the rhizomes and soak what is left for several hours in a solution of 1 tablet of bichloride of mercury in 1 pint of water. It's a good idea to sterilize the soil with this solution or with Chloropicrin before planting in it again.

Tulip fire. Common name given to botrytis blight of tulips (see Botrytis blight). Buying tulip bulbs from reliable sources will generally prevent trouble.

Verticillium wilt. This disease is very much like fusarium wilt except that it usually occurs in cooler weather and causes gradual yellowing and wilting. Many flowers are attacked. Annuals die. Perennials may survive for years, though gradually declining. Destroy infected plants. Treat the soil in which they grew with formaldehyde.

CONTROLLING ANIMAL PESTS

Chipmunks. Chipmunks eat bulbs, and if you have a sizable colony, they will do a lot of damage. Control them by placing Cyanogas (a deadly poison) in their burrows and seal all entrances. Or trap them in Havahart traps.

Dogs. Man's best friend does little, if any, damage to flowers unless you make the mistake of planting them across one of the paths he follows around your property; then he will beat a very visible path right through them. The obvious way to keep this from happening is to stay out of his way. The alternative is to put a low wire fence or an electric fence around the flowers.

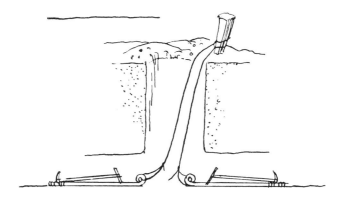

To trap gophers, place two traps in runway on either side of a trench and tie the traps to a stake.

Gophers. Thank goodness we don't have gophers in New England. I well remember a hillside garden my parents had one year in California. A family of gophers took up residence in it, and every time you looked at the garden it seemed as if the pests had dug another hole. Not just a little hole, but a big one with a big mound of dirt alongside. And the plants they damaged and killed by eating the roots and bulbs! Gophers —also called pocket gophers or, in the South, salamanders—are subterranean rodents found in many parts of the country. The only way to control them is with traps or poisoned baits.

Gopher traps, available from a garden-supplies store, are used as in the drawing. First dig a narrow trench between two new gopher holes and perpendicular to the burrow running between them. Then, after attaching flexible wires to two gopher traps, set one trap in the burrow on the right side of the trench and the second trap in the burrow on the left side of the trench. Attach the free ends of the wires to a stake so that the captured rodent cannot make off with a trap. Finally cover the trench rather loosely with a board, and sit back. The gopher is caught— hopefully—when he comes to investigate the sudden light and draft entering the burrow.

To control gophers with baits, cut sweet potatoes, white potatoes, turnips, carrots or beets into ½- by 1-inch pieces and dust them with powdered strychnine alkaloid or thallium sulfate. Open a burrow, as for traps, and place the baits well back in it; then refill the trench. If the gophers are not soon disposed of, make new baits from another vegetable.

Mice.   These little pests make mincemeat of bulbs and may also feed on roots of other plants. Control them with traps or poisoned baits. Bulbs particularly favored by mice should be enclosed in wire mesh boxes (see Chapter 8).

Moles.   Contrary to popular opinion, moles eat grubs, not bulbs. But quite apart from the damage they do to lawns, they cause trouble in flower gardens by digging tunnels which mice then use to reach bulbs. So you should get rid of the moles. Although many ways of doing this have been tried, none is very successful. I've found a steel mole trap about as good as anything. Placed across a burrow, this comes down like a guillotine with spears (instead of a blade) when the miscreant passes underneath.

Rabbits.   Rabbits usually leave flowers alone if they have vegetables or other plants more to their liking for browsing; but without such distractions, you may have problems with them. Unhappily, they are not easily discouraged unless you have a gun or a hungry cat. Putting a foot-high fence around a garden works well enough but doesn't add to the beauty of the garden. Repellents are for the most part a waste of time. For the tenderhearted, a Havahart trap is pretty good; but to get rid of the captured rabbit, you must carry him a mile or so down the road before you release him. He won't return to you; but he will have a happy time in someone else's garden.

Slugs.   These are slimy mollusks without shells. In my garden they don't grow much larger than flies; in California, they're brutes. But regardless of size, when they slither out across a flower garden at night, they do much damage feeding on leaves and flowers. To control them, use pellets, dust, meal or sprays containing metaldehyde. (Some baits also contain arsenic, which increases their effectiveness somewhat but also increases the hazard considerably.) Scatter the dry products around your entire property—not just in the flower garden but also in the thick plantings, such as groundcovers and hedges and lush vegetable gardens, where the slugs congregate during the day. On a sparsely planted property, scatter the baits under planks and stones. Metaldehyde sprays are just as effective as the dry baits but are used primarily when you want to cover a very large area.

Snails. Snails differ from slugs in that they have shells. But this doesn't keep them from doing just as much damage. Control in the same way.

·4·

GARDENING
IN CONTAINERS

There are various reasons for raising flowers in pots, tubs, window boxes, planters and other types of containers. Those that fall under the heading of aesthetics are:

—To let you change your garden around quickly, easily and inexpensively whenever you want it to look different.

—To bring the beauty of flowers right onto the terrace, patio or deck—something that is difficult to do with flowers in beds.

—To place spots of color here and there around the property—wherever you want a bright accent.

—To decorate the exterior walls of the house. This is done usually with window boxes but can also be done by hanging pots on walls much as you hang pictures on interior walls.

—To allow you to grow flowers in spots which are too shady for a permanent planting. This is accomplished simply by moving a pot of flowers into a shady spot for a couple of days, then replacing it with another pot while the first flowers get their strength back in the sun.

Practical reasons for raising flowers in containers are:

—To reduce normal flower-growing chores without cutting down proportionally on your display of flowers. Improbable as it may seem, this is possible because you can readily bring flowers in containers close to where you live your life outdoors. By thus giving prominence to a few flowers, you create the illusion of many flowers. Or, putting it in another way, a few flowers close up in pots often have the impact of numerous flowers in distant beds.

Pots and window boxes filled with geraniums bring glowing color to a quiet flagstone terrace.

—To let you grow flowers where you couldn't grow them otherwise. For example, my eldest daughter and her husband recently bought an old house with a side driveway which is paved right up to the foundations. It's not a pretty arrangement and needs planting of some sort to take the curse off it; yet planting in a bed is patently impossible unless they tear up the driveway. So they have solved the problem simply by standing potted plants on the paving next to the foundations.

A final reason for growing flowers in containers is the least complex of all: They just look pretty. There is a charm and innocence about a container full of flowers that has much of the impact of a baby. We have no difficulty in encompassing and understanding it; and the more we look at it, the better it makes us feel.

CONTAINERS

Anything that is big enough to hold a few inches of soil can be used as a flower container; but I am happy to say I haven't seen too many old bathtubs or washboilers giving service in this way. Generally, people who plant flowers in containers realize that the appearance of the container has a very decided bearing on the beauty of the picture they are trying to create; so there are few bizarre containers to be seen in gardens. On the contrary, most are simple and neat in design. Most also fall into some standard classifications.

Flowerpots.   The choice here is between the ordinary red clay pot, the glazed ceramic pot and the plastic pot. Let's dispose of the last first. It is an excellent container: quite strong, light in weight and very easy to keep clean. But it's a little too artificial and drab in appearance for outdoor use. It just doesn't go with nature.

The old red clay pot, on the other hand, looks well in any garden setting as soon as it loses its initial rawness (which it does quickly). Furthermore, the pot is good because it is porous enough to let the soil "breathe." But on the negative side, it is heavy, breakable and hard to keep clean.

Two ideal plants for containers: geraniums and chrysanthemums.

Glazed ceramic pots are much less standardized than other pots in size and shape. All are designed first and foremost to be decorative. But in addition they are quite durable and cleanable. The main fault with them is that many of them do not provide bottom drainage (this is gardening parlance meaning that they do not have drain holes in the bottom).

Bottom drainage is important in flowerpots—and also in all other types of containers—because it allows moisture to escape and thus keeps the soil from becoming waterlogged. This, in turn, permits plant roots to receive oxygen and guards them against drowning. Note that I didn't say bottom drainage is essential, because it is possible to raise flowers successfully in containers with solid bottoms. But you must change the soil more often, water and fertilize more carefully—and even so, failure ever threatens.

Wooden tubs and boxes. These are usually larger than pots, and for that reason are more often used for shrubs and small trees than for flowers. But if you want them for flowers, go ahead and use them. They should be constructed of redwood or cypress, which resist decay; and when you use them, be sure to raise them about an inch off the paving or ground to allow air to circulate underneath. All ready-built tubs and boxes I have ever seen had drainage holes. If you happen to acquire one that doesn't, correct matters with a drill.

Concrete containers. These come in almost limitless sizes and shapes. I happen to be particularly taken with the big saucer-shaped "dishes" because there are no other containers quite like them and they look delightful when filled with small flowers and placed in a sunny corner of a terrace. But you can find other designs equally pleasing. The containers have a whitish-to-gray, sandy texture. Some have drain holes, but most do not. All are heavy. I don't advise planting them with any idea that you're going to move them around as the spirit pleases. Choose their location before you fill them with soil.

Window boxes. You can buy ready-made metal or fiberglass window boxes—but don't detract from the appearance of your house in this

An old Nantucket house in October. Window boxes crammed with patience are still blooming as bravely as they did in early summer. They will continue until frost.

way. Ready-made wooden boxes are better. Boxes which a good handyman with a sense of proportion builds himself are better still.

Use 1-inch redwood or cypress boards and fasten them together with brass screws. Suit the length of the box to the location. Inside depth should be 8 to 9 inches, inside width at the top of the box, 10 to 12 inches. Drill ½-inch holes at 6-inch intervals in the bottom for drainage. And, whatever else you do, make certain the box is securely anchored to the side of the house. Just the other day I read of a tragic accident in which a little child was killed by a falling window box.

Hanging containers. You can make almost any container into a hanging container by hooping wires, twine or slender chains around it. But the common type sold in most good garden-supplies stores is a wire or plastic mesh basket lined on the bottom and sides with green papier-mâché which is, in turn, lined with sheets of sphagnum moss (sometimes the papier-mâché is omitted). Because the baskets are very light, they must be hooked securely to a terrace roof, tree limb, etc., to keep them from sailing away in a strong breeze.

SELECTING CONTAINERS TO PLACE ON THE GROUND

Hanging baskets and window boxes are eliminated from this discussion.

Regardless of the containers' construction, you must consider these points in selecting them:

1. The size in relation to the size of the flowers above and below ground. This is both an aesthetic and practical matter. Obviously, you don't want to put a great big plant into a little container, or vice versa, because it would look silly. But neither can you put plants such as standard roses and daylilies into small pots because their root systems are too extensive.

There are, to my knowledge, no written rules for fitting pots to flowers; but the following list gives you an idea of which size pot is best for a *single* specimen of certain popular pot plants. The pots referred to are so-called standard pots, in which the diameter equals the depth. "Three-quarter" pots are three-quarters of the standard pot depth; pans—used mainly for small bulbs—are half the standard depth.

Recommended Pot Sizes for Single Flowering Plants

	Diameter (inches)
Begonia, wax	3
Begonia, tuberous	8
Chrysanthemum	6–8
Elephant's ear	18–24
Geranium	4
Hyacinth	4
Lily	5
Marigold, dwarf	4
Patience	4
Petunia	6
Rose, miniature	6–8

2. Whether the potted plants will be in a windy location. If so, the

containers should be heavy and have a broad base; otherwise they will be blown over like tenpins.

3. The weight of the container. I alluded to this before, but it bears emphasis. Many containers are heavy to start with, and when filled with damp soil, they border on the immovable. Yet one of the joys of container gardening is being able to move your plants around to change the scene, follow the sun, etc.

There are, of course, ways to move even the weightiest containers. For instance, you can place them—before they are filled with soil—on small dollies. You can invest in a hand truck like that used by moving men. Or you can slide the container on to a snow shovel or piece of stout canvas and drag it across the ground. Even so, a big concrete tub filled with soil and plants is something to contend with, and therefore—perhaps—something to avoid.

4. Whether the container provides bottom drainage. I've already said you can get along with one which does not. But given a choice between two containers, one with drain holes and one without, take the former.

PREPARING SOIL FOR POTTED PLANTS

An excellent general-purpose mixture consists of 2 parts loam, 1 part coarse sand or vermiculite, 1 part peat moss and $\frac{1}{16}$ part balanced fertilizer or bone meal. Mix together thoroughly.

PLANTING FLOWERS IN CONTAINERS

Unless containers are brand new, scrub all with hot detergent solution and chlorine bleach, and rinse well. This is necessary to destroy bacteria and microscopic insects left over from the previous plants.

Soak all red clay pots, both new and old, for several hours in clean water in order to saturate the pores and prevent them from drawing moisture out of the potting soil.

Cover drain holes in each pot with one or two stones or bits of broken pot (shards). Then cover the entire bottom with a layer of pebbles or small crushed rock. This layer should be about ½ inch thick in containers under 10 inches in diameter; 1 inch thick in larger containers. In containers without bottom drainage, a much deeper layer of pebbles is required. Use a 1-inch thickness in containers under 6 inches across; a layer of 2 inches in those between 6 and 12 inches; and 3 inches in all others.

Fill the container about halfway with soil and firm it slightly. Then set the plant in the center, spread out the roots and fill in around them to within ½ to 1 inch of the container rim. Firm well. Moisten the soil with water and finish with about an ounce of starter solution, a diluted liquid fertilizer. Set small plants aside in a bright but not sunny place for a day or two until they become established enough to resist wilting. Large plants with good root systems can be placed right out in the sun, however.

CARING FOR POTTED PLANTS

Flowers in containers are handled more or less like those in the garden. In some ways they need more attention; in others, less.

Regular, thorough watering is of greatest importance because the soil dries out very rapidly. In hot, dry weather, in fact, some plants—especially those in hanging baskets—may need to be watered daily.

Water as soon as the soil surface is dry. If the container has bottom drainage, apply the water until it starts to trickle out the bottom. In containers without drain holes you just have to guess how much is enough. Underwatering is as bad as overwatering.

If you get weary of the never-ending watering chore, you can simplify it to some extent by mulching the soil in each container with peat moss. Another, more elaborate, trick is to set one container inside a larger container, and fill the space between with damp peat moss or sphagnum moss.

Fertilize each plant lightly about once every six to eight weeks. Use any kind of balanced fertilizer. Liquids, however, are easier to apply and are instantly available to the plant roots.

Repotting of flowers during the summer is rarely necessary. But if a plant for no apparent reason begins to perform with less than normal vigor, it may be because it is rootbound. To determine whether this is the case, rap the sides of the container with a stick to loosen the root ball and slide out the plant. If the ball of earth is covered almost completely with small white roots, replant the plant in the next-size-larger container. You can scrape some of the pebbles off the bottom of the root ball but don't disturb it otherwise. Just set it in the new container, pack fresh soil around it, and apply water and fertilizer.

What to do with potted plants when winter comes is a problem because, except in the warmest climates, they will not survive if they are left standing around the terrace. From Zone 5 southward, containers with bottom drainage which are planted to perennials or hardy bulbs should be set into a trench in the garden. Put a layer of gravel in the bottom of the trench to assure good drainage. The rims of the containers should be level with the soil surface. Fill around the containers with soil, and cover them with several inches of hay or leaves.

Undercover storage should be provided for all plants in undrained containers; all roses; and all perennials and hardy bulbs in Zone 3 and 4. Wait until the plants die down. Then move them, still in their containers, into a place where the temperature holds between 33° and 40°F. They should not have sun and actually do not require light. Water them just enough during the winter to keep the soil from getting bone dry.

Perennials and roses should be repotted the following spring, while they are dormant, to give them some fresh soil to grow on. Slide the root balls out of the pots and scratch off about ½ inch of the soil on the sides and bottom of the balls. Then replant in the same pots with fresh soil mixture. Do not apply fertilizer until growth starts.

Hardy bulbs should be allowed to bloom and die down before they are dug up, divided and repotted in fresh soil.

Don't, however, count on any plants growing in containers to go on and on for years, like those in the garden. The cramped life is debilitating.

LATH SHELTERS

In California and other warm areas with intense sunlight, a number of plants such as tuberous begonias and caladiums cannot survive unless grown in light shade. The easiest way to provide such shade, if you don't have trees, is to erect a lath shelter. This can be a latticed room with sidewalls or simply a latticed roof supported on wires or posts.

For a crude shelter, use snow fencing. But a much more attractive, yet simple, shelter can be built out of 1 × 2- or 1 × 3-inch boards—not

In southern California, a latticed roof—like a lath shelter—shades several enormous amaryllis in pots from the blistering sun.

real laths—nailed to a framework. The boards are laid parallel with spaces between them equal to the width of the boards. This gives a very light shade. For fairly deep shade, reduce the spaces between boards to 1 inch. The roof of the shelter may be pitched, slanted in one direction, or flat; but in all cases, the boards should run north and south so that the sun will come through at different angles throughout the day. If the shelter has lath walls, apply the boards vertically, horizontally or diagonally.

Potted plants inside lath shelters may be placed on the ground, arranged on benches in tiers, or hung from the walls and roof. The plants don't care. The arrangement is usually dictated by the decorative effect you wish to achieve. Lath shelters can be exceedingly attractive—and a great many actually are used to protect not only plants but also gardeners.

·5·
DESIGNING
FLOWER BEDS

I mentioned the many places in which flowers are grown in Chapter 1. But most gardeners—especially new gardeners—raise them in beds, which are often referred to as borders.

Undulating lines of these flower beds, filled with roses, perennials and a few annuals and shrubs, relieve the rigid lines of an almost square corner lot. The pergola is for ornament only.

To be successful, all flower beds must meet several requirements.

1. There must be some reason for them. It's not enough that you want a bed simply to raise a few flowers for cutting. A flower bed is one of the important elements of the property; and in the average small or medium-size property today, all elements should have a purpose, and all should work together to give the property an attractive, cohesive quality.

I remember one development in the town where I used to live which for some reason incorporated the greatest mishmash of flower beds I have ever seen. The residents of the development loved flowers—that was evident in the great number and variety they raised. But the flower beds themselves often didn't make sense. One house had a round bed sitting out in the middle of the front yard like a basketball tossed aside by children after a game. Another had a ribbon of mismatched flowers edging the shrubbery border in front of the house foundations. Another had an irregular bed of flowers surrounding a telephone pole—thus making a feature of the ugly pole.

Obviously this is not the way to make a flower bed—as a whim or an afterthought. On the contrary, you should use the special beauty of a flower bed to contribute to the overall beauty of the property.

You might, for instance, use it to face down a high fence or conceal an unattractive foundation wall. You might use it to edge a walk or driveway. You might use it to mark one area off from another. You might use it as an accent to draw the eye to a particular part of the property. And so forth.

And even if your main aim in having a flower bed is to supply flowers for the dining table, front hall and mantel, you should nevertheless locate and design it with utmost care.

2. The shape of the bed must be related to its location. Flower beds take many shapes. They may be rectangles, squares, diamonds, hexagons, octagons, circles, ovals, half moons, undulating ribbons, rectan-

Sinuous flower bed following the contours of the ground was designed to conceal a definite drop in elevation. The bed also gives the lawn area to the right a feeling of useful immediacy to people sitting on the terrace (not shown, at right) and at the same time adds to the apparent depth of the lawn area to the left. The color scheme of the bed changes with the season.

Beds of white tulips and blue ajuga (a ground cover) form rings around a circular lawn and within a circular wall. The beds are edged with Japanese holly.

gles with scalloped edges. They may have no definable shape at all—be what swimming-pool builders call free-form designs.* But whatever the shape you decide on, it should fit logically into the property and contribute to the appearance of the property.

3. Unless you live in a subtropical climate, the bed should not be in the direct line of view from the room, or rooms, in which you spend most time in winter. This statement may surprise you. "But if I put in a flower bed, I want to see it," you protest. True—but not in winter. In winter, flower beds from Zone 9 northward have nothing to recommend them. They are simply bare ground, sometimes covered with a messy mulch. Beds for roses are even worse.

It is unusual when the view from a house in winter is as attractive as it is in summer. But it should not be unattractive. And for that reason, the all-too-common practice of placing a flower bed in the middle of the view should be avoided. Let a tree, a handsome shrub or a piece of sculpture be the centerpiece, and put the flower bed somewhere else.

* To lay out a bed with curving or irregular edges, string a flexible hose out on the ground.

Never fear: it will not be lost, because in warm weather you spend more time out in the yard and less time looking out the window.

My own garden is a good illustration of what I mean. In winter, when we are indoors, our principal view is of a pretty lawn dominated by two magnificent pin oaks and, behind them, three arborvitaes standing tall and dark against the sky. At the east end of the lawn, behind the oaks, is a stone wall. At the south is our flower garden, but from the house it is only barely visible because it is three feet lower than the lawn and partially obscured by an open iron fence.

In the summer, the picture, in effect, takes a quarter turn. We are outdoors more than we are indoors. We live on the terrace, which is on

This carefully laid out garden is designed primarily for viewing from the house, which is at a higher elevation. In winter the flower beds are empty and unattractive but the owner has compensated for this by giving the entire garden distinctive form and surrounding it with fine trees and shrubs.

This small square garden is divided into sections by paths (not visible here) so the beds can be easily tended. At this season, shasta daisies and white phlox predominate. The informal edging in the foreground is planted with germander.

the north side of the lawn, and our principal view is of the flower beds directly across the lawn.

4. The flower bed must be of a size you can manage easily. Otherwise it becomes a burden rather than a pleasure.

How big is just right? I wish I knew. My most successful flower bed measured 4 by 25 feet. It supplied more and better flowers than any bed I ever had, yet it required little work—which was a good thing because the rest of the property, being new and large, required a great deal.

It seems to me that the only sensible way to get into flower gardening is to start with a small bed—say, one measuring 30 square feet. See how much work it gives you during the first year, and then adjust up or down accordingly.

SIZING A FLOWER BED

Regardless of the types of plant used in flower beds, all beds are laid out in the same way. As noted, the shape of the bed can be anything that suits the location. The length of the bed can also be variable. But in all cases the depth should be limited so that you can tend the flowers and pick them without stepping into the bed among them. I stress this point because it is impossible to walk in a lush flower bed without trampling or otherwise damaging the inhabitants. Furthermore, walking in a bed compacts the soil and impedes plant growth.

The precise depth of a bed depends somewhat on the size of the gardener and the slope of the bed from front to back. As a rule of thumb, if a more or less flat bed is accessible from one side only (for example, if there's a fence at the back of the bed), it should not be more than 30 inches deep—about as far as the average person can comfortably stretch and work. If a bed is accessible from both sides, it should not be more than 60 inches deep.

A vast garden created primarily to provide cut flowers. The rectangular beds, separated by gravel walks, are sized so the owner can easily cultivate them and gather flowers from both sides. The towering flowers behind the roses at left are delphiniums.

If a bed slopes upward at an angle of 45° (which is about as steep as a bed should be if you want to have any space for plants after putting in rocks or timbers to control erosion), it should not be more than 42 inches from the front to the back edges. This is the maximum depth, whether the bed is accessible from one or two sides, because you cannot work in a flower bed from the top side down.

As the slope of a bed decreases from 45°, its depth should also decrease until a point is reached where it becomes possible to work the bed from both sides, not just the low side. I judge this to be when the slope does not exceed 10°.

The height of the surface of the bed is another dimension which should be considered.

In a new flower bed—particularly one to which you have added considerable quantities of humus, gravel, etc.—the soil surface is higher than that of the surrounding area. Within a few weeks, however, the soil settles and the discrepancy is reduced; but it may still be objectionable from an appearance standpoint and because the soil gradually drifts out of the bed. This situation can be corrected by removing enough of the soil from the bed to bring the surface down to within 2 inches of the surrounding area. As I said in Chapter 2, I do not find this slight elevation a problem, especially since it usually decreases with time. On the other hand, there is little doubt that a bed is improved if its surface is about 1 inch *below* the adjacent ground. It looks better. The soil stays in it. And if you put an edging of metal, brick or other material around it, it maintains its crisp lines.

RAISED BEDS

The alternative to this type of more or less level-with-the-surrounding-ground bed is a raised bed—a bed elevated 6 to 24 inches above the ground and confined within masonry or wood walls.

Raised beds are easy to manage because you don't have to bend down so far to reach the soil. You can even sit on the walls around a bed while you work. Of greater importance, flowers in the beds are protected from traffic—dogs, running children and errant grownups. Grass and tree roots cannot encroach upon the beds to compete with the flowers. And if you happen to have a naturally high water table, a

A raised bed planted mainly with petunias is used to relieve the blank wall and reduce its apparent size.

raised bed elevates the plants so that the roots are not constantly immersed.

Aesthetically, a raised bed is often desirable in a flat yard because it gives elevation to the yard. Even better, if placed against a high wall, it makes the wall look lower and less prisonlike. Little wonder that raised beds are especially popular in California, where the small lots are often surrounded by walls.

The dimensions of raised beds are the same as those for normal beds. The soil surface *must* be at least 1 inch below the walls enclosing the bed; and if the drainage is slow, 2 inches are better.

ARRANGING THE FLOWERS

Whether it is raised or level with the ground, a flower bed which is accessible from one side is arranged with the lowest flowers in front, the

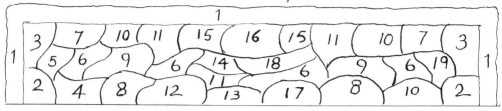

How to lay out a flower bed in clumps and drifts. This plan is for a mixed bed of annuals and perennials. The color scheme is essentially pink, white and blue. 1. White sweet alyssum. 2. Carpathian harebell. 3. Blue petunia. 4. Pink zinnia. 5. Rose phlox. 6. White balloonflower. 7. Yellow snapdragon. 8. Yellow marigold. 9. Blue flax. 10. Rose petunia. 11. Red zinnia. 12. Baby's breath. 13. Rose-pink dahlia. 14. Yellow daylily. 15. Blue veronica. 16. White petunia, 17. Shasta daisy. 18. Pink phlox. 19. Blue salvia.

intermediates in the middle and the tallest at the rear. In a bed accessible from two sides, the tallest flowers are in the center and you scale down from these to the front and back edges.

The flowers are usually arranged in clumps of three, five or seven plants of the same variety. These may be interspersed with a few big single plants which serve as accents. And sometimes there are long drifts of a single variety. If used, edgings around beds may be of a single variety or of two or three varieties of the same species (for example, white, pink and blue petunias).

The clumps, drifts and single plants are grouped together like eggs in a basket or logs in a woodpile. The effect is of a quilt with sizable patches of color blending together. This results from the fact (to re-emphasize the first and third sentences in the preceding paragraph) that the plants in each clump or drift are of the same variety—for example, Blue Bedder salvia in this clump, Rosie O'Day alyssum in this clump and Yellow Climax marigold in this clump. The mistake new gardeners too often make is to buy mixtures of seeds or plants because, even though they clump together the petunias, the marigolds, the zinnias, etc., each clump has flowers of different color and the garden winds up with an overall pepper-and-salt look.

Providing the right spaces between plants within each clump and from one clump to the next is one of the most worrisome jobs for new gardeners. In a note she gave me as I was starting this book, my youngest daughter—the newest gardener in the family—wrote: "And please be sure to tell how much space to give plants." This I have done in the descriptions of favorite flowers in Chapters 6–10. If you should forget these figures while planting a garden, use the following rule-of-thumb suggestions:

Space flowers that grow no more than 6 inches high 6 to 8 inches apart.

Space flowers that grow 6 to 12 inches high 8 to 10 inches apart.

Space flowers that grow more than 1 foot high 12 to 15 inches apart.

Space giant flowers such as cosmos, tithonias and sunflowers 2 to 3 feet apart.

When flowers requiring different spacing are planted next to each other, divide each of the two figures in half and add the answers. The result indicates the proper spacing. Example: If you plant a flower requiring 6 inches of space next to one requiring 12 inches, provide spacing of 3 inches plus 6 inches—9 inches.

If you follow these recommendations, use the higher of the two figures given for each classification of plants if your soil is of average quality and if you provide average care. The closer spacings should be used only if you have good soil, if you keep the plants very well watered at all times and if you fertilize them every four to six weeks with a balanced inorganic plant food.

EDGING FLOWER BEDS

The easiest way to edge a flower bed is to make the bed adjacent to a strip of paving or a wall, or simply to keep a slight trench cut around it with a spade. I don't urge you to do anything more elaborate. But if you do, there are some practical points to think about.

Edging a bed with metal helps to maintain its lines. But the aluminum rolls sold for the purpose are of next to no value. They are so flimsy that when you step on them, they crumple and your crisp lines fade. Semi-rigid steel edging is far superior—and also much more expensive.

Bricks form an attractive edging if buried upright, with the narrow

A tiny flower bed with assorted small perennials is set out from the wall of the house so it will not be in the deep shade of the roof overhang. A raised redwood edging keeps out the gravel on the walk.

Lush strips of candytuft edge two larger borders filled with perennials and tree peonies. The unusual lath house is used for shade-loving potted plants.

The unusual shape of this bed of tulips is derived from the shape of the property at this point. The bed is flanked on both sides and at the near end with similar beds. All are surrounded with dwarf boxwood.

edge parallel to the edge of the bed. Bricks laid flat don't stay in place; and they also tend to topple if buried upright but with the wide side parallel to the bed.

One of the advantages of using bricks for edging is that they greatly simplify mowing grass alongside a bed. This is because one wheel of the mower rolls along the top of the bricks so that you don't have to struggle to hold the machine upright.

When a flower bed adjoins a path or driveway paved with gravel, the edging of brick, flat stones, steel, redwood, etc. between them should be raised about 2 inches above the gravel in order to keep it out of the bed.

An edging is also raised, of course, if a bed is higher than the adjacent ground. In this case, if the bed adjoins a lawn area, the grass next to the edging must be trimmed by hand unless a mowing strip at least 4 inches wide is installed between the lawn and edging, flush with the lawn surface. The mowing strip is made of bricks, stones, concrete, redwood timbers—usually the same material as the edging (except when the edging is steel).

Edgings of evergreen plants—the favorite is dwarf boxwood—have little practical value except to keep trash from blowing out of the flower bed into the adjoining area, or vice versa. They are often used, however, to frame a bed visually, just as a picture frame is used to improve the appearance of a painting. And, to a limited extent, they help to conceal the soil, mulching material, spent bulbs, etc., in the bed. On the other hand, don't overlook the fact that they require considerable maintenance.

·6·

GROWING
ANNUALS

Annuals are plants that come up from seed, bloom and die within a few months (perennials which bloom within a few months of seeding are generally considered to be annuals because they are handled in the same way). The group is large, colorful and accommodating; and it is essential if you want profuse bloom in July and August. No other category of flowers gives as much bloom in the heat of summer.

As container plants, annuals are outstanding because you don't have to worry about carrying them through the winter. But most annuals wind up in flower beds either by themselves or mixed in with perennials, biennials and a few bulbs.

BUYING ANNUALS

If my favorite garden-supplies stores are any criteria, more and more people are buying the annuals they need for their gardens. Certainly this is the easiest way to acquire plants, but it is also the most expensive and the selections offered are somewhat limited. Also, since the plants are identified only with a label, you can't tell exactly what they are going to look like when fully grown.

On the other hand, the plants offered for sale are almost always well grown and, at the start of the planting season, sturdy. But if you wait until late spring before making your purchase, you may be disappointed because the selection becomes even more limited and, worse, the quality of the plants deteriorates because they have been too long confined to small flats. Whenever you buy, take a good look at the condition of the plants. The soil in which they are growing should be damp. The plants themselves should be bright green, well leafed out and not too tall or gawky. Don't pick out a flat of plants just because they happen to have flower buds, which may, in some cases, already be open.

RAISING PLANTS FROM SEEDS

I get a thrill out of raising annuals and other plants from seeds. Watching the tiny green shoots break through the soil surface, put out leaves, stretch upward and finally bloom is to witness a miracle. And though the part I play in the process is insignificant, it is nonetheless deeply satisfying.

If there were no other reasons for raising annuals this way, this one would be enough. But there are other reasons. (1) It is much cheaper than buying plants. (2) You have a wider selection. (3) Since the seed catalogs and the seed packets sold in stores have excellent illustrations, you know what you're getting. And (4) even though it takes about six to ten weeks to bring plants to the flowering stage, the whole process is fun.

Whether you buy seeds from large mail-order seedsmen or in a garden-supplies store, a hardware store or a supermarket doesn't make a great deal of difference. The mail-order houses offer more variety, but the quality in all cases is excellent. Seeds harvested from annuals you have grown yourself may also be of excellent quality (and they also may not be); but their main drawback is that they may not come true— meaning that the plants they produce may not resemble the parent plants. So it is better to stick with commercially grown seeds.

It's also a good idea to buy fresh seeds every year. This is because seeds lose viability with age. True, a high percentage of one-year-old seeds may germinate, but don't count on it. Still older seeds are even chancier.

One question that never occurred to me until one of my daughters raised it is: "How many of the seeds in a packet should you plant?" The answer I gave her was "If the seed is fresh, sow just a few more seeds than the number of plants you want."

This didn't satisfy her. "You mean they'll all come up?"

"Almost, if they are good seeds—and I've never bought any that weren't good. True, there will be a few that won't germinate; and there will also be a few that, although they do germinate, turn into weak little plants. But if you want a dozen plants, you really shouldn't have to sow more than fifteen seeds."

She still wasn't satisfied. "Yes, but how many seeds are in a packet? Bill and I just bought six dollars' worth because we wanted to be sure of having plenty of zinnias and marigolds and so forth. But you make it sound as if we overordered."

"Well, if you were trying to buy a wide assortment of annuals in lots of colors, you probably didn't. But if you were just buying a quantity of plants, you did. I don't know how many flower seeds are in most packets. In the case of some of the newest and choicest varieties, of course, you are told. The catalog says fifty seeds or maybe ten seeds for a dollar; and the packets themselves are labeled with the number of seeds, too. But if the flowers you buy are older varieties, the seeds are parceled out into packets by weight and you don't know how many you have except by counting—which you're not about to do."

"So—" she said—"how many should I plant?"

"Well," I said after hemming and hawing, "you just sort of make an estimate. If I think I want a dozen Primrose Climax marigolds, for instance, I plant a single row of seeds across a four-by-six-inch flat. I don't actually count out the seeds, but they're so big it's easy to make a close guess about what counts as twelve to fifteen. But when I sow tiny seeds, I'm really flying blind. For instance, petunia seeds are so little there's no way of telling how many you sow; so if I want, say, three dozen plants of white petunias, I make two four-inch rows in a flat and sow the seeds as thinly as possible. Usually I wind up with a good many more petunia seedlings than I want, but no matter: when I transplant them to another flat, I save a few more than I really need to compensate for any mortality, and throw the rest away."

"In other words," my daughter said, "you plant a few more seeds than you want plants, but you don't use up a whole packet of seed."

"That's it," I answered. "I think the only time I ever sow a whole packet of annuals is when I start with one that's labeled fifty seeds or whatever. If you sow that entire six dollars' worth of seeds you bought, you'll probably wind up with enough plants to blanket your entire back yard."

"Why don't garden books ever tell you things like that?" she said, getting in the last word. "Six dollars down the drain!"

Where and when you sow seeds depends partly on how anxious you are to have flowers, but mainly on the annuals themselves. Seeds of hardy annuals, such as California poppies and cornflowers, can be sown outdoors in early spring or sometimes in the preceding fall because both seeds and plants have high resistance to freezing weather. Tender annuals such as zinnias and petunias, on the other hand, can be started outdoors only after danger of frost is past; so in order to have early bloom, seeds of these plants are often sown "under glass"—either in the house or in a coldframe or hotbed. (Hardy annuals may also be started under glass.)

SOWING SEEDS OUTDOORS

Hardy and tender annuals are handled in the same way; only the timing is different.

The seeds may be sown in a special propagating bed and then transplanted into the flower bed, or they may be sown in the flower bed where the plants are to grow. The latter procedure eliminates transplanting; and in the case of a few annuals which are hard to transplant, this procedure is essential. But by starting seeds in a propagating bed, space that would be devoted to them in the flower bed can perhaps be filled with early spring bulbs.

In either case, the soil in the seed bed should be turned over, enriched with a little fertilizer (and perhaps humus and lime), pulverized thoroughly and raked smooth. Before sowing the seeds, treat them with a disinfectant to prevent damping-off. Then sow the seeds thinly, with a little space between them so they will be easier to handle later on.

If you are sowing the seeds in a flower bed, scatter them casually across the space you want the plants to fill. In a propagating bed, however, sow the seeds in rows and leave about 6 inches between rows. Scatter a thin covering of soil over the seeds if they are large; but if they are minute, leave them uncovered. Then tamp lightly with a rake and sprinkle with water if the soil is dry.

Keep the soil damp but not sopping during germination and after the seedlings appear. Rip out weeds, but avoid cultivating the soil, since this may dislodge the seedlings. When the seedlings have their first true leaves* and are large enough to handle, thin them out so they will have less competition and more room to grow. Thinning is done by pulling up the plants or by nipping them off at the soil line with your fingernails. In a propagating bed, leave 1 to 1½ inches between the plants you keep. In a flower bed you can thin the plants immediately to the spacing required between full-grown plants; but on the chance that some of the seedlings may die, I thin them twice—first to about half their ultimate spacing and then all the way.

SOWING SEEDS INDOORS

This is the easiest way to get a head start on the season. Seeds started indoors six to ten weeks before the last spring frost (for the mean date of the last spring frost in your community, see the map on pages 96–97) should be ready for planting in the flower bed immediately after the frost.

Sow the seeds in any kind of clean container. I usually use plastic flats measuring approximately 5 × 7 × 1½ inches. But you can use flowerpots, tin cans, plastic food-freezer boxes, deep cake pans, etc.

For soil, use garden soil, ready-mixed potting soil, vermiculite, sand, sphagnum moss or a special seed-starter mix sold under such names as Jiffy-Mix and Redi-Earth. If you use garden soil, it is advisable to sterilize it by baking small batches in a 200° F. oven for two hours. If this is not done, you must treat seeds with a disinfectant to prevent damping-off.

Potting soils are generally sterilized prior to packaging (but check the label) so it is unnecessary to bake them or to treat the seed.

The other mediums are naturally sterile. For this reason, and also because they are inexpensive, for years I used vermiculite, sand or sphagnum moss. But they had one disadvantage: unlike soil, they were devoid of nutrients, so I had to remember to give the seedlings a dose of liquid fertilizer once a week.

---

* The first "leaves" put out by seedlings are actually cotyledons. These differ in shape from the true leaves and eventually wither away. The first true leaves are actually the second leaves to appear.

Then, several years ago, the seed-starter mixes came on the market. I have used these ever since, and I recommend that you do also. Composed of peat moss, vermiculite and fertilizer, they are the perfect growing medium for flowers. You don't have to disinfect seeds. You don't have to feed the seedlings. And the plants grow like weeds.

To grow annuals from seed in one of these special mixes, toss a quantity of the mix into a bucket and add water, stirring until the mix is damp but not so wet that it oozes when you squeeze a handful. Then pack the mix solidly into flats to within ½ inch of the rim. Sow the seeds in rows pressed or scratched in the surface of the mix with the back of a knife. Then sprinkle a little additional mix over large seeds and firm well. Very small seeds are simply pressed into the surface without covering.

If you prefer to devote one flat to a single variety of flower, just scatter the seeds lightly over the entire flat. Several seed growers sell preplanted flats containing seeds of a single variety of annual.

Place the flats anywhere out of the sun until the seeds germinate.

These two small flats of annuals were started at the same time. They demonstrate how much difference there is in the time it takes seeds to germinate and grow. The large plants are red salvia. The plants in the right flat are zinnias. In the same flat, feverfew and nicotiana are barely visible.

When seedlings reach a couple of inches in height, they should be transplanted to give them more space. Each of these flats should have no more than 12 or 13 seedlings after transplanting. The soil is Jiffy-Mix.

Setting them above a radiator—but not directly on the radiator—provides enough heat to encourage early germination.

As soon as the seedlings appear, shift the flats into the sunniest window you have. Keep the soil mix moist at all times. Turn the flats halfway around every day so that the plants do not grow toward the sun and develop a permanent lean.*

When the seedlings are 1 to 2 inches tall, it is time either to thin them or transplant them. Thinning is done if a flat is planted entirely to one variety. In a 5 × 7-inch flat, pull out all but 12 or 13 well spaced seedlings. In other containers, leave each seedling about 2 square inches of space.

Seedlings growing in rows should be transplanted because in a small flat one row doesn't give you very many plants if you thin them out. Fill another flat of the same size with dampened soil mix, firm it, and poke holes for 12 or 13 plants in it with a finger. Then dig up the seedlings in the first flat with a dull table knife. Get all the roots. Carefully pull and shake the seedlings apart, and drop the roots of one into one of the

---

* This phenomenon is called heliotropism.

holes in the new flat, and firm the soil mix around them. Fill the other holes in the same way.

Place the flat in a bright but not sunny spot for a day or two to give the plants time to adjust to their new quarters; then return them to the window. Continue watering the plants and turning the flats until you are ready to move the plants outdoors. They should not require fertilizer if growing in a seed-starter mix; but if you want to force growth, you can give them a little liquid plant food, such as Ra-Pid-Gro.

The plants can be transplanted to the flower bed any time after the last frost; but to prepare them for the move, you must "harden them off" for a week. Start the process by taking the flats from the windowsill and setting them outdoors in a sunny, protected spot for three or four hours. Then bring them indoors again. Repeat this process daily, increasing the outdoor stay roughly four hours each day. Thus, by the end of the week, the plants are accustomed to living outdoors 24 hours a day, and are ready for the flower bed.

Although the foregoing is the time-tested method of raising annuals

Seedlings of annuals and vegetables growing under light. Each fixture holds two 48-inch, 40-watt fluorescent tubes.

Mean date of last 32° F. temperature in the spring. (U.S. Weather Bureau map)

New type of peat container. Hard, thin chips like those in the flat at left swell up into large soft balls when soaked briefly in water. Each ball will nourish a single seedling and will protect the seedling from shock when it is moved into the garden.

from seed indoors, two improvements have been made in recent years.

One of these involves growing the plants under fluorescent light rather than in a sunny window. (This is the only difference in the procedure.) The growth made by the plants is spectacular because the intensity of the light does not vary. Furthermore, since the plants are set directly below the light, they grow straight up instead of at a slant.

The fluorescent fixture used for the purpose can be any inexpensive commercial or industrial unit which hangs from the ceiling by chains so you can adjust it up and down as necessary. It should incorporate two 48-inch, 40-watt tubes. (Anything smaller is a waste of time.) These may be especially designed for plant growing (the best-known brand is called Gro-Lux), or ordinary white tubes, or a combination of the two. Hang the fixture with the tubes about 1 foot above the tops of the flats. I leave the lights burning 24 hours a day, but if you want to save a little current, you can get about the same results on a 16-hour schedule.

The other improvement in seed-growing methods involves the use of containers made of peat rather than plastic flats or other hard-sided containers. Seeds are sown in these and grown in a window or under fluorescent light in the manner described above.

Peat containers are made of peat moss in several designs. One type looks like a conventional flowerpot; another resembles a flat divided into small compartments. To use these, fill them with damp seed-starter mix or any other growing medium.

A newer type of container is a hard, compressed pellet resembling an oversized poker chip. When this is soaked in water, it swells to seven times its size. All you have to do is press seeds into the surface, and your seed-sowing is done.

The purpose of all peat containers is to eliminate the transplanting of seedlings. Two or three seeds are sown in each container and later

A bank of coldframes. The seed bed beneath the sash is surrounded by stone walls. A notched board is used to prop the sash open at different heights.

thinned to a single plant. When this is ready for the flower bed, the entire container is set into the ground, where it disintegrates. Thus the plant is spared the shock that accompanies normal transplanting procedures, and it grows on in the flower bed without any setback.

SOWING SEEDS IN A COLDFRAME

A coldframe is a large, rectangular, bottomless box with a glass top which is used primarily for sowing seeds and raising sturdy little plants prior to the last spring frost. It is thus a substitute for indoor plant growing, and it has the single advantage of permitting you to raise more seedlings than you are likely to have space for in the house.

A coldframe should be built in the autumn so it will be ready for planting in early spring. For simplicity, construct it out of redwood or any other decay-resistant lumber. The standard size is 3 × 6 feet, but you can make it any size to fit the sash you intend to use as the top. The back of the frame (which is 3 feet wide) should be 15 inches high; the front, 9 inches. The 6-foot-long sides taper from 15 to 9 inches.

Standard coldframe sash is made with small glass panes overlapping like shingles. An old window sash or storm window can be used just as well. Or you can make a sash out of polyethylene film or Celloglas. A glass sash is simply laid on top of the coldframe; but if you use a plastic-covered sash, it should be hinged to the back of the frame to keep wind from blowing it away.

Locate the coldframe in an open area where it will get sun throughout the day. It should be set on a north-south axis with the low front aimed southward. Before erecting the frame, turn the soil over to a depth of 1 foot and add humus and lime as necessary. If the weather promises to be warm for a while, you may fumigate the soil to get rid of weeds, nematodes and other pests. Press the frame down into the soil about an inch and bank soil up against the outer sides for several inches.

In the spring, the soil in a coldframe thaws out long before soil in the open. As soon as it loses its chill, mix in about 2 cups of balanced fertilizer and rake the surface smooth and level. You can sow seeds of hardy annuals five to seven weeks before the last frost of the season, but don't start tender annuals until one to three weeks before the last frost.

If you did not fumigate the soil when you built the coldframe, treat the seeds with a disinfectant before sowing them in rows 6 inches apart. Thin the seedlings to 1 inch apart when they are large enough to handle easily. Keep them watered and weeded at all times.

Cover the coldframe with an old quilt or mound of straw at night when the temperature is expected to fall below freezing. The same protection is needed on very cold days; but ordinarily, the more light and sun the seedlings get, the better. Once the seedlings are up and thriving, raise the sash an inch or two on mild, sunny days to keep the plants from wilting in the heat of the frame. In the final week before moving the plants into a flower bed, raise the sash even higher to harden them off.

SOWING SEEDS IN A HOTBED

This is a third way to give annuals a head start. It produces larger plants faster than a coldframe or sunny window; but they are no better than plants grown in a seed-starter mix under fluorescent light.

A hotbed is nothing more than a coldframe with heat. It is built and oriented in the same way. The sides, however, should extend 9 to 12 inches below ground to hold in the heat.

Heating is done with an electric soil-heating cable controlled by a thermostat. For a 3 × 6-foot hotbed, the cable should be about 40 feet long and rated at about 200 watts. It is laid in loops on a 2-inch bed of vermiculite and covered with 1 inch of soil. Over this is laid a piece of wire mesh to protect the cable from accidental damage. And over this goes 4 to 6 inches of soil mixed with humus and a couple of cupfuls of fertilizer.

Sow seeds of hardy annuals in a hotbed six to eight weeks before the last spring frost. Start tender annuals two weeks later. Handle them as in a coldframe.

The soil temperature for tender annuals should start at 70° F. and be lowered gradually, as the plants develop, to 50°. Hardy annuals need a 50° soil temperature from the start. Cover the sash on frigid nights with a quilt or straw, and open it a few inches on warm days. Turn off the heat about two weeks before the plants are to be moved into the flower bed, and open the sash a foot or more during the final week.

One of the newest ways of sowing seeds—in a plastic tape that disintegrates soon after it is covered with soil.

SEED TAPE

One of the newest and most promising—and most expensive—ideas for simplifying plant growing is a narrow plastic tape containing seeds already correctly spaced for maximum growth. Use of the tape not only eliminates the need for thinning seedlings but also makes it easier to plant even the smallest, hard-to-see seeds at the right depth. The tape dissolves with the first watering. Seed tape is used for starting seeds outdoors, indoors or in a coldframe or hotbed. You can cut it with scissors to any desired length—even in half-inch pieces to fit peat pellets.

TRANSPLANTING SMALL PLANTS
TO THE FLOWER BED

Regardless of where they come from—a store, flat, coldframe, hotbed or an outdoor propagating bed—small annuals are transplanted into the garden after danger of frost is past. To prevent wilting, the job should be done on a cloudy day or in late afternoon.

Water the plants well 12 to 24 hours before they are to be moved. The soil should be damp enough to form a ball around the roots but it should not be sopping.

With a small trowel, dig up the plants with a good chunk of soil around the roots. Take pains not to cut or break the roots, and try not to break the soil ball.

In the flower bed, scoop out a hole for each individual plant. It should be the depth of the soil ball and at least twice as wide. Set in the plant, fill in the soil around the roots—but not up onto the stem—and firm it well with your fingers. This should leave a slight saucerlike depression around the plant. Fill this with water, and then fill it again with a starter solution made with a liquid fertilizer such as Ra-Pid-Gro or Miracle-Gro.

During the next couple of weeks, fill the saucer with water whenever the soil looks dry.

Plants growing in peat containers do not need to be treated so carefully since the roots are not disturbed during the transplanting operation. You can move them in the hottest part of a sunny day, because they will not wilt. Just set the container into a hole in the flower bed, firm soil around it and water well.

Transplanting a seedling petunia. Firming the soil around it with the fingers forms a saucer to hold water.

SUMMER CARE OF ANNUALS

Follow the procedure outlined in Chapter 3. In the fall, if an unusually early frost is predicted, you can protect the flowers by covering them with cartons or baskets or by draping old blankets, burlap or sheets of plastic film on stakes over them. Another protective measure is to provide heat in the immediate vicinity of the flower bed with incandescent bulbs strung over the bed or with a charcoal fire in a barbecue brazier.

Later in the fall, when a hard frost finally kills your annuals, pull them up and shake the soil from the roots. Then toss plants that are not diseased on your leaf pile to rot. Chopping them into small pieces with a rotary mower hastens decomposition to some extent.

SELECTING ANNUALS FOR YOUR GARDEN

There are a great many annuals. The long list that follows describes those which are of special value because of their blossoms, foliage, period of bloom, adaptability or general usefulness.

In this alphabetical list—as in the others describing perennials, biennials and bulbs—each genus is registered under the name by which it is best known in this country. In some cases, the common name is given first; the botanical name is italicized and given second (for example: Alyssum, sweet. *Lobularia*); in other cases, the order is reversed (*Ageratum*. Floss Flower). In a few cases, other names which are used are also given (Cornflower. *Centaurea*, Bachelor's Button, Ragged Robin, Blue Bottle). There are also some flowers which are known only by their botanical names (*Cosmos*).

If this is confusing, I beg your indulgence. The best way to identify all members of the plant kingdom is by their Latin botanical names; but people were gardening long before Linnaeus developed the binomial system for classifying and naming plants in the 1700s, and they have always known many plants only by their common names. Be that as it may, if you can't find in the lists a flower under the name you know it by, reference to the index will soon set matters straight.

Favorite Annuals

(The symbol ❋ indicates the very best)

Acrolinium. *Helipterum.* Zones 3–10. 18–24 inches. Daisylike flowers in midsummer up to 2 inches across in white, pink, rose or salmon. They are usually dried for winter bouquets. Sow seeds indoors 4–6 weeks before last frost or outdoors after frost danger is past. Grow in sun, in average soil. Allow 6-inch space between plants.

Ageratum. ❋ **Floss Flower.** Zones 1–10. 3–12 inches. An excellent edging plant also grown in rock gardens and containers. It forms a low mound covered throughout the summer and into the fall with fluffy flowers. These are usually blue but may be pink or dirty white. Sow seeds indoors 6–8 weeks before last frost. Average soil. Needs sun but in hot climates prefers light shade. Plants spread 2 to 3 inches wider than they are high. Allow 6-inch space between plants. In areas with mild winters, sow seeds outdoors in late summer for fall bloom. Elsewhere you can cut back plants in late summer, put them in pots and grow them indoors.

Alyssum, Sweet. ❋ *Lobularia.* Zone 1–10. 3–12 inches. The most popular varieties are very low, mounded plants covered with white, pink or violet flowers. They bloom about 6 weeks after sowing and continue from mid-spring to fall. Like ageratum, this is an excellent edging plant which can also be used in containers, rock gardens and for carpeting large areas. Sow seeds indoors 2–4 weeks before last frost or outdoors at time of last frost. Sun or light shade. Average soil. Allow space for plants to spread to a width at least twice their height.

Amaranthus. Several species known by such common names as Love-Lies-Bleeding, Joseph's Coat, Prince's Feather, Tassel Flower, Flaming Fountain. Zones 3–10. 3–6 feet. Amaranthus is grown for its large, pendent red leaves which are often variegated with white, yellow or green. The plants also have red flowers but these are of secondary importance. Plant at the back of the flower bed or in a shrubbery border.

Sow seeds outdoors after last frost. Grow in sun and average soil. Allow 18-inch space between plants. Apply high-nitrogen fertilizer several times during the summer.

***Anchusa.* Summer Forget-Me-Not.** Zones 1–10. 9–18 inches. Upright, slender-leaved plant with clusters of small, bright-blue flowers throughout the summer. The color is outstanding. Sow seeds indoors 6–8 weeks before last frost or outdoors after last frost. Plant in sun, average soil. Allow 1-foot space between plants.

Arctotis. One species called African Daisy. Zones 3–10. 1–2 feet. Large daisylike flowers in cream, yellow, pink, red or bronze. Very showy and good for cutting. Blooms throughout the summer. Start seeds indoors 4–6 weeks before last frost or outdoors after last frost. Sun. Average soil. Allow 9-inch space between plants.

Aster, China. ❄ *Callistephus.* Zones 1–8. 10–30 inches. This is one of the most colorful annuals but rather hard to grow well. The flowers range up to 6 inches across and have many petals. Some are like stiff pincushions; others like big chrysanthemums. Colors range from white to pink and red; blue to purple.

Sow seeds indoors 4–6 weeks before last frost or outdoors after last frost. Grow in sun in a well-drained, rich, humusy soil. Do not plant in the same location year after year. Allow 10-inch space between plants. Keep plants growing steadily, but don't overwater. Spray with Sevin to control leafhoppers, which spread aster yellows. To avoid the disease known as aster wilt, plant wilt-resistant varieties. However, there is no certainty that wilt-prone varieties will contract the disease.

Baby's Breath. *Gypsophila.* Zones 2–10. 12–18 inches. Upright plant with lance-shaped leaves and profuse white flowers which are larger than those of perennial baby's breath. In the flower bed it is a fine foil for plants with larger leaves and flowers; splendid for cutting. Sow seeds outdoors after last frost and make repeat sowings every six weeks to assure that you have bloom through the summer and fall. Sun. Average soil, which should be limed if it is acid. Allow 6–9-inch space between plants.

Small annual asters (foreground) combined with pink-eyed, white vinca rosea.

Balsam. *Impatiens.* Zones 2–10. 8–36 inches. The balsams have waxy, double flowers in white, pink, red, purple or mixed colors. These are not very large but they are lovely. On taller plants they are tucked in among the large leaves but on dwarf varieties they are held well above the leaves. Sow seeds indoors 6–8 weeks before last frost. Grow in sun or partial shade. Average, humusy soil. Keep well watered. Allow 9–12-inch space between plants.

Basketflower. *Centaurea.* Zones 1–10. 3–5 feet. This is a close relative of the cornflower and is grown in the same way, except that seeds are sown only in the spring, before last frost. The 5-inch pink or rose flowers have a shaggy head surrounded by daisylike petals forming a shallow basket.

Begonia, Wax. ✻ *Begonia semperflorens,* Bedding Begonia. Zones 3–10. 4–18 inches. This fibrous-rooted type of begonia develops into a neat,

A couple of varieties of wax begonia. They are not very showy but they bloom for months on end.

rounded plant with lovely foliage which is covered throughout summer and fall with white, pink or red flowers. The flowers are not good for cutting but they provide a mass of bloom in the garden. Use in edgings, as a carpet in large beds, or in containers.

You can propagate a few plants by taking cuttings of stem tips (see pages 148–49). For lots of plants, sow seeds indoors 3–4 months before last frost. Plant outdoors in sun or partial shade, in average soil containing considerable humus. Allow 9–12-inch space between plants. Water regularly and fertilize lightly every month. Spray foliage with water in dry weather. Pinch stem ends to make plants bushy. In warmest climates, plants can be left outdoors and treated as perennials (which they actually are). In cold climates, stem cuttings taken in late summer will produce indoor pot plants for the winter.

Bells of Ireland. *Molucella.* Zones 2–10. 2 feet. Upright stems surrounded from bottom to top with outward-facing, bell-shaped green flowers with small white centers. Interesting for fresh arrangements; can also be dried. Sow seeds indoors 8 weeks before last frost. Grow in sun and average soil. Allow 1-foot space between plants. Water and fertilize regularly for extra-luxuriant growth.

Blue Laceflower. *Trachymene* or *Didiscus.* Zones 3–8. 18–24 inches. Plant has finely cut leaves and lacy, umbrella-shaped clusters of tiny, insipid blue flowers during the summer. Grow for cutting and drying. Sow seeds indoors 8 weeks before last frost. Sun. Average soil. Allow 9-inch space between plants. Pinch plants to make them bushy.

Browallia. Zones 3–10. 10–24 inches. The browallias are compact, rounded plants suitable for the flower bed and excellent for hanging containers because of their somewhat pendent branches. They are well covered throughout the summer with bell-like flowers to about 1½ inches across. The best color is blue, but white and violet varieties are available. Sow seeds indoors 8–10 weeks before last frost. Plant in sun, in average soil. Allow 10-inch space between plants. You can pot up plants in the fall for continued growth indoors, but flowering will gradually slacken.

Butterfly Flower. *Schizanthus,* Poor Man's Orchid. Zones 1–8. 12–30 inches. Much-branched upright plant with fernlike foliage which is smothered under lovely orchidlike flowers from late spring to midsummer. The flowers have solid background colors of white, pink, rose or violet with gold and other colors superimposed. Use in beds; excellent in containers. Sow seeds indoors 10–12 weeks before last frost. Sun. Average soil. Allow 9-inch space between plants. Pinch to promote bushiness. Spray with water in hot weather.

Calendula. **Pot Marigold.** Zones 1–10. 18–24 inches. Easy, adaptable, upright, branching plant with zinnialike flowers in shades of yellow and orange. Blooms throughout the summer in cold areas; almost throughout the year in warmest areas. Sow seeds indoors 4–6 weeks before last frost, or outdoors after last frost. Grow in sun and average soil. Allow 9-inch space between plants.

Calliopsis. *Coreopsis.* Zones 2–10. 9–36 inches. Slender-stemmed, cosmos-like flowers in yellow, orange and red with dark purplish-brown centers. They bloom continuously in summer and fall if you keep the dead flowers picked off. Easy to grow but a little messy-looking. Sow seeds outdoors after last frost or indoors 4–6 weeks before last frost. Sun. Average soil. Allow 6-inch space between plants for dwarf varieties; 12-inch space for large.

Candytuft. *Iberis.* Zones 1–10. 8–15 inches. Does best in cool climates. Bushy plants with many small, rounded flower clusters in white, pink, red or lilac. Use for cutting, edgings, beds and rock gardens. Sow seeds outdoors where plants are to grow as soon as soil is free of frost and reasonably dry. Needs sun. Average soil. Allow 9-inch space between plants. Repeat sowings at 3-week intervals for a long season of bloom.

Canterbury Bells. *Campanula.* Zones 3–10. 2 feet. Upright plant with loose clusters of large, bell-shaped flowers in blue, pink, lavender, rose or white. They are similar to the more common biennial Canterbury Bells. Use in beds and for cutting. To have flowers in midsummer, sow seeds indoors 8–10 weeks before last frost. Grow in sun. Average soil. Allow 1-foot space between plants. Keep dead blooms picked off.

Cineraria. ❀ *Senecio.* Zones 7–10. 8–15 inches. These are very beautiful flowers but unfortunately they are easily grown outdoors only in cooler,

Candytuft forms little mounds of color. The feathery plant at left is gilia.

Cockscomb plumes always make a brilliant spot of color in the garden. These are fire-engine red and yellow.

more humid parts of the far West—around San Francisco, for example. The large, daisylike blossoms borne in clusters in late winter and spring range from white through red to blue and purple. The colors are rich and are frequently highlighted by contrasting eyes. Use in beds, in mass plantings and in containers.

Although cinerarias are easily grown from seed, they must be started in the summer or early fall and carried over the winter in a place where they will be safe from frost. It is therefore better to buy plants and set them out in the garden as soon as all frost danger is past. Grow in shade in rich, humusy soil. Allow 1-foot space between plants. Don't let the soil dry out.

Clarkia. Zones 2–10. 1–4 feet. These flowers make their growth in cool weather. They bloom in the spring in California; in summer, elsewhere. The plants are slender and upright; they bear showy, cup-shaped or, more often, double flowers in white, rose, pink and purple. Sow seeds in early spring where plants are to grow. In frost-free areas you can sow seeds in the fall. Partial shade. Average, well-drained soil. Allow 9-inch space between plants. Water regularly.

Cockscomb. *Celosia.* Zones 2–10. 10–36 inches. Cockscomb is a flamboyant flower—usually a bright red but frequently yellow and sometimes orange or silvery white. In the plume type of cockscomb, the blooms resemble feathery plumes. In the crested type, they look like big, much distorted rooster combs. The latter are odd but not pretty.

Sow seeds indoors 8 weeks before last frost or outdoors after last frost. Sun. Average soil. Allow 15-inch space between plants. Needs little attention. Thrives in heat.

Coleus. Painted Nettle. Zones 5–10. 1–3 feet. Slender plants grown for their brilliant foliage. Large oval leaves are red, maroon, green, yellow, pink or any combination of these colors. Use in flower beds, shrubbery borders or containers. Sow seeds indoors 8–10 weeks before last frost or take stem cuttings from established plants and root them in a glass of water. Plant in strong light but not sun. Both sun and deep shade retard coloring. Average soil. Allow 6–9-inch space between plants. Fertilize every month with high-nitrogen fertilizer. Pinch back stem ends frequently to discourage the legginess to which the plants are addicted. If flower buds appear, remove them at once to maintain bushy growth.

Cornflower. ❄ *Centaurea,* Bachelor's Button, Ragged Robin, Blue Bottle. Zones 1–10. 1–3 feet. Favorite flower for wearing in buttonholes —if that's being done any more. It's also good for cutting and makes a nice display in the garden from late spring through summer if you keep the dead flowers picked off. The plant is slender, upright and has narrow, gray-green leaves. Fluffy flower heads as much as 1½ inches across in blue, white, pink, red or violet. Sow seeds where plants are to grow before last spring frost. You may also sow them the preceding fall. Give sun and average soil. Allow 6-inch space between plants.

Cosmos. ❄ Zones 2–10. 3–7 feet. One of the largest flowers in the garden and also one of the easiest and most obliging. A many-branched plant with carrotlike foliage and flat, daisylike flowers up to 6 inches across in rose, pink, white, yellow or orange. Sow seeds indoors 6–8 weeks before last frost or outdoors after last frost. Sun or light shade. Average soil. Allow 3-foot space between plants for varieties over 4 feet tall. These should also be staked, for while they have strong, thick stems, they are so large that they are easily knocked down in storms.

Cosmos grows to huge proportions but the flowers are gentle and useful in the garden and for picking.

Cuphea. **Cigar Flower.** Zones 6–10. 1 foot. Compact plant as wide as it is high, with tubular flowers which are bright red with a dark ring just below the mouth and with white lips. A familiar pot plant, it can also be effective in the flower bed. Sow seeds indoors 8 weeks before last frost. You can also start with stem cuttings from houseplants. Grow in sun or light shade in average soil. Allow 1-foot space between plants. Pinch branch ends to promote bushiness.

Cynoglossum. **Chinese Forget-Me-Not.** Zones 2–10. 15–30 inches. A biennial usually grown as an annual. It's a bushy plant with sprays of small blue, white or pink flowers. Blooms in summer in most areas, but in spring where summers are hot. Sow seeds indoors 8–10 weeks before last frost or outdoors several weeks before last frost. You can also sow the seeds in the fall if winters are not too severe. Grow in sun or light shade in average soil. Allow 9-inch space between plants.

Daisy, African. *Dimorphotheca,* Cape Marigold. Zones 2–10. 1 foot. Excellent plant for hot climates. Compact, free-flowering plant with 3½-inch daisies in white, yellow, salmon or orange. Sow seeds indoors 8 weeks before last frost. Plant in full sun: flowers close in shade or even in cloudy weather. Average soil. Space 9 inches apart.

Daisy, Blue. *Felicia* or *Agathaea.* Zones 5–10. 1 foot. Slender, branched plant with daisylike flowers with sky-blue petals and yellow centers. Grow in containers or in beds protected from wind. Sow seeds indoors 6–8 weeks before last frost. Sun. Average soil. Allow 1-foot space between plants.

Daisy, Swan River. *Brachycome.* Zones 1–10. 12–18 inches. Lacy-foliaged plant producing hundreds of 1-inch daisies in blue, white, rose or bicolors from late spring to midsummer. Use in rock gardens, flower beds or as a ground cover. Sow seeds indoors 8 weeks before last frost or outdoors after last frost. Sun or light shade. Average soil. Allow 6-inch space between plants.

Daisy, Tahoka. *Machaeranthera.* Zones 6–10. 18 inches. Bushy plant with fernlike leaves and 2-inch daisies with lilac-blue petals and large yellow centers. Fine for cutting. Sow seeds outdoors about three weeks before last frost. Grow in sun, average soil. Allow 9-inch space between plants.

Dusty Miller. ❄ ***Centaurea.*** Zones 1–10. 8–18 inches. This plant is grown for its lovely chiseled leaves. Depending on the variety, these are silvery-gray or silvery-white. The plants also have pretty yellow or purple flowers, but these are of minor importance. Use as edgings in the rock garden, in containers, or in beds as a foil for green-leaved plants. In cold climates sow seeds indoors 8–10 weeks before last frost. In warm climates, sow seeds outdoors after last frost. Give plenty of sun and average soil. Allow 6-inch space between plants. Remove flower heads and cut plants back slightly after flowering.

Emilia. **Tasselflower,** Paint Brush. Zones 3–10. 18–24 inches. Easy, erect annual with loose clusters of ½-inch red or yellow flowers suggestive of small round paintbrushes. Use in beds and for cutting. Sow seeds outdoors after last frost. Sun. Average soil. Allow 9-inch space between plants.

Euphorbia. Zones 3–10. Succulent plants grown for their colored foliage. One called Snow-on-the-Mountain is an erect 2-foot plant with light-green, oval leaves at the bottom and almost white leaves at the top. Another euphorbia called Annual Poinsettia or Mexican Fire Plant grows to 3 feet and has upper leaves blotched with bright red. Both plants are handled in the same way. Sow seeds indoors 6–8 weeks before last frost or outdoors after last frost. Grow in sun in average soil. Allow 1-foot space between plants. Needs to be watered only in long dry spells. The juices of the plant are poisonous.

Everlasting, Winged. ***Ammobium.*** Zones 2–10. 3 feet. Bushy plant with prominent wings on the branches; cottony, white leaves, and chaffy, silvery-white flowers in summer. The latter should be picked just before they mature and dried for winter bouquets. Sow seeds outdoors about 2 weeks before last frost. Grow in sun in average, well-drained soil. Plants grow well in extremely sandy soil. Allow 1-foot space between plants.

Feverfew. ***Chrysanthemum.*** Zones 4–10. 6–24 inches. This is a perennial which is usually grown as an annual for its mass of small white or yellow summer flowers. Use the compact dwarf varieties for edgings; the taller plants in the flower bed for cutting and continuous color. Sow seeds indoors 6–8 weeks before last frost or outdoors just before last frost. Grow in sun in average, well-drained soil. Allow 6-inch space between plants for low varieties; 1-foot space for others. In mild climates, plants will survive the winter.

Flax. *Linum.* Zones 2–10. 18 inches. A slender, upright plant with gray-green foliage and innumerable small, slightly cupped, scarlet flowers throughout the summer. The flowers are open for one day only but they keep on coming one after the other. Sow seeds outdoors several weeks before last spring frost, or sow them in the fall. Plants need full sun, average soil, little attention. Allow 6–9-inch space between plants.

Four-O'Clock. *Mirabilis,* Marvel of Peru. Zones 3–10. 20–36 inches. Branching plant with white, pink, red, yellow or lilac flowers about 1 inch across and trumpet-shaped. On sunny days they open late in the afternoon and close the following morning; on cloudy days they are open all day. They bloom from midsummer on. Sow seeds indoors 6–8 weeks before last frost. Grow in the sun in average soil. Allow 1-foot space between plants.

Gaillardia. ✽ **Blanket Flower,** Gay Flower. Zones 1–10. 10–24 inches. Old gaillardias were daisylike flowers. Newest varieties, called Lolli-pops, are very double flowers like fat balls and as much as 3 inches in diameter. They are yellow, orange or red and in many cases two-toned. Sow seeds indoors 6–8 weeks before last frost or outdoors after last frost. Plant in average soil in a sunny spot. Allow 1-foot space between plants.

Gazania. Zones 5–10. 9–15 inches. A mounded plant with white-and-green, deeply cut leaves and daisylike flowers up to 3 inches across. The profuse blossoms, appearing in the summer, are white, yellow, pink or red. The plants are good for edging and massing. Sow seeds indoors 6–8 weeks before last frost or outdoors after last frost. They need total darkness to germinate. Plant in sun in average soil. Give each plant space equal to its ultimate height.

Geranium. ❈ *Pelargonium.* Zones 3–10. 12–18 inches. Favorite plant with handsome leaves and large, round clusters of red, pink or white flowers throughout the summer. It is usually grown in containers and window boxes but makes a splendid show planted in masses in beds. The most commonly grown geraniums are those known as zonal, or garden, geraniums. These have more-or-less round leaves with scalloped edges and frequently with attractive zones of color. The other commonly grown geraniums are ivy geraniums with trailing stems and ivy-shaped leaves, and scented geraniums with leaves in many delightful shapes.

You can raise geraniums from seeds but it's a slow job, since germination may take up to 8 weeks. For this reason, it's better to start with scarified seeds, which should germinate in 2 weeks. In any case, sow the seeds indoors about February 1, and when the seedlings appear, transplant them before they get their true leaves to individual small pots. Then, when they are 6 inches high, transplant them again to larger pots. Move them outdoors after last frost.

The other way to grow geraniums for outdoor use is to take cuttings from houseplants in early February. These should have five leaves. Remove the three bottom leaves and root the cuttings in rooting medium in a plastic bag (see Chapter 7); then move them into pots and shift outdoors after last frost. To grow plants for indoor bloom in winter, follow the same procedure with cuttings taken from your garden plants in August.

Geraniums require sun, but in our hottest climates they should have some shade in the summer. They grow in average soil which has good drainage. Water only when the soil has dried out to a depth of about ½ inch; then water heavily. Apply a little liquid fertilizer every month. Do not remove buds when plants are small, since this delays flowering. Keep dead blooms picked off. Allow 9–12 inch space between plants.

Geraniums are actually perennials and in Zones 9b–10 can be treated as such. Pinch stem ends frequently and keep dead flowers picked off. Cut plants back hard in spring. But don't be surprised if flower production gradually peters out. That's why it is generally wise to keep producing new plants and handling them as annuals.

Gilia. Zones 6–10. 8–30 inches. This is a Western native which does particularly well in that area. The species called Blue Thimble Flower has funnel-shaped blue flowers in small, dense clusters. Another called Bird's-Eye Gilia has loose clusters of deep-violet flowers with yellow throats. The showy plants are good in the flower bed and excellent for cutting. Sow seeds outdoors 2–3 weeks before last frost. Grow in full sun in average soil. Allow 9-inch space between plants.

Globe Amaranth. *Gomphrena.* Zones 3–10. 9–24 inches. Branching plant covered from midsummer on with large cloverlike blossoms in white, pink, red or purple. Used for cutting and especially for drying. Sow seeds outdoors after last frost. Grow in sun and average soil. Allow 1-foot space between plants.

Godetia. **Satin Flower.** Zones 2–10. 10–18 inches. Branching plant with single or double satiny flowers in white, pink or violet. They are showy in the garden and very good for cutting, since the blossoms last for several days. Plants do best along the northern Pacific Coast and in similar cool climates. Sow seeds outdoors about a week before last frost. Grow in partial shade in average soil. Allow 9-inch space between plants.

Heliotrope. *Heliotropium.* Zones 3–10. 15–30 inches. Old-time favorite grown chiefly for its fragrance, but its large, round clusters of blue, violet or sometimes white flowers are not to be scorned. A good plant for the border, it is also grown in pots outdoors and in. In warm climates it is handled like the perennial that it actually is. Elsewhere it is usually grown as an annual.

The seeds, which are slow to germinate, can be sown at any time in flats in a warm spot. If you intend to use the plants in the flower bed, sow seeds indoors 10–12 weeks before the last frost. Grow in sun or partial shade outdoors. Average soil with humus added. Allow 15–18-inch space between plants. Don't let the plants dry out but don't overwater either. Feed once a month. Take stem cuttings in July and pot them up for winter bloom indoors. As the plants develop, move them into larger pots so the roots will have plenty of room to expand.

Honesty. *Lunaria,* Money Plant. Zones 3–10. 18–30 inches. Honesty is a biennial usually grown as an annual. It is not a very pretty plant while growing, but it is prized for its round, flat, silvery, parchmentlike seed-pods. These are dried on the slender stems for winter bouquets. Sow seeds indoors 8 weeks before last frost. Grow in light shade in average soil in an out-of-the-way place. Allow 1-foot space between plants.

Kochia. **Burning Bush,** Summer Cypress, Mexican Firebush. Zones 2–10. 3 feet. Upright, oval plant that resembles a needled evergreen shrub. It has light-green foliage which turns bright red in the fall. Use it for a temporary hedge or as a background for small flowers. Sow seeds indoors 8 weeks before last frost, first soaking them in water for 24 hours. Grow plants outdoors in full sun in average soil. Water regularly and apply high-nitrogen fertilizer several times during the summer. Allow 12–15-inch space between plants.

Larkspur. ✿ *Delphinium.* Zones 1–9. 1–5 feet. Beautiful white, blue, pink or red flowers in tall, dense spikes from late spring to midsummer. Plant them in small groups or, better, masses at the back of the flower bed. Marvelous for cutting. Easily grown, particularly in cooler climates. Sow seeds where plants are to grow as soon as the soil can be worked in the spring. You can also sow them in the late fall. Grow in full sun in average soil containing extra humus. Fertilize when you thin plants, allowing 9 inches of space, and again just before they start to bloom.

Lavatera. **Tree Mallow.** Zones 2–10. 2–5 feet. A plant very similar to the hollyhock. It has 4-inch flowers in white, pink or red in mid- and late summer. Plant it at the back of the flower bed. Sow seeds outdoors after last frost. Give full sun, average soil. Allow 1-foot space between plants. Pick off dead flowers to assure continuing bloom.

Layia. **Tidytips.** Zones 3–10. 8–18 inches. Useful annual for the sunny or semishaded garden. 2-inch, fragrant yellow daisies with small white petal tips bloom from late spring into the fall. Sow seeds outdoors after last frost. Average soil. Allow 9-inch space between plants.

Linaria. **Toadflax,** Baby Snapdragon. Zones 2–10. 8–18 inches. Mounded plant covered with snapdragonlike flowers in almost every color from mid-spring through the summer. Makes a colorful show when planted in large groups. Sow seeds outdoors 2–3 weeks before last frost. Grow in sun in average soil. Allow space equal to height of the variety you plant.

Lobelia. Zones 1–10. 4–8 inches. Pretty little mounded plant for use in edgings, beds, rock gardens or containers. The flowers are usually blue with white centers but rose and white varieties are available. They bloom in the summer. Sow seeds indoors 8–10 weeks before last frost. Grow outdoors in partial shade and average soil. Allow 6-inch space between plants.

Love-in-a-Mist. **Nigella.** Zones 2–10. 1–2 feet. Very airy plant with leaves like fine grass blades and cornflowerlike summer flowers in white, pink, red, blue or purple. These are followed by ornamental papery seed capsules. Both flowers and capsules are good for bouquets; the plants are fine foils for those with coarse foliage. Sow seeds outdoors in the spring as soon as the soil is workable. Grow in sun and average soil. Allow 8-inch space between plants.

Lupine. **Lupinus.** Zones 3–10. 18–36 inches. Annual lupines have lovely leaves divided into many fingers and upright spikes of blue, white or pink flowers during the summer. Nick the seeds with a knife before sowing. Sow indoors 6–8 weeks before last frost, or outdoors after last frost. Grow in sun in average soil which has very good drainage. Allow 1-foot space between plants.

Marigold. ❋ *Tagetes.* Zones 1–10. 6–36 inches. A garden without marigolds? It's hard to imagine. These are indispensable flowers. All the large-flowered types (and that includes most varieties) make a brilliant show in beds. The dwarfs are superb edging plants. All are handsome in containers and excellent for cutting. What's more, they are easy to grow; they start blooming soon after sowing; and as long as you keep the spent blossoms picked off, they will keep on blooming until frost.

Most blossoms are double, but a few dwarf varieties are single. Yellow and orange are the usual colors; bronze-red and mahogany-red are not uncommon, however.

These large marigolds were making as bright a show in early November as they did in July.

For early bloom, sow seeds indoors 4–6 weeks before last frost. Then transplant to a sunny spot in the garden. The soil need be no better than average but should be well drained. Allow 6-inch space between plants for dwarf varieties; 15 inches for large. To promote bushy growth, pinch off the growing tips once or twice when plants are young. Fertilize soon after plants are set out and again after they start to bloom. Water in dry weather. In windy locations, large plants should be staked.

Mexican Sunflower. *Tithonia.* Zones 3–10. 4–8 feet. This is a massive, rather coarse plant, which makes up for these shortcomings by producing 4-inch flowers similar to single dahlias in sensational tones of rich orange. Appearing throughout summer and fall, they have a peculiar fascination for monarch butterflies. Sow seeds indoors 8 weeks before last frost. In warm climates they can also be sown outdoors after last frost. Grow plants in full sun in average soil. Allow 3-foot space between plants. Provide sturdy stakes to hold plants upright against wind and storms. Water only in long dry spells; this is an excellent plant for desert regions.

Mignonette. *Reseda.* Zones 2–10. 12–18 inches. A somewhat sprawling plant with loose spikes of greenish flowers which add little to the appearance of the garden but contribute immensely to its fragrance. Sow seeds outdoors where the plants are to grow about a week before last frost. Make a second sowing in early summer so you will have bloom into the fall. Grow in partial shade in all except very cool regions, where full sun is necessary. Average soil. Allow 1-foot space between plants.

Monkeyflower. *Mimulus.* Zones 2–10. 6–18 inches. Monkeyflowers are perennials grown as annuals. They are rather floppy plants with trumpet-shaped flowers during the summer in red, yellow, orange or bicolors. Sow seeds indoors 8–10 weeks before last frost. Grow in sun or partial shade in average soil which is kept damp. Plants do particularly well along the edges of streams or ponds or in hanging containers which are watered every day. Allow 9-inch space between plants.

Nasturtium. ❋ *Tropaeolum.* Zones 1–10. 1–3 feet. Popular annuals with bright-green leaves and fragrant single or double flowers in orange, red, yellow or mahogany throughout the summer and into the fall. Plant in beds or containers; use 3-foot varieties for covering stumps, rocks or fences. Sow seeds outdoors where plants are to grow after last frost. Give full sun. The soil should be of average to poor quality but with excellent drainage. Allow 9-inch space between plants. Don't fertilize, but water in dry spells. To control aphids, which are a common pest, spray with malathion or apply a systemic poison.

Nemesia. Zones 2–8. 6–18 inches. Dainty plant with clusters of small tubular flowers in almost every color, which bloom during the summer. Use in masses in beds, and in containers. Sow seeds indoors 8–10 weeks before last frost so they will be well grown by the time hot weather comes. Grow in sun in rich, moist soil. Allow 8-inch space between plants. Pinch stem ends to make for bushier growth.

Nicotiana is a useful fill-in plant with a pleasant fragrance.

Nemophila. Zones 2–10. 6 inches. One variety, Baby Blue Eyes, has cup-shaped blue flowers with white centers. Another, Spotted Nemophila, has white flowers with purple lines and dots. Use for edgings or ground covers, or grow in containers. Sow outdoors before last frost. Sun or light shade. Average soil. Allow 9-inch space between plants.

***Nicotiana.* Flowering Tobacco.** Zones 2–10. 8–30 inches. This is an accommodating flower with a profusion of fragrant blossoms in white, pink, red or lime-green. These appear in the summer and have long, slender tubes with star-shaped faces. Plant in large groups in the flower bed. Sow seeds indoors 8 weeks before last frost. Grow in sun or partial shade in average soil. Allow 1-foot space between plants.

Patience. ❊ ***Impatiens.*** Zones 3–10. 6–24 inches. These are ideal plants for partially shaded borders and also for growing in containers in light shade. The green, bushy plants are covered from mid-spring to fall with phloxlike blossoms up to 2 inches across. Once available in only a few colors, the flowers now come in white, many shades of pink and red, tangerine and purple. Most blossoms are single, but doubles are available.

Sow seeds indoors 8–10 weeks before last frost. Grow in partial shade in well-drained, average soil. Allow 6–9-inch space between plants, depending on their height. Fertilize twice during the growing

Patience does better in the shade than any other annual. This bed, which is also planted with coleus and a few tuberous begonias, is mulched with chopped bark.

season and keep watered. In the fall you can cut plants back, pot them up and continue to grow them in a sunny window during the winter. But for best results, take stem cuttings in late summer and propagate new plants for winter enjoyment.

Petunia. ❋ Zones 1–10. 1–2 feet. If you were able to grow only one annual flower, the petunia would be your first choice. In terms of flower shape and color it offers more than any other genus. And wherever it is used—in beds, window boxes or containers, or as cut flowers in a vase—it makes an excitingly beautiful show.

Some of the single flowers have star-shaped faces, some are round, some are ruffled and some have lacy fringes. The double flowers are ruffled all over. Colors range right through the spectrum, missing only green. True, the yellows and oranges are below par; but the reds, pinks, blues, purples and whites are gorgeous. For good measure, there are entrancing bicolors.

Although some petunias form reasonably compact plants, all spread —some to a considerable distance. The latter, especially suited to window boxes and hanging baskets, are called cascade or balcony petunias. Those used in borders are known as bedding petunias.

Petunia seed is minute, and you should take pains to sow it thinly. Do not cover it with soil; just press it lightly into the surface. For the earliest bloom, start seeds indoors 8–10 weeks before last frost. Move the plants outdoors as soon as the weather is reliable. Plant them in full sun or very light shade. The soil should be of average quality, but well drained. Allow each plant a 1-foot space. Pinch the young plants back several times to make them bushy. Fertilize them after they are established outdoors and again about a month later. Water regularly. Pick off dead flowers and stems promptly. If the plants get too rangy as summer nears the end, cut them back 50 percent to encourage new growth.

One of the very best annuals: petunias. But to keep them blooming like this, you must pick off the spent blossoms faithfully.

Phlox, Drummond. ❄ ***Phlox drummondii.*** Zones 2–10. 6–18 inches. Topnotch flowers for beds and edgings and also for cutting. Flat, five-petaled flowers sometimes more than 1½ inches across are borne in showy clusters on erect stems. There are whites, pinks, reds and purples, sometimes with contrasting centers. Sow seeds indoors 8 weeks before last frost or outdoors after last frost. Grow in the sun in rich, humusy, well-drained soil. Allow 6-inch space between plants for dwarf varieties, 9 inches for tall. Pick off dead flowers to prolong bloom from mid-spring through the summer.

Pinks, China. ❄ ***Dianthus.*** Zones 2–10. 6–12 inches. Gay little white, pink, red or lavender flowers borne in profusion during the summer on erect stems. Some are singles; some, doubles. Some have plain edges; others have fringed edges. All are showy in beds or edgings. Sow seeds indoors 8–10 weeks before last frost. Grow in sun in average, well-drained soil. Allow 6-inch space between plants. Keep spent flowers picked off.

Poppy, California. ***Escholtzia.*** Zones 1–10. 8–24 inches. Many-branched plant with 2-inch single or double cup-shaped flowers in yellow, orange, pink, red or white. They bloom from mid-spring to mid-autumn, provided you pick off dead flowers at once. If you will remember to do this, the poppies can be grown in a flower bed; otherwise they should be broadcast on hillsides and other naturalized areas. Sow seeds outdoors where plants are to grow as early in the spring as possible; or sow them outdoors in the fall. Thin to give each plant 9 inches of space. Give sun and average soil.

Poppy, Mexican Tulip. ***Hunnemannia.*** Zones 6–10. 2–3 feet. A perennial grown as an annual. Bushy plant with nicely chiseled foliage and yellow cup-shaped flowers with crinkled petals from midsummer till fall. Plant in large groups in beds. Excellent for cutting because they last a week if you cut them before they open completely and burn the stems at the cut. Sow seeds outdoors where plants are to grow 2 weeks before last frost. Grow in sun in average, well-drained soil. Allow 9-inch space between plants. Don't overwater.

Poppy, Prickly. ***Argemone.*** Zones 6–10. 2–3 feet. Does particularly well in the Southwest. It has prickly leaves and large, showy, yellow or white flowers in the summer. Sow seeds outdoors where plants are to grow after last frost. Give sun and average soil. Allow 1-foot space between plants.

Poppy, Shirley. *Papaver.* Zones 1–10. 18–36 inches. Lovely papery single or double flowers on slender stems start blooming in mid-spring and continue to midsummer if you keep spent blooms picked off. In dainty tones of red, pink, white or salmon—often with a suffusion of a second color. Sow seeds outdoors in early spring before the last frost; can also be sown in the fall if winters are mild. Don't cover the seeds; just water them in well. Grow in sun in average, well-drained soil. Allow 9-inch space between plants.

Portulaca. **Rose Moss,** Sun Plant. Zones 2–10. 6–8 inches. If you want a bright patch of color, this is a good flower to plant; but it is useless otherwise. Flowers are profusely borne on creeping stems during the hottest part of the summer. They have a general resemblance to miniature single or double roses; available in white, pink, red or yellow. They open only during the day. Sow seeds outdoors where plants are to grow after last frost. Sun. Average soil. Thin to 6 inches apart.

Salpiglossis. **Velvet Flower,** Painted Tongue. Zones 1–10. 2–3 feet. Upright plant with sticky leaves and pretty petunia-like flowers in yellow, red, mahogany or blue. The petals are intricately streaked with contrasting colors. Blooms in summer. Good for beds and cutting, but plants are hard to get started. Sow seeds indoors 8–10 weeks before last frost. Put several seeds in a small peat pot and thin to one seedling before planting outdoors. This reduces transplanting shock. Grow in full sun in rich, humusy soil. Allow 9-inch space between plants. Pinch out stem ends to promote branching. Don't overwater.

Salvia, Blue. ❋ *Salvia farinacea* and *Salvia patens.* Zones 3–10. 30 inches. Blue salvia is nowhere nearly as well known as red salvia—probably because it doesn't make its presence known so forcefully. But it is a superior plant. The gray-green leaves on thin, upright stems contrast nicely with foliage of other flowers in the border. The slender spikes of flowers in several lovely shades of blue appear throughout the

Two salvias. The lower one at left is a lovely dusty-pink form of the familiar red salvia. The tall one at right is blue salvia, a more delicate and useful plant in every way.

summer until long after the first frost. They are favorites of all flower arrangers.

Blue salvias are perennials usually grown as annuals. Sow the seeds indoors 8–10 weeks before last frost. Grow in average soil in the sun. Allow 9-inch space for each plant. Stake plants if in a windy location.

Salvia, Red. ❄ ***Salvia splendens,*** Scarlet Sage. Zones 3–10. 8–36 inches. There is nothing more brilliant in the garden than a bed of red salvia. The flower spikes borne above bushy green plants are fire-engine red—so red, in fact, that it is hard to use this plant in a border with anything else. However, there are several lovely varieties in much more subdued shades of rose, pink, white or purple. All bloom from summer till frost. Sow seeds indoors 8–10 weeks before last frost. Plant in average soil in the sun; however, non-red varieties also do well in partial shade. Allow 6-inch space between plants for dwarf varieties; 12–18 inches for all others.

Sanvitalia. Zones 3–10. 6 inches. Little trailing plant with numerous 1-inch daisylike flowers with short yellow petals and large purplish-black centers. Blooms from mid-spring through summer. Use in rock gardens or flower beds. Sow seeds indoors 6–8 weeks before last frost or outdoors after last frost. Sun. Average soil. Allow 9-inch space between plants.

Scabiosa. **Sweet Scabious,** Pincushion Flower. Zones 2–10. 18–36 inches. Long-stemmed flowers with largish, somewhat twisted outer petals surrounding a mound from which the stamens protrude like pins in a pincushion. White, pink, rose, blue, purple. Blooms in summer. A good bedding and cutting flower. Sow seeds indoors 6–8 weeks before last frost or outdoors after last frost. Grow in average soil, which should be limed if acid. Sun or partial shade. Allow 1-foot space between plants. Keep dead flowers picked off.

Snapdragon. ❅ *Antirrhinum.* Zones 1–10. 6–36 inches. These are sensational plants—a must in every garden. They have beautiful forms; their colors—white, cream, pink, red, yellow, orange or lavender—are vivid. Use them in flower beds in small clusters as accent plants, or use them in great masses. Use the dwarf varieties for edgings, window boxes and rock gardens.

Large varieties have thick spikes of flowers which open over a period

Snapdragons combine lovely color with interesting form; but they often need help to grow as straight as this.

of time from the bottom up. They are a flower arranger's dream. On dwarf varieties, the flower clusters are much shorter, but so numerous that they almost hide the attractive slender green leaves. Bloom extends throughout the summer until after the first frost.

Snapdragons are actually biennials but are usually grown as annuals. Sow the seeds indoors 8–10 weeks before last frost and take pains to turn the flats so the plants do not grow on a slant. Move outdoors into full sun in well-drained, humusy soil. Allow 1-foot space between plants for tall varieties; 6 inches for dwarf. Fertilize twice before flowering starts. Pinch stem ends to make for bushier growth. Because the tall plants tend to flop when young, it's advisable to stake them until they fill out.

In areas with mild winters, cut plants down after they stop flowering and cover with a little salt hay to carry them over the winter.

Spiderflower. *Cleome.* Zones 2–10. 3–5 feet. An oddly attractive plant for the back of the flower bed. It has strong-smelling, compound leaves

Tall-growing spiderflower makes an odd outline against the sky. The flowers in the foreground are dwarf hollyhocks.

from which arise tall stalks that put out a new whorl of pink, white, purple or orange flowers every day. The flowers, which bloom throughout the summer, have long, protruding stamens and are succeeded by very long, slender seed capsules surrounding the stalks. Sow seeds outdoors after last frost. Grow in sun and average soil. Allow 18–24-inch space between plants. Pick off old seed capsules before they open; otherwise the plants will self-sow all over your garden.

Star of Texas. *Xanthisma.* Zones 6–10. 18 inches. Bushy plant with daisylike flowers with pointed yellow petals from spring till fall. Not well known, but useful if you live in a dry climate. Sow seeds outdoors 2–3 weeks before last frost. Grow in sun and average soil. Allow 9-inch space between plants.

Statice. *Limonium*, Sea Lavender. Zones 2–10. 18–36 inches. Interesting plant with large basal leaves above which are borne numerous stems with airy flower clusters in almost all colors. On most varieties the flowers appear at the tops of the stems, but in *Limonium suworowii* the flowers surround the stems from top to bottom. Bloom period is from late spring through the summer. Effective in flower beds and arrangements and very popular for drying. Sow seeds indoors 6–8 weeks before last frost. Grow in sun in average, well-drained soil. Allow 12–15-inch space between plants.

Stock. *Mathiola.* Zones 2–10. 12–30 inches. These are lovely, very fragrant annuals but they are not easy to grow. They do best in cool weather. The flowers are borne in large, dense spikes of white, pink, red, blue or purple. Use in beds and for cutting. Small varieties are good in large containers or window boxes. Some varieties bloom only 7 weeks after sowing; most take longer. The evening-scented stock is an 18-inch plant which opens its flowers only at night.

Sow seeds indoors 4–6 weeks before last frost and keep in a cool (under 65° F.) room. Transplant into individual small pots when seedlings have six leaves. Move outdoors after frost danger is past. Put in a sunny spot in well-drained, very fertile, humusy soil. Allow 6–9-inch space between plants for small varieties; 12–15 inches for large. Fertilize monthly. Water regularly but don't overdo it. Pinch out side stems to produce very large flower spikes.

Strawflower. *Helichrysum.* Zones 2–10. 18–30 inches. The most popular everlasting used for dried winter arrangements. Upright plant with numerous papery blossoms in pink, red, orange, yellow, white or purple. Plant in an out-of-the-way corner of the flower bed, because it does not contribute much to the beauty of the bed. Blooms during the summer. Sow seeds outdoors after last frost. Give sun, average soil. Allow 9-inch space between plants. Water sparingly.

Sunflower. *Helianthus.* Zones 1–10. 15 inches–10 feet. Strong, coarse plants with huge daisylike flowers. These are usually single and yellow, but some are double and chrysanthemumlike. Other colors are chestnut-red and a very pretty white, shading to yellow, next to a black center.

Giant sunflowers: not very pretty, but a marvelous conversation piece. When the seeds in the black centers of the flowers ripen, birds will come flocking.

Small varieties are planted in the flower border or used for screens. The mammoth Russian sunflowers with blossoms 1–2 feet across are usually relegated to the vegetable garden or an out-of-the-way part of the yard because they are anything but handsome.

Sow all sunflower seeds outdoors where the plants are to grow after the soil is warm and frost danger is about over. Grow in full sun. The soil need be of only average quality, but if you want maximum growth, make sure it is well drained and well reinforced with humus. Allow 1-foot space between plants for dwarf varieties; 3 feet for large. Although plants are quite drought-resistant, water regularly and fertilize several times during the summer. Pinch back smaller varieties to make them bushier. Stake tall varieties. As the seeds of the giant varieties ripen, cover the heads with cheesecloth to keep off the birds.

Sweet Pea. ❊ *Lathyrus.* Zones 1–10. 8 inches–5 feet. Ever popular flower with lovely clusters of fragrant flowers in white, pink, red, salmon, blue or purple. Small bush varieties such as Bijou, Americana and Knee-Hi don't need to be staked. Large vining types must be given some sort of trellis or other support to grow on. Time of flowering also varies. Some types, such as Americana and Galaxy, bloom in the summer. Others such as Cuthbertson bloom in the spring. The so-called "early-flowering" types bloom in winter and are grown outdoors only in frost-free areas (the seeds are sown in September).

To raise spring- and summer-flowering sweet peas, sow the seeds outdoors where the plants are to grow as soon as the soil is workable. The seeds should be planted 2 to 3 inches deep. Plants need full sun. They will get along in average soil if it is well drained and fertilized several times during the growing season; but you will get better results by preparing the soil to a depth of 12–18 inches, by mixing in plenty of humus and a handful of bone meal or half a handful of balanced fertilizer per cubic foot of soil.

Give each bush-type plant 1 foot of space; vining types, 6 inches. Stake vining types when they are about 4 inches tall. Water during dry spells. Keep flowers picked.

Sweet Sultan. *Centaurea.* Zones 1–10. 2–3 feet. A relative of the cornflower and grown in the same way—but sow seeds only in the spring.

The fragrant 2-inch flowers look like flattened thistles. They come in white, red, shades of lavender-pink and sometimes yellow. Use in the flower bed. Excellent for cutting.

Torenia. **Wishbone Flower.** Zones 3–10. 1 foot. Bushy plant with pretty, oddly shaped 1-inch flowers which are usually two shades of blue and with a yellow blotch in the throat; but white-and-yellow and blue-and-white forms are available. Blooms throughout summer and fall. Use in beds, edgings, containers and rock gardens. Sow seeds indoors 8 weeks before last frost. Plant in average soil in sun or partial shade. Allow 6-inch space between plants.

Venidium. **Monarch of the Veldt.** Zones 6–10. 2–3 feet. A fine but little known annual with handsome, deeply cut gray-green leaves and 4–5-inch daisies with rich orange petals and purple-black centers. Showy in the border during the summer, and good for cutting. Sow seeds indoors 8–10 weeks before last frost or outdoors after last frost. Give sun and average, well-drained soil. Allow 1-foot space between plants. Fertilize sparingly and keep rather dry.

Verbena. ❋ Zones 1–10. 6–12 inches. Bushy, spready plant with sizable clusters of delightful little flowers in white, pink, red, salmon, blue or purple; these often have contrasting eyes. The flowers are borne from mid-spring till frost. Use in edgings, ground covers, rock gardens and containers. This is a perennial grown as an annual. Sow seeds indoors 8–10 weeks before last frost. Transplant to small individual pots. Then move into the garden in full sun and average soil. Allow 9–18-inch space between plants. Remove dead flowers. In very mild climates plants will survive the winter.

Vinca rosea. **Madagascar Periwinkle.** Zones 5–10. 8–18 inches. Useful plant with dark-green leaves and numerous flat five-petaled flowers up to 1½ inches across from summer through fall. The flowers are usually deep pink but may be white with or without pink eyes. Use the tall bush type in the flower bed; dwarf varieties in edgings or containers; and creeping types, which spread as much as 2 feet, as ground covers or in hanging baskets. This is a perennial usually grown as an annual. Sow seeds indoors 8–10 weeks before last frost. Transplant to individual pots. Then plant out in average, humusy soil when the weather is warm. Grows best in sun but also takes some shade. Allow 9-inch space between all except creeping varieties, which need 15 inches. Water regularly. Will survive the winter in warm climates.

Xeranthemum. Immortelle. Zones 2–10. 2–3 feet. A slender plant with sparse leaves and fluffy, papery flowers in white, pink, red or purple. The flowers are used for dried arrangements. Blooms in summer. Sow seeds outdoors after last frost. Sun. Average soil. Allow 9-inch space between plants.

Zinnia. ✿ Zones 2–10. 6–36 inches. Zinnias share with petunias and marigolds the honor of being our most popular annual flowers. And with good reason: the large-flowered varieties are spectacular. All varieties are useful, and all are easy to grow.

Mammoth zinnias are a mainstay in every annual garden.

The flowers come in every color except blue. Some are two-toned. In size they range from 1 inch to as much as 7 inches across. And in shapes they range from tidy little buttons, ever so stiff and proper, to big, shaggy, chrysanthemumlike heads.

Flowering starts in early summer and continues until frost. Use plants in beds, edgings and containers; and have plenty of vases handy to make bouquets for every room in the house.

Sow seeds indoors 6 weeks before last frost. Move into a sunny location outdoors. The soil need be of only average quality but should be well drained and humusy. Allow dwarf plants 6–9-inch space; large varieties, 1 foot. When plants are small, pinch the stem ends to make them bush out. Water regularly. Fertilize soon after planting out and again when plants start to bloom. Keep flowers cut. Dust with sulfur (except in hottest weather) to prevent mildew.

·7·

GROWING
PERENNIALS

If you love flowers, you will sooner or later grow perennials. Most new gardeners, it is true, shy away from them for the first few years. But eventually they realize that the flowers have many pluses and no minuses.

Peonies—some open, some about ready to open—provide glowing color and fragrance and serve as an excellent background throughout the growing season for smaller plants.

For one thing, the group is made up of numerous lovely flowers; and there are several which have no equals.

For another, some perennials are in bloom long before annuals even start to form buds; at least one continues blooming long after most annuals have been struck down by frost; and several bloom in the winter. Thus they extend the normal growing season at both ends; and while they may not be so spectacular as annuals in midsummer, they nevertheless provide much color even at that time.

In the third place, perennials are permanent. They may cost a bit more than annuals to start with, but in the long run they are cheaper because they go on and on for years. Furthermore, this permanence tends to save work for the gardener. I don't want to overstress this point because it is difficult to determine whether annuals require more work than perennials or vice versa.

Finally, perennials are useful not only in the flower bed but also in other types of plantings in which annuals and bulbs and roses have little place.

PERENNIALS IN FLOWER BEDS

Although there are old-time gardeners who plant flower beds entirely to perennials, most people today build beds in which perennials are mixed with annuals and perhaps biennials and bulbs. This gives you the best of everything. And it is also easier this way to keep the bed bright with color and fragrance throughout the growing season.

Laying out and developing a flower bed with a mixture of flowers or with perennials only is done in the same way that you lay out a bed for annuals only (see Chapter 5). There is only one rather small, special problem to think about: Some early-blooming perennials disappear after their flowers have faded. The leaves and stems die and you are left with a bare patch of earth and an empty hole in your blanket of color. Obviously you should not and cannot plant a replacement on top of the departed; but there is no reason why you should not move a potted plant into the gap. The more usual alternative is to plant annuals rather close around the perennial and let them fill the hole as they grow up and out.

Large-leaved hostas and feathery astilbes—perfect plants for shady locations.
Phlox and globe thistles grow in a sunny spot out from under the shade tree.

PERENNIALS AS GROUND COVERS

Ground covers are low-growing plants used instead of grass to cover areas where grass either will not grow or cannot be grown because you can't keep it mowed. Although most plants used for ground covers are shrubs or vines, some are perennials. The following are among the best:

Perennials Used as Ground Covers

Alternanthera
Germander
Hosta
Ice Plant

Though almost too steep to climb, this California hillside does not erode, because it is covered with lavender ice plants. In the middle of the day thousands upon thousands of blossoms make a sheet of color. The plants beside the wall are mainly succulents.

Lamb's Ears
Lily-of-the-Valley
Phlox
Queen's Tears
Sedum
Snow-in-Summer

When using perennials as ground covers, it is imperative to prepare the soil in the area with care because it should support vigorous growth with minimum attention year after year. You must, accordingly, dig the soil deeply, as for a flower bed, enrich it with humus and bone meal,

Moss pinks (creeping phlox) cover a sunny bank. These are pale blue and white and obviously go well together. But many gardeners let their enthusiasm for great masses of color ruin the effect.

and add whatever other materials the situation requires (see Chapter 2).

Only one variety of perennial should be planted in any one area, since the purpose of a ground cover is to create a blanket of green leaves and a blanket of flowers of a single shape and color. Space the plants as in a flower bed. Until they spread to cover the bare soil, keep them weeded (weeds are the worst pests in a ground-cover planting); then apply and maintain a mulch of peat moss or other organic matter. Fertilize the planting early every spring with bone meal or a slow-release balanced inorganic fertilizer. This should be enough for the year. But water regularly during dry weather.

PERENNIALS AS EDGINGS

Edgings are used not only in flower beds but also along walks and driveways and sometimes in the front of shrubbery borders. Perennials which are ideal for this purpose are the following:

Perennials Used in Edgings
Arabis
Armeria
Aster
Basket of Gold
Campanula
Candytuft
Dusty Miller
Germander
Hosta
Lamb's Ears
Pink
Snow-in-Summer

Perennials used in edgings should be handled like those in flower beds.

Two views of an unusually well-designed, well-planted wall garden crammed with perennials. The early spring color scheme is mainly white and yellow, but flowers of other colors are used as accents.

ROCK GARDENS

These are specialized gardens which should be undertaken only after you have studied several created by experts. They are very difficult to do well, and many people who try them wind up with little more than an ugly rock pile.

Enthusiasts build rock gardens in various forms, identified by such names as glacial moraine, scree, alpine lawn, rocky pasture and heath. But the only type of rock garden a novice should attempt is one resembling a natural rock outcropping on a hill.

In this, all the rocks are of the same type and color—for instance, all gray granite or red sandstone—and all tilted in the same direction. Some of the rocks stick out higher aboveground than others, but in all cases a larger part of the rock is belowground than above. The rocks are separated from one another by winding strips of soil, and it is in these strips that you plant flowers. Some of the strips should also be wide enough to serve as paths and surfaced with gravel or chopped bark.

The design of a rock garden is not the only thing you must worry about. Construction is also complicated by the fact that the rocks used should be large. Old-time rock gardeners maintained that if you can move a rock yourself, it is too small for a rock garden. If you consider that a 12 × 12 × 12-inch rock averages 170 pounds, the enormity of building an attractive, true-to-nature rock garden becomes clear.

Happily, planting the rock garden is not difficult. Purists to the contrary, you can use any low-growing perennials you like. Small bulbs are also excellent, and a few annuals can be added for good measure.

WALL GARDENS

A wall garden resembles a retaining wall built of stones and with small perennials growing in the chinks. It is much less difficult to design and build than a rock garden.

The face of the wall should be approximately 2 feet in front of a slope. Dig a trench at least 6 inches deep, and preferably 12 inches, and fill it with well-compacted small stones or crushed rock. Build the wall up from this frost-resistant base with flat rocks which are no more than 1 foot deep (from front to back). The face of the wall should slant backward 2 inches in each 1-foot rise; and the rocks themselves should slant slightly backward to resist pressure from the ground behind.

As you lay the rocks, fill in the space behind them with good soil containing plenty of humus and bone meal. The soil should be mixed with stones about the size of baseballs in the proportion of 3 parts soil to 1 part stone. Scatter more soil (without stones) in the horizontal and vertical chinks between the rocks. Plant your flowers in this. The crowns* of the plants should be 1 inch back from the face of the wall,

---

* The top of the root from which plant stems grow.

and the roots should be spread out in the soil and sprinkled with water before the next rocks are laid. Pour additional water into the newly added soil behind the rocks.

The wall should not exceed 3 feet in height. Anything higher might be dislodged by the pressure of the sloping ground.

When you reach the top of the wall, fill in the space behind it with about 2 inches of crushed stone or thin flat rocks.

Perennials suitable for planting in a wall garden are trailers, such as basket of gold, and those which form small tufts, such as violas. More plants of the same kind are usually planted in a narrow bed at the base of the wall. And the same plants plus additional larger species are planted just behind the top of the wall.

BUYING PERENNIALS

What has been said about buying annuals applies also to perennials. But whereas annuals are usually sold in small flats by local garden-supplies stores, perennials are usually sold as single plants, and not too many are to be found locally.

The principal and best sources of perennials are the large nurseries that sell by mail. These charge about 90 cents up for a single small plant, which will in most cases bloom the same year. If the plant should die, it will usually be replaced without charge.

Order perennials from mail-order firms as early as possible in the winter after the catalogs arrive, because the supply is sometimes limited. In addition, an early order may earn you a discount or bonus. The plants will be shipped to you in the spring when it is safe to put them in the ground. Each plant is wrapped individually (unless you order several of the same variety, in which case they are bundled together) in damp sphagnum moss or excelsior and plastic film. They should be planted in the garden soon after they arrive; but if this is impossible, as it sometimes is, you can leave them in their wrappings for several days. Make sure, however, that the inside wrappings are damp; if not, sprinkle them with water and rewrap the plastic in order to hold in moisture. Keep the plants in a sunless, cool (but not freezing) place until you are ready to plant them.

RAISING PERENNIALS FROM SEEDS

The majority of perennials are easily propagated this way, but since most need a year or more to develop before they come into bloom, the timing is less critical than with annuals. Sow the seeds outdoors any time after the last frost—but the sooner, the better, since it gives the plants more time to develop. Put them in a propagating bed or a cold-frame or unheated hotbed with the top removed. The seeds are handled much like annual seeds: Sow in rows 6 inches apart and thin or trans-plant the seedlings, after they have their true leaves, to about 3 inches apart. Keep watered and cultivate lightly to control weeds and aerate the soil. The alternative is to apply a mulch, preferably of grass clip-pings, after thinning. Fertilize lightly after thinning and every four to six weeks thereafter with a balanced plant food.

Transplant the plants to a flower bed (or any other location) either in early fall or early the following spring. If you transplant in the fall, give the plants a half cupful of starter solution and do not fertilize again until spring. When the soil freezes, cover it with a mulch of leaves, hay, etc., to prevent repeated thawing and freezing and thus keep the plants from being heaved out of the ground.

The few perennials that bloom fairly soon after seed-sowing can be handled in the same way. If you want bloom the first year, however, sow the seeds—like annuals—indoors under fluorescent light or in a hotbed; then move them into the flower bed as soon as the danger of frost has passed.

RAISING PERENNIALS FROM DIVISIONS

This is the most common and by far the simplest way of propagating perennials. The method involves nothing more than dividing large es-tablished plants into smaller rooted sections, which are planted directly in the flower bed. The job is done either in early spring or in the autumn after growth has died down.

How often perennials need to be divided depends on the species and also on the care they are given. Every three years is the normal sched-ule. But a few perennials, notably chrysanthemums, should be divided annually. Others should be divided every other year or only every four or five years. And a very few, such as peonies, are happier if you let them go ten years or more. Your best guide is the plants themselves. As perennials grow older, they increase in girth and begin to take up more room than you care to give them. In addition, the roots at the center of the plants lose vigor, and instead of putting up a solid mound of leaves and flowers, the plants become somewhat doughnut-shaped. The time to make divisions is just before these two things happen.

Divisions are made in four ways after the plants are dug up from the flower bed and the roots are washed off under a hose. Pull small plants apart with your fingers. Use a knife and/or hand fork on larger plants. Separate plants which develop huge mats of intertwined roots—daylilies, for example—by driving two spading forks into them, back to back, and pushing the handles apart. If this doesn't work, or you don't happen to have two forks, simply chop the roots apart with a sharp spade.

Whichever technique you use, save only the roots—with stems attached—at the outer edges of the root ball. These are young and vigorous and will develop within several months into big, healthy plants with abundant bloom. The roots at the center of the root ball should be discarded.

Replant the divisions in the flower bed as soon as possible after they are made. They should not be allowed to dry out. If you have more plants than you need, wrap the leftovers in damp newspapers and give them to your friends.

The roots of some perennials form such tight clumps that the only way you can divide them is to drive a spade through them.

How to make a stem cutting. After a short length of stem is cut from a plant, the lower leaves are removed, the stem is dipped in a rooting powder and is then stuck into the damp rooting medium in a large plastic bag which will hold in moisture around it.

PROPAGATING PERENNIALS BY STEM CUTTINGS

This is a good way to produce a great many plants; it is also a good way to produce only one or two plants if the perennial is too small to be divided or if it belongs to somebody else.

Stem cuttings, also called slips, are 2- to 4-inch pieces of stem taken from the tip ends of mature stems. Cut off the pieces ¼ inch below a leaf and then pull off all but three or four of the upper leaves. If you are making a number of cuttings, sprinkle them with water and place them in a plastic bag until all are ready.

The cuttings are rooted in damp vermiculite or sand. For just a few cuttings, pour 3 to 4 inches of the rooting medium into a large plastic bag; for lots of cuttings, put the rooting medium into a wooden flat. Poke holes in the rooting medium with a sharp pencil. They should be about 1 inch apart and 1 inch deep. Then dip the bottom ends of the cuttings in a hormone rooting powder to stimulate root development, drop them into the holes and firm the rooting medium around them. When all the cuttings are in place, sprinkle them very lightly with water.

To keep the cuttings from wilting and dying, they must be covered tightly with plastic film to hold moisture around them. Tie the tops of plastic bags shut with string. To cover a flat, bend stiff wires over the top and stretch a large sheet of plastic film over this, around the ends and under the flat. Tack securely. Try not to let the plastic touch the cuttings.

Place the cuttings in a warm, bright but sunless spot. Check them daily to make sure the moisture has not escaped and also to make sure the cuttings are not mildewed. If there is not enough moisture, add a little water to the rooting medium and see that the plastic is tightly sealed. If some cuttings are mildewed, rip them out and spray the rest with a fungicide.

After two or three weeks, open the plastic very slightly and leave it open to let in air. Roots should be developed about two weeks later. Check this by digging up one of the cuttings. Don't pull it out.

As soon as the cuttings are rooted, transplant them to the flower bed or a propagating bed and give them a little starter solution.

RAISING PERENNIALS FROM ROOT CUTTINGS

This is another way to produce lots of plants, but it's a slow process and I recommend it only for perennials such as Oriental poppies with large, fleshy roots that grow more or less straight down.

Dig the plants up in the fall; cut off a few of the vigorous outer roots; and cut these into pieces 3 to 4 inches long. To differentiate between the top and the bottom of each piece, make the cut at the top straight across, that at the bottom on a slant.

For a rooting medium, use a mixture of 3 parts soil to 1 part peat moss. Pour this to a depth of about 6 inches into large flowerpots or wooden boxes. Plant the cuttings with the top end about ½ inch below the soil surface, and firm the soil around them. The cuttings should not touch one another.

Store the cuttings over the winter in a coldframe. In late spring, after stems and leaves are well developed, transfer the plants to a propagating bed. Then move them into the flower bed in the fall.

PLANTING AND CARING FOR PERENNIALS

When transplanting small perennials you have raised from seed indoors, follow the directions for transplanting annuals. Larger perennials need not be handled with quite so much care because they have strong root systems, and at the time of transplanting they usually are showing very little green growth. It is therefore unnecessary to wait for a cloudy day or until late afternoon to move them; but you should give them water and then about a half cupful of starter solution after they are in the ground.

If you move established perennials from one part of the garden to another, and when you replant large divisions, be sure not to neglect the preparation of the soil just because of the plants' size. Dig it deeply and mix in fresh peat moss and a little bone meal before scooping out the planting holes. Then firm the soil well around the plants, but don't cover the crowns unless the directions given for individual perennials call for this.

For how to care for perennials, see Chapter 3. All perennials should be fertilized in early spring and once again in late spring. Those which bloom in summer and fall can be fertilized a third time between July 15 and August 15 in colder climates, two or three weeks later in warm climates.

In the spring, cultivate lightly around perennials so air and moisture can get down to the roots and also to mix in fertilizer, but take pains not to injure the roots. Maintenance of an organic mulch throughout the growing season is highly advisable.

When plants die down, cut off the tops and add them to your leaf pile to decompose if they are not diseased. Be sure to mark the locations of the plants with labels. Protection over winter is not required in our coldest and warmest climates—but in moderate areas, where the soil alternately freezes and thaws, you can keep plants from being heaved out of the ground by covering them and the soil around them with a light mulch of hay, salt hay or evergreen boughs after the ground is frozen. (Of course, if you maintain a summer mulch, there is no need to pile on additional covering.)

Favorite Perennials

(The symbol ❋ indicates the very best)

Acanthus mollis. **Bear's Breech.** Zones 6–10. 3–4 feet. Striking plant with huge, deeply cut, glossy leaves at the base and an 18-inch spike of tubular white or pinkish-lilac flowers in early summer. A good border plant, but because the roots spread far and wide, it's a better idea to use it where these can be confined or restricted—in a raised bed, for instance, or in a terrace planting pocket. Propagate by seeds, root cuttings or annual division in the spring. Grow in sun or partial shade. Average soil. Allow 4-foot space between plants. Watch out for slugs and snails.

Achillea. **Yarrow,** Milfoil. Zones 2–10. 8–48 inches. Easygoing plant with attractive, usually fernlike, aromatic foliage and sizable clusters of small pompon flowers throughout the summer. White, yellow, pink or red. Use in the flower bed and for cutting. Dwarfs are good in rock gardens. Grow from seeds or divisions in spring. Plant in full sun in average soil. Allow 1-foot space between plants.

Adonis. Zones 5–9. 9–12 inches. Uncommon plant with beautiful yellow flowers in early spring. These suggest a cup-shaped cosmos. Use in the rock garden or flower bed. Propagate by seeds or by division in spring. Grow in sun in rich soil. Allow 9-inch space between plants. Plant disappears in summer after it has bloomed, so be sure to mark its location.

Air Plant. *Kalanchoe* or *Bryophyllum.* Zones 9b–10. 3 feet. A succulent which produces tiny plants in the scallops of the leaves. Greenish-red, lanternlike flowers in summer. Can be grown in beds but is best in containers on a terrace, because the fallen leaves will sprout new plants if they come in contact with the ground. Propagate by potting up the plantlets. Grow in sun or partial shade. Average soil with plenty of humus. Allow 1-foot space between plants.

Alternanthera. Zones 9b–10. 15–24 inches. Several plants grown for their red or sometimes creamy-yellow foliage. The dense clusters of white flowers appearing in summer and fall are of minor value. Use the plants in the border or as a ground cover. Propagate by stem cuttings or division in the spring. Grow in sun in average soil. Allow 2-foot space between plants. Keep pruned to prevent legginess; or, if you wish, you can shear the plants frequently and hold them at a height of about 6 inches.

Anchusa. **Alkanet,** Bugloss. Zones 4–10. 3–5 feet. Large, spreading coarse plant with small, bright-blue forget-me-not-like flowers in clusters in the summer. Effective in the back of the flower bed. Propagate by seeds or by division in spring. Sun or light shade. Average soil. Allow 3-foot space between plants.

Anemone, Japanese. *Anemone hupehensis.* Zones 6–10. 2–3 feet. Graceful plant with slender stems rising from the foliage and bearing saucer-shaped flowers as much as 2½ inches across in late summer and early fall. White, pink or rose. Grow in a shrubby border or naturalized planting. Propagate by seeds, root cuttings or spring division. Plant in partial shade or sun. Average soil with plenty of humus added. Allow 1-foot space between plants. Don't divide too often.

Anthemis. **Golden Marguerite,** Ox-Eye Chamomile. Zones 5–10. 24–30 inches. Anthemis has feathery, light-green leaves and profuse yellow daisies with yellow centers on long stems. Blooms from summer into fall. Use in beds and for cutting. Propagate by seeds or by division in spring. Give sun, average to poor soil. Allow 1-foot space between plants.

Arabis. **Rock Cress.** Zones 2–10. 6–9 inches. Spreading, gray-leaved plant with white or pink flowers in early spring. Use in the rock garden or wall garden or as an edging. Propagate by seeds or by division in spring. Sun or partial shade. Average soil. Space 1 foot apart. Cut back after blooming and when it becomes overgrown, because it will try to take over your entire garden.

Armeria. **Thrift,** Sea Pink. Zones 4–9. 2–6 inches. This plant forms a

Silver mound artemisia is a fluffy blanket of silvery gray—an excellent foil for green-leaved plants.

cushion of stiff grasslike leaves which are topped by delightful bright-pink double flowers on short stems. Blooms in late spring and early summer. Use in edgings, beds, rock gardens and containers. Propagate by seeds or by division in spring. Needs sun and average, well-drained soil. Allow 6-inch space between plants for *Armeria caespitosa*; 1 foot for the spreading *Armeria maritima*.

Artemisia. Zones 2–10. 1–4 feet. There are several species of artemisia, all characterized by gray or whitish foliage. But the low-growing varieties such as Silver Mound and Silver Frost are especially desirable because they form compact, feathery-foliaged clumps which are excellent for edgings and can also be used to good effect as a foil for other perennials and annuals. They are attractive from spring to fall. Propagate by division. Plant in sun. Average soil with excellent drainage. Allow 1-foot space for small varieties.

Aster. ❊ **Michaelmas Daisy.** Zones 1–10. 6 inches–5 feet. Outstanding perennial which produces great masses of small daisylike flowers usually from late summer until after light frost, but, in a few cases, earlier. Colors range from white through pink and red to blue and purple. Use tall, erect varieties toward the back of the flower bed; small varieties which form dense, rounded clumps in the foreground and for edgings. You will be delighted with them all.

Propagate asters by seeds or by division in spring. Plant in full sun. They need only average soil but will grow more luxuriantly if you mix in plenty of humus and a couple of light doses of fertilizer. Allow 9–12-inch space between plants for small varieties; 24 inches for large. The latter need to be divided every year because they spread rapidly. Pinch stem ends to promote bushy growth.

Astilbe. **False Spirea.** Zones 3–9. 18–36 inches. Charming plant for the flower bed or large containers. It has pretty chiseled leaves and feathery plumes of tiny white, peach, red or lilac flowers on slender stems in late spring and early summer. Good for arrangements. Since the best astilbes on the market today are hybrids, these must be propagated by division in the spring; otherwise they will not come true. Plant in sun or partial shade. The soil should be rich, humusy and moist. Allow 1-foot space between plants.

Aubrieta. **Purple Rock Cress.** Zones 6–10. 4–6 inches. A spreading, early-spring-blooming plant with gray-green foliage and tiny pink, red, blue or purple flowers in great profusion. Use in the rock and wall gardens. Propagate named varieties by stem cuttings taken after bloom. Mixtures can be raised from seeds. Plant in sun in cool and temperate climates; in light shade in hot climates. Average soil. Allow 1-foot space between plants. After flowering, cut off blossoms and straggly leaf shoots and feed lightly.

Baby's Breath. ❊ ***Gypsophila.*** Zones 2–10. 3–4 feet. Few flowers have the airy, delicate grace of baby's breath. The slender-leaved, many-branched plant is a cloud of tiny white flowers in late spring and early summer. Bristol Fairy, with little double flowers, is the outstanding variety. Use in the flower bed and for cutting. Sow seeds outdoors after last frost or buy plants. Sun. Average soil. Allow 3-foot space between plants. Don't disturb plants any more than necessary by dividing or deep cultivating.

Balloonflower. *Platycodon.* Zones 4-10. 1–2 feet. Erect, many-stemmed plant with numerous flowers in the summer. These start out as white, blue or light-pink balloonlike buds and then open to 2-inch bells with 5 points. Propagate by seeds or division in the spring. Sun or light shade. Average, well-drained soil. Allow 9-inch space between plants for small varieties; 12–18 inches for large. Stake taller varieties because the stems flop badly. Keep spent flowers picked off to prolong bloom. Mark location of plants in the fall before they die down, because they disappear entirely in the winter and are late to come up the next spring.

Baptisia. **Wild Indigo,** False Indigo. Zones 5–10. 4–5 feet. Baptisia is a vigorous plant with attractive leaflets arranged finger-fashion and upright, loose spikes of dark-blue pealike flowers in early summer. These are followed by inflated seed pods. Use in the flower bed. Both flowers and seedpods are nice in arrangements. Propagate by seeds or by division in spring. Sun. Average soil. Allow 30-inch space. Pick off dead flowers to prolong bloom.

Basket of Gold. *Alyssum.* Zones 3–10. 1 foot. Popular spring perennial used in rock gardens, edgings and chinks in dry walls. The gray-green foliage is almost completely hidden under yellow flowers. Propagate by division in spring or fall or by seeds. Sun. Average soil. Allow 1-foot space between plants. Cut the stems back about a third after flowering to prevent lanky growth.

Beebalm. *Monarda,* Bergamot. Zones 3–7. 2–3 feet. You may not like the fact that beebalm attracts bees, but it is also attractive to hummingbirds—and that makes it a delight. Furthermore the flowers, like spidery daisies, are charming, in shades of red, pink, purple or white; they appear in midsummer. Both the flowers and leaves smell like mint. Use in flower beds and for cutting. Propagate named varieties by division in spring; mixtures by seeds. Plant in partial shade or sun in average soil that holds moisture. Allow 1-foot space between plants and keep the roots cut back so they don't spread beyond that.

A handsome clump of bird of paradise growing in a circular plant pocket in the middle of a California terrace.

Bergenia. Zones 5–10. 9–20 inches. Plant is grown mainly for its large, rounded, glossy leaves, which are evergreen in milder climates. Nodding clusters of white, pink or rose flowers in early spring. Use in shrubbery borders and under trees. Propagate by seeds or by division in spring. Plant in partial shade in average, humusy soil. Space 12–18 inches apart. Water regularly. Watch out for slugs and snails.

Bird of Paradise. *Strelitzia.* Zones 9b–10. 3–5 feet. Spectacular plant with long-lasting orange, blue or white flowers resembling birds. These come on long straight stems and appear off and on throughout the year. The leaves are long, wide, leathery straps. Grow in the border or in big containers. Propagate by seeds or by division in late winter when the plants are crowded. Grow in sun, or in light shade in the hottest climates. Average soil with plenty of humus. Allow 3-foot space between plants. Keep watered. Fertilize every month.

Bleeding Heart. *Dicentra.* Zones 1–10. 1–3 feet. Pleasant but not showy plant with pretty foliage and little red, pink or white flowers on long, slender stems. These usually appear in mid-spring and usually last to about midsummer. Use in flower or shrubbery borders. Propagate by seeds or by division in spring. Plant in partial shade in rich, well-drained, humusy soil which retains moisture. Allow 1-foot space between plants. Plants usually disappear after flowering, so mark their location. In hottest areas, where they are short-lived, make new divisions annually.

Boltonia. Zones 4–10. 2–6 feet. Boltonia is similar to the hardy aster but grows larger and has somewhat smaller flowers in clusters. They are white, pink, lavender or blue, with yellow centers. Propagate by seeds or by division in spring. Sun. Average soil. Allow 2-foot space between plants for small varieties; 3 feet for large. Keep roots cut back and divide annually; otherwise the plants will outgrow the garden.

The flowers grow in such thick clusters on this clump of bleeding heart that the stems droop.

Bugbane. *Cimicifuga,* Snakeroot. Zones 3–10. 3–6 feet. Statuesque plant with glossy, dark-green, much-divided leaves and dense white flower spikes in late summer or fall, depending on the species. Use at the back of a flower bed, as a screen or in a naturalized setting. Propagate by division in the spring. Plant in partial shade in moist, rich, humusy soil. Allow 2-foot space between plants for smaller varieties; 3 feet for large. Don't disturb plants too often.

Butterfly Weed. *Asclepias,* Orange Milkweed. Zones 4–8. 2 feet. This is a milkweed with rigid stems and big, flat clusters of orange flowers in late summer and fall. They attract butterflies. Use in the flower bed. Propagate by seeds or by division in spring. Full sun. Average soil, but does well in very sandy soil. Allow 1-foot space between plants.

Campanula. ❀ **Bellflower.** Zones 2–8, though some do well in zones 9 and 10 in California. A large, important and very useful group of perennials blooming in the summer and, in some cases, in late spring. All are propagated by seeds or by division in spring. Grow in sun or partial shade in average soil. Allow 9–15-inch space between plants, depending on their height. Pick off dead flowers to prolong bloom. Outstanding species include the following:

Carpathian Harebells. These form rounded mounds to 1 foot high. Blue, white or purple cup-shaped flowers. Use in beds, edgings, rock gardens or containers.

Peach Bells. Slender, 3-foot plants with big, bell-shaped blue or white flowers. Use in the border.

Milky Bellflowers. To 5 feet. Another border plant with broad, bell-shaped white or pale-blue flowers in drooping clusters.

Bluebells of Scotland. Bell-shaped, blue to lavender flowers in loose clusters. Plants to 20 inches high and variable in shape. Use in beds or rock gardens.

Candytuft, Perennial. *Iberis.* Zones 4–10. 1 foot. Evergreen plant with neat foliage which is covered in mid-spring with white flowers. Use in beds, rock gardens or edgings. An extremely good low-growing plant. Propagate by seeds or division in the spring. Plant in sun or partial shade. Average soil. Allow a 2-foot space, but the plant can be kept smaller. Trim it somewhat after flowering to keep it from straggling.

Cardinal Flower. *Lobelia.* Zones 4–10. 2–4 feet. Stiffly upright plant with loose spikes of 1-inch flame-red flowers from midsummer on. Grow in the flower bed in a large clump or, better still, a mass; or naturalize next to a stream or pond (where the plant grows in nature). Propagate by seeds or by division in spring. Partial shade. Average, humusy, moist soil. Allow 9-inch space between plants. Don't let the plants dry out.

Cardinal's Guard. *Pachystachys.* Zones 9b–10. 5 feet. Large, lustrous-leaved plant with tubular scarlet flowers in a spike. Blooms in summer and fall. Propagate by young stem cuttings in the spring. Plant in partial shade in average soil. Allow 2-foot space between plants.

Chinese Lanterns. *Physalis.* Zones 5–10. 2 feet. Grown for its bright-red, 2-inch-long fruits, which resemble Chinese lanterns. These ripen in late summer; are often dried for bouquets. White flowers in early summer are inconspicuous. Grow in the border or a large container. Propagate by seeds or annual division in the spring. Sun or partial shade. Average soil. Allow 1-foot space between plants. Watch out that the plant doesn't get away from you; its roots spread rapidly.

Christmas Rose. *Helleborus.* Zones 5–8. 18 inches. Unusual, distinctive evergreen perennial with large, glossy, compound leaves divided finger-fashion into 7 to 9 sizable leaflets. Five-petaled flowers more than 2 inches across appear about Christmastime in mild climates, somewhat later in colder areas. These start out white or greenish-white and gradually turn purple. They are long-lasting and good for cutting, and on established plants there are many of them. Plant near the house in a

The Christmas rose blooms in the snow. The large, compound evergreen leaves are beautiful the year round. (Photo by Stern's Nurseries)

foundation or shrubbery border. Purchase plants. Grow in a place that gets a little sun in winter but none in summer. Soil should be of average or better quality, well drained, humusy and not acid. Allow 1-foot space between plants. Water regularly. Fertilize lightly a couple of times a year and topdress with peat moss in early fall. Don't move or divide plants.

Chrysanthemum. ❋ Zones 3–10. 1–4 feet. A garden is hardly a garden without chrysanthemums. They are essential not only because they fill the garden with color when almost all other perennials have stopped blooming and most annuals are petering out but also because of their innate beauty. They come in every color except blue and green. In shape they range from tiny buttons through huge football mums to large, flattish blossoms with spoon-shaped petals. Small plants form dense, rounded mounds; large ones are bushy and erect.

There are so many varieties to choose from that you'll have trouble working your list down to manageable proportions. One thing you must remember, if you live in a very cold climate, is that you should select plants which have been developed, as at Cheyenne, Wyoming, specifically for winter hardiness.

Although you can raise chrysanthemums from seed, don't waste time trying; there's no telling what will come up. Buy rooted cuttings or divisions before July; or if you wish to wait until August or September, you can buy full-grown plants that are blooming. (One of the unusual things about chrysanthemums is that they can be transplanted while in bloom. This means that, if you don't have space for them in your flower bed during the summer, you can raise them in a nursery or in pots and then move them into the bed in the fall.)

Chrysanthemums must be grown where they get at least 6 hours of sunlight per day. Allow 12–15-inch space per plant. The soil need be of only average quality but should be deeply dug, well drained and humusy. Give each plant a handful of balanced fertilizer a couple of weeks after planting, and another handful when it is a foot tall.

To make plants bushy, pinch the tips of all stems when they are 6 inches high. From then until August 1, pinch all stems every time they make an additional 6 inches of growth. If you want very large flowers instead of many flowers, remove all but 4 to 6 stems per plant and retain only one bud per stem.

Keep plants watered. Spray with an all-purpose spray every two weeks. When frost threatens, cover plants with boxes, burlap, plastic sheets, etc. After plants finally die down, cut them to the ground and cover them with about 4 inches of salt hay. In the coldest climate zones, if you have not planted extremely winter-hardy varieties, it is advisable to dig up the plants and put them in a coldframe over winter.

Most chrysanthemums should be divided every spring, but those that bloom fairly early in the summer need to be divided only every other spring.

Cinquefoil. *Potentilla.* Zones 1–10. 1 foot. The cinquefoils are neat, spreading plants with strawberrylike leaves and single or double flowers something like roses from mid-spring through summer. They are useful in the flower bed or rock garden, and are good for cutting. Buy new hybrid varieties with yellow, orange or pink flowers and propagate them by division in the spring. Grow in sun. Average soil. Allow 12–18-inch space between plants.

Columbine. ❉ *Aquilegia.* Zones 1–10. 2–4 feet. Columbine is a must not because it is showy but because of its grace and delicacy. The leaves are fernlike. The curiously shaped intricate flowers are borne well off the ground on slender stems. They come in every color of the rainbow. Appearing in considerable numbers from mid-spring to early summer, they are delightful for arrangements and add a fairyland quality to the flower border. (*See photo page 162.*)

Propagate by seeds sown in early spring while the soil is cool (germination will not take place otherwise). Also propagated by division in the spring. Grow in sun or partial shade in average, well-drained soil to which you should add a good quantity of humus. Allow 9–12-inch space. If you cut off spent flowers promptly, you may get a second period of bloom. If seedpods are allowed to open, plants will self-sow.

Coneflower, Purple. *Echinacea.* Zones 3–10. 3 feet. Vigorous plant with stout stems topped by large daisies in shades of red or white with drooping petals and big, pincushionlike centers. Plant at the back of the border for display and cutting in late summer. Buy new varieties and propagate them by division in the spring. Plant in sun or partial shade. Average soil. Allow 12–15-inch space between plants.

Coral Bells. *Heuchera.* Zones 5–10. 18–30 inches. Coral bells form low mounds of scallop-edged leaves from which rise many long, slender stems with loose sprays of tiny red, pink or white flowers. The bloom period is from late spring through summer. Propagate by seeds or by division in spring. Sun. Humusy, well-drained, average soil. Allow 9-inch space between plants.

Coreopsis. **Tickseed.** Zones 2–10. 1–3 feet. Yellow, single or double, daisylike flowers are borne throughout the summer on slender stems which tend to sprawl. Use in beds and for cutting. Propagate by seeds or division in the spring. Sun. Average soil. Allow 12–18-inch space between plants. Keep spent flowers picked off.

Cornflower, Perennial. *Centaurea,* Mountain Bluet. Zones 2–8. 2 feet. Similar to the more common annual cornflower but with blue blossoms 3 inches in diameter in early summer. Good in beds and for cutting. Propagate by seeds or by division in spring. Sun. Average soil. Allow 1-foot space between plants.

Cranesbill. *Geranium.* Zones 5–10. 4–18 inches. This is the true geranium, not the plant commonly called geranium (which is really a pelargonium). It has attractive dissected leaves and five-petaled, cup-shaped pink, rose, blue or purple flowers to 3 inches across. Not showy but pretty. Depending on the variety, it blooms in late spring or summer. Use in the flower bed or rock garden. Propagate by division in spring. Give sun, average soil. Allow 9–12-inch space between plants.

Cupid's Dart. *Catananche.* Zones 3–10. 2 feet. Gray-leaved plant with 2-inch blue summer flowers resembling double daisies. Effective in the flower bed; excellent for cutting and drying. Propagate by division in the spring or by seeds. Sun. Average, well-drained soil. Allow 9-inch space between plants. In coldest climates, mulch with salt hay in winter.

Daylily. ✿ *Hemerocallis.* Zones 2–10. 15 inches–5 feet. Very popular, showy, easy perennial for planting in clumps in the flower bed or in

The distinctive flowers of the columbine dance in the slightest breeze.

Yellow daylilies are as attractive in back of a wall as in front of it. The blossoms are fleeting but there are many of them.

masses along walls, fences, etc. The big lily-shaped flowers up to 6 inches across are borne on sturdy smooth stems above large clumps of sword-shaped leaves. Many shades of yellow, orange, pink, red or purple; also bicolors. The flowers open for only one day, but each plant produces so many that bloom lasts for a long time. Normal time of bloom is summer, but if you pick varieties carefully, you can prolong the season from mid-spring to early fall.

Buy new hybrid varieties and propagate them by division in the spring. You can't be sure what you will get from seed. Plant in sun or very light shade. Average soil which is well drained. Rich soil should be avoided. Allow 1–2-foot space, depending on the height of the plant. Water in dry spells.

Delphinium. ❋ Zones 1–10. 18 inches–8 feet. The delphinium's flower spikes are probably the most spectacular sight in any flower bed. Under best conditions, on the Pacific Coast, these are 4 to 5 feet long—towering above everything else. Even the spikes of the smallest varieties are worthy of exclamation points!

Most people associate delphiniums with the color blue, but there are also rich purples, deep reds, lavender and white. Bloom starts in mid- to late spring and extends into the summer; then, if you're lucky, you will get a second round in the autumn.

To the average gardener, the most desirable varieties are the enormous Pacific and English hybrids. Unfortunately, while these will grow almost everywhere in the United States, they achieve their full size only in California and other areas with cool summers. So if you live elsewhere, it is well to pass by these varieties until you have had more experience with the genus. This does not mean you will be disappointed with the smaller varieties. Try the Belladonna, Bellamosa or the Connecticut Yankee hybrids.

Propagate delphiniums by seeds or by division of established clumps in the spring. Plant in bright sun in an area with good air circulation. The soil must be rich, humusy, well drained and not acid. Make sure the crowns of the plants are set just above the soil surface. Allow 12–18-inch space between plants. Fertilize in early spring. Water regularly. Apply an all-purpose spray every two weeks. Stake plants when they reach 18 inches. After first bloom dies down, cut the stalk just below the bloom. Apply a second dose of fertilizer. Then when new growth put up from the base is 9 inches high, cut the old stalks to the ground. New flowers should appear in the fall, but will not be so spectacular as the spring flowers.

Doronicum. **Leopard's Bane.** Zones 4–10. 1–3 feet. Doronicum puts out countless 2-inch yellow daisies in early or mid-spring. These make a brave show in the flower bed, rock garden or wall garden, and are very good for cutting. Propagate by division after flowering. Plant in sun or partial shade and in average, humusy soil. Allow 9–12-inch space between plants. Because the attractive heart-shaped leaves disappear in the summer, keep clumps small so you don't wind up with gaping holes in the flower bed.

Dusty miller has fernlike silvery-gray foliage that is often used for contrast with other flowers. In the foreground are several clusters of verbena's tiny bright-eyed blossoms.

Dusty Miller. *Cineraria* or *Senecio.* Zones 6–10. 8–12 inches. Plant with finely cut, woolly white leaves and pretty yellow flower clusters from midsummer to fall. Use in edgings or the rock garden, or as foils for other plants in the flower bed. Propagate by seeds or by division in spring. Sun. Average soil. Allow 18-inch space between plants. Shear plants when they begin to look leggy.

Erigeron. **Fleabane. Zones** 6–10. 6–24 inches. Asterlike flowers with yellow centers and white, pink or lavender petals. Blooms in summer and early fall. Use large varieties in the border; small in the rock garden. They are good cut flowers. Divide in spring. Sun or partial shade. Average soil with good drainage. Space dwarf varieties 9 inches apart; others 1 foot. Cut back somewhat after flowering.

Eryngium. **Sea Holly. Zones** 6–10. 2–3 feet. Handsome plant with rigid, deeply cut, spiny-edged leaves and odd metallic-blue flowers with thimblelike centers surrounded by spiny petals. Blooms in mid- and late summer. Plant in the border; use in arrangements. Good dried. Propagate by seeds sown where the plants are to grow or by root cuttings. Sun. Average soil. Allow 1-foot space between plants.

Eupatorium. **Hardy Ageratum,** Mist Flower. Zones 4–10. 15 inches. A close relative of the annual ageratum but a bit larger. Blue flowers in late summer and fall. Divide in the spring. Plant in sun or light shade. Average soil. Allow 1-foot space between plants.

Evening Primrose. *Oenothera.* Zones 3–10. 1 foot. This is the best perennial evening primrose. Use it in the border or rock garden. It is a prostrate plant with fragrant, cup-shaped, 4-inch yellow flowers which open at night from late spring through midsummer. Propagate by seeds or by division in spring. Plant in sun in average, well-drained soil. Allow 1-foot space between plants.

False Dragonhead. *Physostegia.* Zones 6–10. 2–4 feet. A very good perennial for the border and cutting, this puts up a cluster of slender green bud spikes. The buds then open from the bottom up to display pretty tubular flowers in white or pink. These appear from midsummer till fall. Use in masses. Propagate by division in the spring. Sun. Average soil. Allow 1-foot space between plants. Stake tall varieties. Cut back roots so they won't run throughout the garden.

Filipendula. **Dropwort.** Zones 4–8. 15–24 inches. The base of this plant is a neat, low mound of fernlike foliage. Well above this, on rigid stalks, are large, informal, airy clusters of little white blossoms. These appear in midsummer and not only add to the beauty of the flower bed but are also fine for cutting. Propagate by division in the spring or by seeds. Give sun and average, moisture-holding soil. Allow 1-foot space between plants.

Flax. *Linum.* Zones 3–10. 2 feet. Delightful, slender plant with gray-green foliage and small, shallow-cupped, light-blue flowers throughout the summer. A splendid garden filler. The flowers last only a day but keep on coming. They close at night or in the shade. Sow seeds outdoors after last frost and transplant to the flower bed in the fall or early next spring. Plants can also be divided. Grow in full sun, average soil. Allow 9–12-inch space between plants.

Foxtail Lily. *Eremurus,* Desert Candle. Zones 6–8. 4–12 feet. This slender giant has a clump of long straplike leaves at the base. Out of this rise sturdy stems which are surrounded for more than half their length by closely spaced, bell-shaped flowers of white, pink or yellow. The graceful tapering spires bloom in late spring and early summer. Thanks to a stout root system, there is no need to spoil the appearance of the plants by staking. Use tall varieties at the very back of the flower border or silhouetted against a wall or evergreen trees. Small varieties easily fit into the border and are good for cutting.

Buy plants and don't disturb them once they are planted. Plant in the autumn in a sunny spot with rich, well-drained soil. Allow 12–18-inch space between plants for small varieties; 3 feet for large. After flowering, mark location of plants because they disappear completely until the next spring.

Gaillardia. **Blanket Flower.** Zones 2–10. 1–3 feet. Easygoing perennial covered with big daisylike flowers in yellow, orange and red shades. Usually bicolored. Bloom throughout the summer. Propagate by seeds or by division in spring. Named hybrids, the best varieties, must be divided if you want your new plants to look like the old ones. Plant in sun; average, well-drained soil. Allow 1-foot space between plants.

Gas Plant. *Dictamnus,* Dittany, Fraxinella. Zones 3–8. 30 inches. The gas plant gets its name because on hot summer nights the flowers emit a volatile oil which ignites if you hold a match nearby. This is one reason to put in the plant—but a more valid one is that it is very effective in the border. The foliage is leathery and handsome and has a lemon fragrance. Upright spikes of white or rose-pink flowers bloom in late spring and early summer.

Sow seeds in the fall in a nursery bed. Plants appearing the next spring should be allowed to grow where they are until the following spring, when they are transplanted to the border. They should not be disturbed thereafter. Grow in sun in rich soil with good drainage. Avoid overwatering. Pick off seedpods before they open.

Gayfeather. *Liatris,* Blazing Star. Zones 3–10. 2–6 feet. Accent plant for the border. It has long, slender, white or purple flower spikes rising in late summer from a thick basal mass of grassy foliage. The flowers in the clusters are tiny and spidery. Propagate by division in the spring or by seeds. Plant in sun or light shade. Almost any soil will do if well drained. Allow 1-foot space between plants. Water in dry spells.

Germander. *Teucrium.* Zones 6b–10. 1 foot. A shrublike perennial with small, shiny leaves and unimportant rosy-purple flowers in summer. It is much like boxwood and is usually used as a substitute for it in low hedges and edgings. It can also be used as a ground cover. Propagate by division in spring or by seeds. Sun. Well-drained, average soil. Allow 1-foot space between plants. Can be sheared or left to grow naturally.

Gerbera. **Transvaal Daisy.** Zones 8–10. 18 inches. Extremely beautiful single or double daisies up to 4 inches across from spring through fall. White, pink, red, yellow and countless lovely shades in between. Use in a bed; perfect for cutting. Propagate by fresh seeds sown after the temperature reaches 70°, or make divisions in late winter. Grow in sun. The soil should be rich and well drained. Allow 2-foot space between plants. Be sure that the crowns of the plants are never covered with soil. Water whenever the soil dries out. Fertilize every 6 weeks during the growing season.

Geum. Zones 4–10. 1–2 feet. The leaves of this bushy perennial are divided into numerous pretty leaflets. The brilliant red, orange or yellow flowers bloom late spring through the summer if you keep the dead blossoms picked off. There are singles, semidoubles and doubles. Use in the flower bed and for cutting. Propagate by seeds or by division in spring. Plant in sun or light shade in rich soil with good drainage. From Zone 6 northward plants need to be mulched in winter. In warmest zones they are evergreen.

Globeflower. *Trollius.* Zones 2–10. 1–2 feet. Three-inch yellow flowers are globular at the start; open out to resemble large, rather flat buttercups. They bloom from late spring to late summer. Very attractive foliage. Use in beds and for cutting. Propagate by seeds or by division in spring. Partial shade. Rich, humusy soil. Allow 1-foot space between plants. Keep well watered.

Globe Thistle. *Echinops*. Zones 3–10. 4 feet. Plant with coarse, spiny, deeply cut leaves from which striking 2-inch blue thistlelike flowers rise on strong, straight stems. Blooms in midsummer. A real eye-catcher, it should be used in large clumps in beds. Also excellent for cutting and drying. Propagate by seeds or by division in spring. Sun or partial shade. Average, well-drained soil. Allow 2-foot space between plants.

Gloriosa Daisy. *Rudbeckia*, Coneflower. Zones 2–10. 1–3 feet. Rather coarse plant producing big summer daisies with backward-drooping petals and prominent dark centers. Single flowers are white, yellow, red or mahogany; double flowers are yellow. Use in the border and for cutting. Easily grown from seeds or can be divided in the spring. Sun. Average, well-drained soil. Allow 12–18-inch space between plants. Keep flowers picked. Tall varieties need staking in windy locations.

Though perennials, gloriosa daisies are often grown as annuals. In this case, sow seeds indoors 6–8 weeks before last frost.

Goatsbeard. *Aruncus*, but often identified as *Spiraea* or *Astilbe*. Zones 3–8. 3–5 feet. If a goat's beard grew upward, it would look exactly like this plume of small white flowers. They bloom in early summer. The foliage is feathery and attractive. Propagate by seeds or by division in spring. Grow in partial shade in good, humusy soil that holds moisture. Allow 2-foot space between plants.

***Heliopsis*.** Zones 5–10. 3–4 feet. Upright plant with coarse foliage and yellow or orange sunflowerlike blooms from summer till fall. Good for cutting. Use in beds. Propagate by seeds or by division in spring or stem cuttings in summer. Sun. Average soil. Allow 30-inch space between plants.

***Hepatica*. Liverleaf.** Zones 4–8. 4–6 inches. A charming almost evergreen plant for a shady garden—preferably a rock garden or wild garden. Small six-pointed lavender, blue, white or rosy flowers in very early spring. Propagate by seeds or division after flowering stops. Humusy soil. Allow 6-inch space between plants.

Dainty hepaticas welcome spring at the base of a stone wall in a hillside shrubbery planting. The flowers at right are coming up through an evergreen fern.

Hibiscus. **Rose Mallow.** Zones 5–10. 3–8 feet. One of the giants of the garden, this tall, straight, big-leaved plant has handsome flat flowers like dinner plates measuring as much as a foot across. Available in white, pink, red or bicolors, it blooms through the summer until frost. Use at the back of the border. Propagate by seeds or division in the spring. Grow in full sun or light shade. Moist soil, but it doesn't have to be especially rich. Allow 2–3-foot space between plants.

Hosta. ✳ **Funkia,** Plantain Lily. Zones 5–10. 1–5 feet. There are few handsomer foliage plants. The plants themselves form neat mounds. The leaves are large, heart-shaped, strongly veined, in shades of green and in many cases marked with white or cream. The flowers resemble little nodding lilies and appear in the summer in loose sprays on long stems. They are not overly brilliant but they are attractive. Blue, lilac or white. Use plants in shrubbery borders, under trees and in luxuriant edgings and ground covers.

Hostas are sometimes grown from seeds but are usually propagated by division in the spring. Normally planted in light to heavy shade where few other perennials grow, they also do well (but not every variety) in sun. Average, humusy soil. Allow 1–2-foot space between plants, depending on ultimate height. Water regularly; feed twice a year. Don't divide plants too frequently.

Ice Plant. ✳ Zones 8b–10, but does much better in California than anywhere else. 3–12 inches. All perennial ice plants were at one time identified by the botanical name *mesembryanthemum*; but they are now split up into many genera. All are evergreen succulents with fleshy leaves and daisylike flowers in many colors. These bloom in spring, summer and fall. The flowers open at midday; they close at night and in cloudy weather.

The plants are particularly useful for controlling erosion on slopes,

Hostas are grown primarily for their fine foliage, but the flowers are pretty, too.

but are also used to cover big areas in beds. When the flowers are open, they form a solid blanket of brilliant color. Plants belonging to the *Lampranthus* genus are the most colorful; those belonging to the *Drosanthemum* genus are best for planting on steep slopes.

The best way to propagate ice plants is to divide them into small rooted sections in the spring; but you can also cut off fat leaves when the plants are making active growth, let the cut ends dry for about ten days, and then stand them upright in sand and keep them in light shade with only a little water until they root. Grow ice plants in full sun. The soil can be average to poor. Allow 1-foot space between plants. Water sparingly. Fertilize lightly in early spring and after flowering stops.

Incarvillea. Zones 6b–10. 1–2 feet. Handsome plant with compound leaves above which large, trumpet-shaped, red, rose or yellow flowers are borne in clusters of up to a dozen. They are grown in flower beds and containers. Propagate from seeds or by division in spring. If seeds of *Incarvillea variabilis* are started indoors 8–10 weeks before last spring frost, the plants will bloom the first season; consequently, this species can be grown in all climate zones. Give a sunny location and average soil with plenty of humus. Allow 1-foot space between plants.

Lamb's Ears. *Stachys.* Zones 3–10. 12–18 inches. A foliage plant used in edgings and ground covers. The soft, thick leaves are white, woolly and dense. Stalks of purple flowers in summer. Propagate by seeds or by division in spring. Sun or light shade. Average soil. Allow 6-inch space between plants.

Lenten Rose. *Helleborus.* Zones 6–10. 18 inches. Very similar to the Christmas rose and grown in the same way. Handsome compound, evergreen leaves with leaflets arranged finger-fashion. Two-inch flowers ranging from purple to brown, rose to white; some spotted with red. They bloom in late winter and continue past Easter.

Lily-of-the-Valley. ❋ *Convallaria.* Zones 2–7. 8 inches. Perennial used as a ground cover in partial shade. Also planted in shrubbery borders in clumps. Excellent for cutting. Upright sprays of tiny white bell-shaped

Lilies-of-the-valley form an excellent, sweet-smelling ground cover in partial shade.

flowers in spring are marvelously fragrant. Plants have neat, upright elliptical leaves.

Lily-of-the-valley is grown from small upright roots known as pips. You can have as many of these as you want simply by dividing clumps of plants in fall or early spring. Plant pips 1½ inches deep in the shade. Soil should be humusy, well drained, fertile. Space pips 4 inches apart. Fertilize in early spring. Dig up, divide and replant every 4 to 6 years. This isn't an absolute necessity, but big clumps sometimes die out otherwise.

Linaria. Toadflax. Zones 3–10. 2–3 feet. Rather wispy plant with small gray-green leaves, but effective when planted in big clumps in beds. Flowers like small snapdragons on slender spikes in summer. These are blue, pink or yellow. Propagate by seeds or by division in spring. Sun. Average soil. Allow 9-inch space between plants.

Lobster-Claw. Heliconia. Zone 10. 6–8 feet. Bright-red flowers borne in upright spikes in early summer resemble lobster claws or the perennial bird of paradise. They are strange and flamboyant, stand out above the luxuriant foliage. Use in the back of the flower bed. Propagate by division in late winter. Grow in sun or partial shade. Rich, humusy soil. Allow 2–3-foot space between plants.

Lupine. ✳ *Lupinus.* Zones 1–9. 2–5 feet. In late spring, an established bed of lupines suggests a miniature forest of stately cedars in just about every pastel color imaginable. Even a single plant will make you stop to stare, so lovely is the compact, well-shaped flower spike. The leaves are also attractive, with numerous bright-green leaflets arranged like the spokes of a wheel.

Lupines grow best in areas with fairly cool summers—near the oceans or Great Lakes, for example. Propagate by division in early

Lupines have dense flower spikes in pastel colors and charming leaves with leaflets arranged like umbrella ribs. The fat iris buds are just about to open.

spring, or sow seeds where plants are to grow in the spring. In either case, stick to the hybrid varieties called Russell lupines. Give plenty of sun, average soil with good drainage and considerable humus. Allow 9–12-inch space between plants. Because lupines are legumes, which put nitrogen into the soil, fertilize with a plant food low in nitrogen but rich in phosphorus. Water regularly. Leave as much foliage on the plant as possible when cutting flowers. Pick off dead flowers promptly. Don't divide or move plants any more than you can help.

Lychnis viscaria splendens flore-pleno. Zones 2–10. 12–18 inches. Lychnis has been a favorite perennial for generations but most species are coarse, unexciting things. This new variety, which has no common name, is something else again. A compact, bushy plant with grasslike leaves, it puts up a dozen or more spikes of pretty double rose-pink flowers in summer and early fall. Use it in beds or the rock garden. Very good for cutting. Divide plants in spring. Sun. Average soil. Allow 1-foot space between plants.

Lythrum. **Purple Loosestrife.** Zones 2–10. 2–4 feet. Very hardy plant with lance-shaped leaves and covered with lovely spikes of pink, rose or red-purple flowers in summer and fall. Use in beds, for cutting, or along edges of brooks and ponds. Propagate by seeds or by division in spring. Sun or light shade. Average soil but preferably moist and humusy. Allow 2-foot space between plants.

Maiden's Wreath. *Francoa.* Zones 6–10 in California. 2–3 feet. Plant forms a large clump of crinkled leaves above which graceful white flower spikes appear in summer. Good for cutting. Propagate by division in spring. Grow in half sun, half shade—as in a lath shelter. Average soil. Allow 1-foot space between plants.

Marguerite. *Chrysanthemum,* Boston Daisy, Paris Daisy. Zones 9–10. 2–3 feet. This is a rather difficult but vigorous plant which puts on a fine display of yellow or white daisies in the summer. Use it in the flower bed and for cutting. Let professionals propagate plants for you. Plant in sun in average soil. Allow 1–2-foot space between plants. Pinch stem ends to make young plants bushy. Keep dead flowers picked off. Plants should be replaced every 2 to 3 years. Actually, best results are obtained by treating marguerite as an annual. If you do this, you can use it as far north as Zone 4.

Meadow Rue. *Thalictrum.* Zones 4–10, but dies out quickly in warmest areas. 3–5 feet. Top-notch perennial with lovely fernlike or columbine-like leaves and clusters of white, yellow, pink or lavender flowers in summer. In some varieties the clusters are very airy; in others, dense. But all are charming in the border and good for cutting. Propagate by seeds or by division in spring. Sun or partial shade. Humusy, well-drained, average soil. Allow 1–2-foot space between plants, depending on size.

Monkshood. *Aconitum,* Aconite. Zones 1–10. 3–5 feet. Monkshood bears a resemblance to delphinium and has blue or violet, helmetlike flowers in tall spikes in summer. Use it in the shaded border or under trees. Note that all parts of the plant are poisonous if eaten, but not to the touch. Propagate by seeds or by division in spring. Rich, humusy soil. Allow 1-foot space between plants. Keep watered. Disturb as little as possible. Since the plant disappears in the winter, be sure to mark its location so you don't dig it up accidentally.

Nierembergia. **Cup Flower.** Zones 6b–10. 3–6 inches. Perennial for edgings, fronts of beds, the rock garden and containers. Spoon-shaped leaves. Cup-shaped flowers to 1 inch across in white, violet, blue or purple, bloom in summer. Propagate by seeds or by division in spring. Sun or light shade. Average soil with plenty of humus. Keep moist. Allow 6-inch space between plants.

Pearly Everlasting. *Anaphalis.* Zones 3–8. 2 feet. This plant is covered with small pearly-white button flowers in late spring and has woolly gray-green foliage. Use it in the border to contrast with more common plants; also in the rock garden. Flowers are excellent for cutting and drying. Propagate by seeds or by division in spring. Sun, but takes light shade also. Average, well-drained soil. Allow 1-foot space between plants. If you cut back plants after flowering, you may get a second bloom. Mulch with salt hay in winter in coldest climates.

Penstemon. **Beard-Tongue.** Zones 3–10. 18–48 inches. The penstemon genus is large and varied. The best of the species are erect plants with slender leaves and handsome tubular flowers in loose spikes. Usually available in vivid shades of red and blue, but also to be had in white, pink, rose and purple. Bloom in summer. Use in beds and for cutting. Propagate by seeds or by division in spring. Sun or very light shade. Average soil, well drained. Allow 1-foot space between plants. Water regularly in summer. Don't let flowers go to seed.

Some of the prettiest penstemons are the Sensation and Giant Flora-dale hybrids. These can be grown as annuals if you sow seeds indoors 8–10 weeks before last frost and move plants outdoors after frost danger is past.

Peony. ❋ *Paeonia.* Zones 3–8. 2–4 feet. Peonies are among the most beautiful and rewarding of all perennials. They form large, handsome clumps of foliage which mingle well with other flowers in the border and serve as a backdrop for them. And in middle and late spring they produce enormous, very fragrant flowers that brighten every garden scene and are ideal for cutting. Most of the flowers are very double, but there are also semidoubles and singles. Usual colors are white, pink and red. Yellow is available but uncommon.

Peonies are divided in late summer or fall and planted at that time. The eyes, or buds, in the crowns should be buried 1–1½ inches deep. The plants need full sun; fertile, humusy, well-drained soil. Allow 2–3-foot space between plants. Fertilize in very early spring and about the time plants start to bloom. Don't let them dry out. Spray every fortnight in the spring with zineb to prevent botrytis blight. For extra-large flowers, pick off the side buds on each main stem. As a rule, plants should not be divided more than once every ten years, and they can go much longer than this.

Phlox ❋ Zones 4–10. There are several excellent species of phlox but until you become a specialist, you'll be happy with just two. Summer phlox are tall (2–4 feet) upright plants which put out great rounded clusters of flat-faced flowers from summer into fall. In various shades of white, pink, red or purple, they make a brilliant show in the flower border and are superb for cutting.

Peony blossoms are among the showiest and most fragrant in the flower garden.

Garden phlox blooms through most of the summer. The flower trusses will be extra large if you reduce the number of stems in each clump to a total of six or eight.

Moss pinks are 6-inch plants which spread to form enormous mats that are blanketed in early and mid-spring with small white, pink, red or blue flowers. They are used in rock and wall gardens and for ground covers; and you couldn't ask for a more colorful display. Unfortunately, it is often a distasteful display because many gardeners put clashing colors side by side.

Always propagate phlox by divisions made in the spring. If you use seeds, the plants will not come true. Plant in full sun in a place with good air circulation. The soil for summer phlox should be fertile, humusy and well drained. Moss pinks do well in average soil provided it has excellent drainage. Allow 1-foot space between plants for summer phlox; 8 inches for moss pinks. Fertilize twice in the spring. Water regularly. Spray summer phlox when you spray roses or fruit trees with the same insecticide-fungicide. Keep dead flowers picked off. Divide clumps every three years. Moss pinks need less attention but should be divided and replanted when they begin to look ratty.

Pink. ❋ *Dianthus.* Some varieties called Carnations. Zones 2–10. 4–24 inches. Another large and variable genus with charming single or double flowers in white, pink, red or purple, blooming in late spring or summer. Many are fragrant.

Use small compact varieties such as Tiny Rubies in the rock garden or edgings. Use larger, somewhat spreading types such as the cottage or grass pinks in edgings or big drifts. Use border carnations, also called Clove Pinks, in large clumps in the flower bed for display and particularly for cutting.

Propagate pinks by seeds; by division in early spring or fall; or by stem cuttings in summer. Plant in full sun. The soil should be of slightly better-than-average quality and well drained. Allow 9-inch space between plants except for the smallest varieties, which need only 6 inches. Spray carnations regularly with zineb in damp weather. Mulch with salt hay in winter in coldest climates.

Polemonium. One species called Jacob's Ladder. Zones 2–10. 9–18 inches. Slightly cup-shaped, blue summer flowers in loose clusters above

Pinks are soft and feathery and make a bright clump of color. They are associated here with coral bells and campanulas.

fernlike foliage. Use in the bed or rock garden. Propagate by seeds or by division in spring. Sun or partial shade. Average soil. Allow 9-inch space between plants.

Poppy, Himalayan. *Meconopsis.* Zones 2–8. 2–5 feet. An unusual flower and worth trying if you live along the seacoast or in any other cool, humid climate because it has beautiful blue, 3–4-inch poppies with yellow centers. Blooms in summer. Plant in the flower bed or shrubbery border. Grow from seeds. Partial shade. Average soil but must be acid and must contain lots of humus. Allow 18-inch space between plants. Plants probably will not live long.

Poppy, Iceland. *Papaver.* Zones 1–10. 18–24 inches. Wiry-stemmed plant with cup-shaped flowers up to 4 inches across in white, pink, red, yellow or orange. Blooms in summer. Propagate by seeds sown outdoors where plants are to grow as soon as ground can be worked in the spring (you will have bloom that summer). Give full sun and average, very well-drained soil. Allow 9-inch space between plants.

Poppy, Matillja. *Romneya.* Zones 7b–10. 4–8 feet. California native with deeply cut gray-green leaves and delicate, crinkled, fragrant poppies 5–9 inches across in summer. They have white petals and yellow centers. Use in a large border, against a wall or in a naturalized setting. Good for cutting. Propagate by seeds sown in individual peat pots. Sun. Average soil with excellent drainage. Allow 2-foot space between plants. Water sparingly. Keep spreading roots cut back but don't disturb plant otherwise.

Poppy, Oriental. ❋ *Papaver.* Zones 2–8. 2–4 feet. Best of the poppies. Not too long ago Oriental poppies were simply brilliant orange flowers. Now they have been so hybridized that you can get them in white, pink, red, orange or lavender and to almost a foot across. They bloom in mid- and late spring. Plant them in clumps or masses for a spectacular display. Excellent for cutting if you sear the stem ends over a flame before

New varieties of Oriental poppy are much less gaudy than those of yesteryear. These are a soft pink.

putting them in water. You may also dip them for one minute in boiling water.

Oriental poppies can be grown from seeds but won't come true. Propagate by root cuttings taken in late summer and planted 3 inches deep with the top end up. Grow in full sun in average soil with good drainage. Space 1 foot apart. Water regularly. Plants disappear after flowering, so mark their location.

Poppy, Plume. *Macleaya* or *Bocconia.* Zones 6–9. 6–8 feet. A spectacular plant which doesn't look much like a poppy. The leaves are large and deeply lobed. The small white flowers are borne in erect plumelike clusters in the summer. Use at the back of the border or as a screen. Propagate by root cuttings or division in spring. Sun or partial shade. Rich, humusy soil. Allow 2-foot space between plants. Keep watered and fertilize heavily.

Primrose. ❋ *Primula.* Zones 5–10 but does best in cool, humid areas. 6–36 inches. There is no particular reason why primroses should not be used in flower beds but they usually are planted in woodland areas, informal shrubbery borders and along the edges of streams and ponds, because they need partial shade and cool, moist soil. Be that as it may, they are charming plants. They have crinkled bright-green leaves in large clusters at the base. Small flowers in every color of the rainbow except green rise above the foliage on stems of varying length, depending on the species. The flowers are usually in clusters but may be solitary; they are usually pointed upward but may be pendulous. Spring is the season of bloom.

Propagate primroses by seeds or divisions made after flowers fade. The soil should be fertile and contain plenty of humus. Keep it moist. Allow 9-inch space between plants for all but the largest varieties, which need 12. Fertilize plants before they bloom and side-dress with peat moss after bloom. Mulch with salt hay in winter.

Pulmonaria. **Lungwort.** Zones 6–10. 6–12 inches. Spreading plant with elliptical leaves and profuse small royal blue, funnel-shaped flowers in early and mid-spring. Use in beds, rock garden or massed under trees. Propagate by seeds or by division in the fall. Will grow in sun but does

Primroses like partial shade. Here they grow in a little rocky, seminatural pocket by a garden pool.

even better in the shade. Average soil. Allow 9-inch space between plants.

Pyrethrum. *Chrysanthemum,* Painted Daisy. Zones 1–10. 1–3 feet. Bushy plant with fernlike foliage and single or double daisies in white, pink or red. Plants bloom in mid-spring; and when they stop, if you cut them back hard and feed them, they should bloom again in the summer. Use in beds. Perfect for cutting. Propagate by seeds or by division in spring or fall. Double-flowered varieties should always be divided, since they may not come true otherwise. Sun. Average soil with humus and good drainage. Allow 1-foot space between plants.

Queen's Tears. *Billbergia.* Zone 9b–10. 12–18 inches. Queen's tears is an epiphyte—a plant that normally grows on trees. It has spiny, pineapple-like leaves and gaudy blue, red, pink or yellow flowers in spikes in the spring. It is propagated by cutting off the suckers that form at the base. If grown in borders or containers or as a ground cover under trees, plant in an equal mixture of soil and sand, or sand and peat moss. Allow 1-foot space between plants. An alternative way to grow it is to tie the plant to a tree limb or slab of bark and wrap sphagnum moss around the roots.

The plant needs partial shade. Water sparingly in the winter; but when it is making growth, pour water regularly into the rosette of leaves, which serves as a reservoir. A plant growing on a tree should also be sprinkled all over with water.

Rehmannia. Zone 10. 2–3 feet. Plant with large toothed leaves above which are borne beautiful big tubular flowers that are rosy-purple on the outside, yellow and red inside. Blooms from mid-spring to mid-autumn. Good for beds and cutting. Propagate by division in late winter. Needs partial to rather deep shade. Rich, humusy soil. Allow 1-foot space between plants. Keep well watered.

Salvia. Zones 6–10. 3–4 feet. The best of the perennial salvias have slender spikes of blue flowers through much of the summer and into the fall. Use in the border and for cutting. Propagate by seeds or by division in spring. Sun. Average, well-drained soil. Allow 1-foot space between plants. Protect with salt hay in coldest areas.

Scabiosa. **Pincushion Flower.** Zones 3–10. 18–24 inches. Similar to annual scabiosa. Three-inch flowers with large, twisted outer petals and a pincushionlike mound of smaller petals and stamens in the center. Blue or white. Blooms through the summer in beds. Good for cutting. Propagate by seeds or by division in spring. Sun. Average, humusy soil with good drainage. 1-foot space between plants. Remove faded blooms.

Sedum. **Stonecrop.** Zones 4–10. 9–18 inches. There are many, many sedums. Most are creeping plants with tiny flowers which are used as ground covers. But there are several erect species—*Sedum sieboldii, S.*

spectabile and *S. telephium*—which are very desirable in the flower bed and containers. These have attractive thick, succulent leaves and rather big clusters of pink or red flowers in late summer or fall. Propagate by division in spring or by stem cuttings in summer. Plant in sun in average, well-drained soil. Allow 9-inch space between plants.

Shasta Daisy. ❃ *Chrysanthemum.* Zones 2–10. 18–30 inches. Enormous white daisies with yellow centers which are sometimes almost hidden by the petals. In addition to single flowers, there are now doubles—some with twisted petals or crested centers. They bloom from late spring to fall. Plant lots of them in the flower bed and use them for cutting. Propagate by seeds or by division in spring. Best grown in sun, but doubles may also be grown in light shade. The soil should be fertile, humusy and well drained. Allow 1-foot space between plants. Water in dry weather. Keep spent flowers picked off. Divide every year or two.

Sidalcea. **Miniature Hollyhock,** False Mallow. Zones 4–8. 18–36 inches. Hollyhock-like plant with hollyhock-like flowers of purple, pink or white in spikes. Blooms all summer. Use in beds. Propagate by seeds or by division in spring. Sun. Average soil. Allow 9-inch space between plants. Water in dry weather. Divide every three years.

Sneezeweed. *Helenium.* Zones 3–10. 1–4. Free-flowering plant with rather coarse foliage and daisies up to 2 inches across from late summer till frost. They are yellow, copper or red, with dark protruding centers. Use in beds and to supply cut flowers. Propagate by seeds or by division in spring. Sun. Average to poor soil with excellent drainage. Allow 1-foot space between plants except for the tallest varieties, which need 18 inches. Keep dead flowers picked off.

Snow-in-Summer. *Cerastium.* Zones 4b–10. 6 inches. Creeping plant which forms a large mat that is covered with star-shaped white flowers in mid- and late spring. Good in the rock garden, wall garden, as an edging for flower beds or as a ground cover in a shrubbery border. Propagate by seeds or by division in spring. Sun or light shade. Average, well-drained soil. Allow 12–18-inch space between plants. Divide every 2 or 3 years.

Statice. *Limonium,* Sea Lavender. Zones 2–10. 30 inches. Plant with handsome leaves at the base and an airy flower mass which may be as much as 3 feet across. The little flowers are pink or lavender, bloom in mid- and late summer. The effect in the border is delightful, and the flowers are equally delightful for cutting and drying. Propagate by seeds or by division in spring. Sun. Average, well-drained soil will do, but if you enrich it with plenty of humus and loam, the flower masses will be just that much larger. Allow 2-foot space between plants. Don't disturb too often.

Stokes Aster. *Stokesia.* Zones 6–10. 12–18 inches. Erect plant with large flowers like China asters. These are as much as 5 inches across, have big, flat outer petals with fringed tips and a mound of tiny, twisted petals in the center. Lavender-blue, blue or white. Blooms from mid-summer on. Use in beds or containers. Nice for cutting. Propagate by seeds or by division in spring. Sun. Average soil with perfect drainage. Allow 1-foot space between plants. Mulch with salt hay in cold climates in winter.

Sundrops. *Oenothera.* Zones 3–10. 2 feet. Bushy plant with cup-shaped, 1½-inch yellow flowers throughout the summer. It is a close relative of the evening primrose, but unlike that plant, it blooms during the day. Grow from seeds or by division in spring. Plant in sun in average, well-drained soil. Allow 1-foot space between plants.

Tritoma. *Kniphofia,* Red-Hot Poker. Zones 5–10. 2–4 feet. Plant forms a big clump of grasslike leaves and produces stiff, brilliant flower spikes on tall stems in the summer. These resemble a poker or bottle brush. Colors range from white through yellow to red. There are also bicolors. Use in beds and for cutting.

The best tritomas are hybrids, which must be propagated by division in the spring. You can, however, sow seeds and take what you get. Plant in full sun in average soil with good drainage. Protect from wind. Allow 18-inch space between plants. Mulch with salt hay in winter in coldest climates.

Valerian. *Kentranthus* or *Centranthus,* Valeriana, Jupiter's Beard, Garden Heliotrope. Zones 4–10. 3–4 feet. A coarse plant requiring close control, but very ornamental in beds and naturalized settings. It is covered throughout the summer with rounded clusters of fragrant rose or white flowers which are good for cutting. Propagate by seeds or by division in spring. Sun or light shade. Average to poor soil. Allow 1-foot space between plants. Keep spent flowers picked off to prolong bloom and prevent self-sowing. Watch out that roots do not run wild.

Veronica. **Speedwell.** Zones 2–10. 6 inches–4 feet. Variable perennials covered in most cases with slender, curving, sharp-pointed spikes of small flowers. These are usually blue but may be pink or white. Bloom in summer. Use in beds and for cutting. Low-growing, spreading varieties which form large mats are excellent in the rock garden, or for edgings or ground covers.

Propagate by seeds or by division in the spring. Popular hybrid varieties should always be divided. Grow in sun and average soil with extremely good drainage. Allow 9–12-inch space between plants for taller varieties; 6–9 inches for spreading varieties. Keep flowers picked.

Viola. **Tufted Pansy.** Zones 2–10. 6–12 inches. Small plant with miniature pansies in almost every color throughout the summer. Use in beds or rock gardens. Propagate by seeds or by division in the spring. Sun or partial shade. Average soil with humus. Allow 6-inch space between plants. Pick off spent flowers to prolong bloom and keep plant from getting ratty-looking. Violas grown in Zones 2–5 should be treated as annuals, as they are not winter-hardy in these areas. Sow seeds outdoors as soon as the soil can be worked.

Virginia Bluebells. *Mertensia.* Zones 2–10. 18–24 inches. Recommended for shady beds. In early spring, small clusters of pendulous trumpet- or bell-shaped blue flowers hang from the ends of the leafy flower stalks. The entire plant then dies down and disappears until next spring, so be sure to mark location. Propagate by seeds or by division in early spring or fall. Grow in light to fairly deep shade. Fertile soil with plenty of humus. Allow 9-inch space between plants.

Yucca. **Adam's Needle,** Spanish Bayonet. Zones 6–10. 5 feet. When yucca is in bloom in midsummer, it's a very decorative plant for the back of the flower bed or in naturalized plantings by itself; but when not in bloom, it is rather untidy. The plant has a large basal cluster of tough, sword-shaped leaves that remain green throughout the year. From the center rises a stout stem with a loose cluster of rather big, bell-shaped, creamy-white flowers. These last for several weeks, but unfortunately the plant does not always bloom every year.

Propagate by seeds or pieces of the root. Grow in full sun in average to poor soil which must be well drained. Allow 18-inch space between plants.

Left to its own devices, yucca springs up along the roadside and in fields; but it's also a good candidate for the back of a flower bed or a shrubbery border.

·8·

GROWING
BIENNIALS

The biennials comprise a small group which includes a disproportionately large share of favorite flowers. Use and grow them like perennials.

Raise biennials from seeds which are sown in an outdoor propagating bed or open coldframe in May or June. Transplant into the flower bed, or wherever the flowers are to bloom, in the fall or early the following spring. In cold climates, mulch the ground around the plants after it freezes.

When blooming stops, rip out the plants and discard them. They will do no more for you.

Favorite Biennials

(The symbol ❈ indicates the very best)

Canterbury Bells. ❈ *Campanula.* Zones 2–10. 2–3 feet. This is one of the prettiest campanulas. It has large single or double bell-shaped flowers as much as 2 inches across in open clusters in late spring and early summer. These are blue, violet, lavender, pink or white. One popular variety is called Cup-and-Saucer Flower because it has a cup resting in the middle of a wide, more or less flat saucer. Use in the flower bed and for cutting.

Plant in sun or partial shade. Average, well-drained soil. Allow 15-inch space between plants.

Daisy, English. *Bellis.* Zones 1–10. 6 inches. Nice little plant for beds, edgings and naturalizing. It is well covered in spring and early summer with small single or double daisies in white, pink or red. A perennial, it is usually treated as a biennial. It may also be treated as an annual if you start seeds indoors 8–10 weeks before last frost. Plant in partial shade in average soil. Allow 6-inch space between plants. Don't let plants go to seed, because they self-sow freely, and double flowers revert to single flowers.

Evening Primrose. *Oenothera.* Zones 3–10. 3–5 feet. Erect, unbranched plant with fragrant, cup-shaped yellow flowers about 2 inches across. They bloom at night in the spring and early summer. Plant in the sun in average soil. Allow 1-foot space between plants. Self-seeds and can become a nuisance.

Forget-Me-Not. *Myosotis.* Zones 1–10. 6–12 inches. Easily grown biennial for planting in masses in beds or for use in edgings. It is covered from early spring to summer with tiny bright-blue flowers. For earliest bloom, handle as an annual. For later bloom, sow seeds outdoors in the spring as soon as the soil can be worked.

Forget-me-nots grow in sun or partial shade in average soil. Allow 4–6-inch space between plants. Water regularly. If you allow plants to go to seed, they will self-sow all over the place.

Foxglove. ❊ *Digitalis.* Zones 2–10. 3–6 feet. Spectacular plant with great spikes of big, tube-shaped, pendulous flowers in white, pink, red, yellow or lavender. The newest English varieties are the prettiest because the flowers almost completely surround the stems, whereas in older varieties they are mainly on one side of the stems. The flowers open in late spring and early summer. If possible, mass them in the flower bed. Excellent for cutting.

Foxgloves prefer light shade but will grow in sun. The soil should be of average quality and well drained. Allow 12–18-inch space between plants. A new strain of foxgloves called Foxy will bloom the first year if you sow seeds indoors 8–10 weeks before last frost.

Breath-taking cinerarias and tulips brighten a California garden in early April.

Iris is a mainstay of every garden.

LEFT Pale-pink Oriental poppies—a far cry from the brilliant orange usually associated with this perennial.

BELOW Daffodils show off especially well against a dark background.

OPPOSITE Red and white peonies with blue campanulas

Petunias, dwarf sunflowers and feverfew bloom early in a large mixed border.

These lupines have been allowed pretty much to spread and fend for themselves—to the gardener's great reward.

Phlox and zinnias distract from the view of an interstate highway.

Always rewarding, petunias come in almost infinite colors and color combinations.

Three outstanding roses. TOP J. S. Armstrong; CENTER Peace, the champion of champions; BOTTOM Queen Elizabeth.

OPPOSITE Roses in June— a sight to make the heart throb.

At noon the flowers of ice plants open to compete in brilliance with the sun.

Tall spires of foxglove stand out above a neat perennial border in the spring.

Hollyhock. *Althaea.* Zones 3–10. 5–8 feet. Old-fashioned favorite with white or double flowers loosely clustered up and down sturdy, erect stems. White, pink, red, yellow or purple. Blooms in summer. Most effective when grown in front of a wall or backdrop of evergreens. Plant in sun. Average soil is satisfactory but rich soil will result in better plants. Allow 9–12-inch space between plants. Stake plants to hold them upright against wind and heavy rain.

Mullein. *Verbascum.* Zones 3–10. 2–5 feet. Handsome plants with gray-green foliage and big, straight spikes of summer flowers in yellow, white, pink or purple. Plant at the back of the border. Although mullein is actually a perennial, it is usually best handled as a biennial and grown from seed. If you put in new named varieties, however, you must propagate new plants every year by root cuttings. Grow in sun and average, well-drained soil. Allow 12–18-inch space between plants, depending on their height.

Pansy. ❋ *Viola.* Zones 2–10 but does best in cool climates. 8 inches. Pansies are among the most colorful of all flowers. Their large, round, flat faces come in just about every hue except green, and in many color combinations. They bloom early and continue until the temperature goes above 60° F. Use them in the foreground of your flower beds, as edgings anywhere, in containers. They are also superb cut flowers.

There are several ways to raise pansies but the simplest is to sow the seeds outdoors in midsummer and to transplant to a nursery bed when the seedlings are big enough to handle. Fertilize them at that time. After the ground freezes in the fall, cover with salt hay. Move the plants into their final place in the garden early the following spring. Space them 6–8 inches apart. Keep dead flowers picked off to prolong bloom.

At all stages during their growth cycle, pansies need a rich soil containing lots of humus. Grow them in light shade. Keep moist at all times.

Sweet William. *Dianthus.* Zones 2–10. 6–24 inches. Showy, easy biennial with big clusters of small, flat, single or double flowers in white, pink, red or bicolors. They bloom from mid-spring into early summer and make a stunning display in the border if grown in a mass. Use

A clump of pansies around the base of a rural mailbox.

dwarf varieties in edgings. Grow in sun in average soil. Allow 9-inch space between plants. Don't save plants that come up from self-sown seeds, because the colors are poor.

Wallflower. *Cheiranthus.* Zones 5–10. 1–2 feet. Spring-blooming favorite with clusters of fragrant flowers in various shades of yellow, red or brown. Use it in the wall garden, rock garden or flower bed. Generally grown from seeds, but named varieties should be propagated by stem cuttings after flowering stops. Plant in sun or light shade. The soil need be of only average quality but must have perfect drainage. If you are at all doubtful about this, plant the flowers on soil mounds. Allow 1-foot space between plants.

·9·

GROWING
BULBS

I think the reason most people have a special affection for bulbs is that some of them pop out of the ground and bloom so early in the spring. At the very moment that I write, for example, I am keeping daily track of the growth the daffodils and tulips in the border under our bedroom window are making. Spring arrived officially two days ago; but the first half of March was unusually mild and the bright-green leaves are already well up. One clump of daffodils is even beginning to show swelling buds. Before these bloom, however, the crocuses in the lower garden will have opened their gay little cups. It is all very exciting. I have watched the same thing happen year after year after year, but it never ceases to thrill me. And I am happy—but not surprised—to see that it thrills my children and their little children in the same way.

Not all bulbs bloom in the spring by any means. But the early birds have somehow invested the entire contingent with magic—magic which they well deserve. Bulbs are beautiful. Bulbs are dependable. And most of them—but especially those that stay in the ground the year round—are easy to grow.

But at this point I must interject a technical comment: Not all bulbs (which is the popular term for bulbous plants) really grow from bulbs. Some grow from corms; some from rhizomes; and some from tubers. Botanically speaking, these three structures are quite different from bulbs, and they are also different from one another—but the differences are important mainly to the scientist. In the plant descriptions that follow I specify whether a plant grows from a bulb, corm, rhizome or tuber because I want the descriptions to be accurate. But beyond that I follow the popular practice of calling everything which comes up from a fleshy root a bulb.

There is, however, another difference between bulbs which we can't gloss over so easily: some can be grown outdoors the year round in cold climates. These are known as hardy bulbs. Some can be grown outdoors the year round only in warm climates. And some can be grown outdoors the year round in warm climates and can also be grown outdoors in cold climates, but only if you plant them in the spring and dig them up in the fall. The last two groups are known as tender bulbs.

WHERE TO USE BULBS

This is a versatile group of plants. As is true of other flowers, of course, some varieties are not considered suitable for every purpose. (Gardening is full of traditions about plant uses.) But the possibilities are legion, even so. There is just one thing to remember in all cases: always plant bulbs in groups of the same variety. The smaller the flowers, the more bulbs you need per group.

In flower beds.   Flower beds are rarely devoted exclusively to bulbs. (The most notable exceptions I can think of are beds which fanciers fill with giant dahlias and other beds which numerous Californians and New Englanders fill with tuberous begonias.) But bulbs are very commonly planted in beds with annuals and perennials, and this is a splendid way to use them.

The only problem is that, if you place bulbs that live outdoors the year round in among other flowers, there is danger that when they are dormant you will injure them or unearth them while cultivating the other flowers. This means that you must mark the location of bulbs very carefully (and remember that one stake in the middle of a clump is not enough; mark the edges of the clump as well). The only alternative is to limit yourself to bulbs which for one reason or other usually escape mistreatment. Most iris, for instance, do not entirely disappear at any time of year. Tulips are usually (or at least should be) planted deeper than gardeners dig when cultivating beds.

In shrubbery borders.   The smaller kinds of bulbs are particularly good here. They come up, give color to the border, disappear—and while you may miss them, they don't leave a big hole in the planting as they do in a flower bed. (In a flower bed, bulbs take up space which you may not be able to fill with other flowers when the bulbs die down. In a shrubbery border, on the other hand, there are always empty spaces between shrubs, so disappearance of bulbs doesn't create a new problem.)

In ground covers.   This is a charming way to use many of the bulbs, though I can't say exactly why. The ground cover complements the bulbs, and vice versa, and neither does the other any harm. One of the interesting things about the arrangement is the way the bulbs spear up through a thick evergreen ground cover as if it didn't exist. In the same situation, annuals and perennials rarely make the grade.

In rock gardens.   I doubt that I have ever seen a good rock garden without bulbs. They just seem to go together.

In containers.   There is nothing much prettier than a hanging container spilling over with tuberous begonias—unless it is just an ordinary red clay pot crowded with yellow daffodils—unless it is . . . why go on? Bulbs are splendid in containers of all kinds, but most of them lose vitality if you keep them incarcerated for more than a year.

For naturalizing.   The bulbs listed below lend themselves especially well to naturalizing, and there isn't any happier sight in the world when they are in radiant bloom under a blue, blue sky. More than that, bulbs handled in this way are so undemanding that it is almost unbelievable. I know many naturalized bulb plantings which have been neglected for years, yet the flowers bloom on as well as they did originally—and with never an accusing glance at the gardener.

The one thing naturalized bulbs require is that you allow them to ripen their foliage and die down after they have bloomed. In this respect they are no different from other bulbs (see discussion on page 210). But fulfilling this requirement sometimes raises problems because, if the bulbs are in a grassy area, you can't mow the area until it resembles a

A small, well-laid-out dooryard garden in Natchez, Mississippi, is ablaze with tulips in early March.

hayfield. So think twice—not about naturalizing bulbs, but about where you naturalize them.

Bulbs for Naturalizing

Anemone
Bulbocodium
Camassia
Crocus
Cyclamen
Dogtooth Violet
Daffodil
Fritillaria
Glory-of-the-Snow
Grape Hyacinth
Iris
Mariposa Lily
Oxalis
Puschkinia
Scilla
Snowdrop
Snowflake
Star of Bethlehem
Sternbergia

BUYING BULBS

If you're looking for lots of different genera and species of bulbs, and lots of different varieties of the same species, you must buy by mail from the few companies that sell bulbs and almost nothing else. Even the best of the local outlets offer only a limited line of merchandise; and the big "all-purpose" mail-order houses which sell seeds, perennials, shrubs, etc., as well as bulbs, offer even less.

The other outstanding sources of bulbs are the growers who specialize in only one or two or three genera. Offhand, for instance, I can think of two eminent Pacific Coast firms, one concentrating on lilies, the other on tuberous begonias. Firms like these also sell by mail.

Happily, the bulbs available from all sources (except a few cut-rate mail-order outlets) are of good quality. I think bulbs from the specialists are the best, but the margin of superiority is not great. This is because the majority of the bulbs sold in the United States are grown in Holland, and the canny Dutch are not about to lose a big market by undercutting quality. Neither are the one-kind-of-bulb American specialists. But you are likely to find the terminology used to describe the size of bulbs confusing, because growers and merchandisers can't agree on it. In some cases, the biggest bulbs are called Top Size; in other cases, Exhibition Size; and in still other cases, First Size. Price is a better indicator, at least when you are comparing bulbs sold by one firm.

PROPAGATING YOUR OWN BULBS

The bulbous plants are reproduced in many ways, and, as a rule, you don't have to provide much help. In fact, some genera are so exuberant about propagating their tribe that you will reach a point where you can't use any more and must give them away to neighbors and friends. And then they, too, become oversupplied and you start throwing bulbs into the trash. To me, this is painful—partly because I hate to discard anything capable of producing so much beauty and partly because of my built-in streak of thrift. But I manage it somehow, and so does everybody else.

Bulblets. Flowers growing from true bulbs reproduce themselves by dividing naturally into additional small bulbs known as bulblets, or offsets. This may or may not happen the first year after you plant a bulb; that depends on the size of the bulb to start with. If it is small, it will fatten up for a year or two. But when it reaches a certain size, it divides into two or sometimes three bulbs that are slightly smaller than the original but still of flowering size. To propagate the plant at this stage, wait until the flowers have faded and foliage has died down. Then dig up the bulbs, break them apart and replant them.

If you don't propagate a plant when the bulb first divides itself, it will continue to multiply year after year until it forms a large clump containing scores or even hundreds of bulblets, most of which are too small to bloom. All can be propagated, however, by digging up the clump after the foliage has died, separating the bulblets according to size, and planting them in a propagating bed, leaving them until they reach flowering

A clump of daffodils in sore need of division. It produced only ten rather small blossoms. When dug up (below), it turned out to be a mass of small bulbs.

Compare the bulbs produced by the overgrown, undivided clump shown opposite with the big bulbs produced by a single daffodil bulb planted three seasons previously. When planted, each of the big bulbs will have flowers the first year; but it will take most of the small bulbs a couple of years to reach flowering stage.

size. (The larger bulbs in the clump are replanted in the garden, where they will probably bloom the following year.)

The proper time to plant bulblets in a propagating bed depends on the genus. If the flowers are grown outdoors the year round, plant the bulblets immediately after they are separated. Otherwise store them in a cool, dark place until the following spring.

Bulbils. In contrast to bulblets, which are produced below ground, bulbils are small bulbs produced above ground. They are found in some lilies on the stems just above the leaf joints. They are also found in the flowers of some alliums.

Harvest bulbils when firm, just before or after they fall to the ground, and plant them 1 inch deep in a propagating bed. In two or three years they will grow into bulbs of flowering size.

The little round, dark marbles at the base of the leaves of this tiger lily are bulbils. They can be harvested and planted in a propagating bed to produce big bulbs.

Cormels. A cormel is to a plant growing from a corm what a bulblet is to a plant growing from a true bulb: a small offset which can be used to produce a corm of flowering size.

After a cormous plant has bloomed and died down, dig it up and set it aside in a shady, not-too-cold-not-too-hot place until the soil clinging to it dries and can be shaken off. You will then find that the original

The old gladiolus corms have withered away but have left behind new, even larger corms, plus dozens of cormels which can be grown to blooming size in several years.

corm has shriveled away almost to nothing but has left in its place a new larger corm plus a number of cormels about the size of peppercorns or peas. Break the old corm from the new one and throw it away. Pick off and collect the cormels.

If your cormous plants are tender—and most are—store the new cormels and corms over winter and plant them in the spring. (Hardy plants, however, should be replanted at once.) Plant the cormels in a propagating bed about 1 inch deep.

Divisions.   Plants growing from tubers and rhizomes are propagated by cutting the fleshy roots into pieces with a knife. Each of the new pieces must contain at least one bud, or growth tip. After dusting the cut surfaces with powdered sulfur, plant the pieces in the garden where you want them to grow. They will often flower the same year. The time to make divisions varies between genera, but spring is favored for most.

Seeds.   It is so easy to propagate bulbs in the ways described above that few bother with seeds. But this method is a possibility in many cases. Follow the directions for growing annuals from seeds. Start the seeds indoors in late winter or outdoors after danger of frost has passed.

Stem cuttings.   A few bulbs can be reproduced by young stem cuttings. Handle them like perennial cuttings.

HOW TO GROW HARDY BULBS

The hardy bulbs are listed below. All bloom in the spring unless noted otherwise.

Hardy Bulbs

Allium   *spring and summer*
Anemone
Belladonna lily   *summer*
Bletilla   *summer*
Brodiaea
Bulbocodium
Camassia   *spring and summer*
Crocus   *spring and fall*
Cyclamen   *spring and summer*
Daffodil
Dogtooth Violet
Fritillaria
Glory-of-the-Snow
Grape Hyacinth

How to divide an iris rhizome. The old, worn-out roots which had formed the center of the clump have been discarded. The vigorous outer roots are then cut into sections, each with a fan of leaves.

Hardy Bulbs (cont.)

Hyacinth
Iris   *spring and summer*
Lily   *spring and summer*
Lycoris   *summer and fall*
Mariposa Lily
Puschkinia
Scilla
Snowdrop
Snowflake
Star of Bethlehem
Sternbergia   *fall*
Tulip
Winter Aconite

Except for bletilla and lycoris, which are planted in the spring, and iris, which is planted immediately after it has flowered, all the hardy bulbs are planted between late summer and whenever the ground freezes. This gives most gardeners at least three months to get the job done. Actually, the earlier that you plant, the better, because it gives the bulbs more time to start developing roots. But I have set out daffodils in December after the ground has frozen and thawed again, and watched them come up and bloom on schedule the next spring.

Planting depth is given in the descriptions of the bulbs beginning on page 218. All figures indicate the depth from the soil surface to the *top* of the bulb. If you happen to forget the figures while working in the garden, a good rule of thumb is to cover a bulb with soil equal to three times the height or width of the bulb—whichever is greater. If you also forget the rule of thumb, please at least remember that it is better to plant bulbs a little too deep than too shallow. Deep planting discourages bulbs from multiplying and forces them to concentrate on putting out flowers of maximum size.

Planting is a tedious operation, but you can console yourself that it doesn't have to be done often. If you are planting a few individual bulbs in prepared ground, use a trowel to dig the holes. But if you are planting clumps, scoop out a big hole for all the bulbs; set them in place; shovel the soil back over them, and firm it. An alternative method is to use a dibble—a short, stout, round stick with a point. Push this into the ground to the proper depth (if the dibble doesn't come with marks indicating planting depths, mark it yourself, starting 1 inch above the place where the dibble starts to taper to a point). Then drop a bit of loose soil into the hole to make a flat bottom; if this is not done, the air pocket under the bulb will retard root development. Then drop in the bulb and push the soil back over it. Whichever method you use, make sure that you plant all bulbs of the same variety at exactly the same depth if you expect the flowers to bloom at the same height.

Some bulbs (noted in their descriptions) are favorites of mice and chipmunks tunneling through the ground—frequently via mole runs. If you know you have a lot of these pests, you will save yourself mild anguish and expense by protecting the bulbs at the time you plant them. If the planting is large, surround the entire bed with a 1-foot-wide strip of ½-inch galvanized wire mesh sunk into the ground. Small clumps of bulbs are protected by planting in mesh boxes like that illustrated.

Half-inch galvanized wire mesh cut and partially folded to make a mouse-proof enclosure for bulbs. The edges of the mesh must, of course, be wired together.

In most parts of the country it is unnecessary to water newly planted bulbs because rains are frequent. But in dry areas, wet the bed thoroughly with a sprinkler after planting.

In cold climates, cover new bulb plantings the first year with a 2- or 3-inch mulch of leaves, hay or evergreen boughs. Apply this after the ground freezes. Continued protection in other years is not needed.

Fertilize bulbs, whether newly planted or established, once a year when they start to make growth. Use bone meal or a balanced fertilizer, such as 10–10–10. Simply sprinkle a little on the soil and scratch and water it in.

If the weather is dry, water bulbs deeply now and then while they are making growth and until two weeks after the flowers have faded. From then on, it is best to withhold water so the plants will die down naturally.

As soon as flowers begin to fade, cut them off or, if you prefer, cut off the entire stalk. But don't touch the leaves. They must be allowed to remain until they die down naturally and can be pulled off with a very slight tug. This nourishes the bulb and restores the strength which is sapped from it by the flowering process. If you don't like the looks of the floppy leaves, however, you may fold them down half way and fasten them with a rubber band.

Sometimes the gardener finds it necessary to get spring bulbs out of the garden right after they have bloomed so he can put in something else. This is especially true in beds which are planted solidly to bulbs. To save the bulbs, dig them up promptly with all the foliage intact and heel them in in some place out of the way to finish their normal growing season. Heeling-in is done by digging a trench to about two-thirds the depth that the bulbs are normally planted, then setting the plants in on a slant, and filling the trench with soil so the tops of the leaves protrude to approximately the right length. Water well. The dead leaves can be pulled off when they have withered away. In the fall, dig up the bulbs and replant them in the bed. They will bloom again, though not as well as the first year.

After flowering, the leaves of the daffodils were bent over and tied with a rubber band to make a neater garden.

How often you separate hardy bulbs depends on whether you want to increase your bulb supply and/or on how well the bulbs are doing. As bulbs proliferate by producing offsets, the flowers gradually get smaller; and eventually flowering may stop altogether. This process is not so noticeable in the small bulbs such as scillas and grape hyacinths but is very obvious in daffodils, tulips and hyacinths. It follows that if you want flowers of maximum size, you should separate and replant the larger genera about every three to five years. Note, however, that such frequent division is usually necessary only if you failed to plant the bulbs to the proper depth in the first place.

NATURALIZING HARDY BULBS

Naturalizing bulbs is fun, but nowhere nearly as easy as it looks.

To begin with, the collection of bulbs which are sold as inexpensive "naturalizing mixtures" are not at all the right things to start with. Although these are collections of one genus (usually daffodils or crocuses), they are made up of different varieties; consequently, when you plant them together in a corner of the lawn or in a grove of trees, they produce a pepper-and-salt effect. In nature, plants do not arrange themselves in this way. On the contrary, one variety of plant spreads over a large area before another variety takes over. To naturalize bulbs effectively, therefore, you should buy them in large lots of a single variety and plant them in the same way.

Plant the bulbs in informal clumps and drifts as you might expect them to grow on their own. This doesn't mean putting a clump here and another there around the edges of the yard. I remember when I tried that arrangement once, long ago, I was called down mildly by an expert. "The clumps are informal, yes. But do you really think nature could manage such a contrived arrangement? She'd probably have the entire lot of bulbs in one big drift. Not a solid, evenly spaced drift like sand on the beach, but a drift with some bulbs tight together and others spread far apart—as rocks appear in a glacial moraine."

This description suggests the way that naturalized plantings are best laid out. Decide first where they should be—say, in a little swale or beside a pond or around the edges of a clump of trees. Then put all the bulbs in a large bucket, stand at one end of the planting area, and toss the bulbs from the bucket with a mighty heave. Plant each bulb exactly where it lands.

The time-honored way of planting naturalized bulbs is to drive a pick or mattock into the ground, rock it back and forth to open a hole, drop in a bulb, and close the hole by stepping on it. This is supposed to be the fast way to plant large numbers of bulbs—and I have never found one any faster. But it isn't as easy as it sounds; and you rarely make holes as deep as they should be—for daffodils, anyway. As a result, the daffodils multiply and dwindle away. So I recommend this method only for the tiny bulbs such as crocuses and scillas.

For daffodils, use a plug cutter—a cylindrical tool which is pushed into the ground and pulled up with a plug of soil and sod. (It's just like a cookie cutter with a very long blade.) You can then drop the bulb directly into the hole and replace the plug; but more vigorous growth will be achieved by first filling the hole with an inch or two of good soil mixed with a little peat moss and bone meal.

Two good naturalized plantings of daffodils here and on the next two pages. In summer, both areas are heavily shaded, but the trees leaf out late enough to let the flowers complete their normal spring bloom period.

HOW TO GROW TENDER BULBS
IN COLD CLIMATES

The bulbs in this category are listed below. All bloom in the summer.

Tender Bulbs

Achimenes
Acidanthera
Agapanthus
Anemone
Begonia, Tuberous
Caladium
Calla Lily
Canna
Crinodonna
Crinum
Crocosmia
Dahlia
Elephant Ear
Gloriosa
Gladiolus
Ixia
Jacobean Lily
Lapeirousia
Oxalis
Peruvian Daffodil
Pineapple Flower
Ranunculus
Sparaxis
Tigridia
Tritonia
Tuberose
Zephyr Lily

Most of these bulbs should be planted outdoors where they are to grow after all danger of frost is past. A few such as tuberous begonias and caladiums, however, may be started indoors in pots or flats and then transplanted outdoors after frost.

Plant in prepared soil like the hardy bulbs. Water as necessary during the growing season and for about two weeks after the flowers fade.

One way to store bulbs over winter: in a plastic bag filled with vermiculite.

Fertilize at time of planting or when the growth appears, and again lightly just before flowering.

Allow the foliage to die down naturally before digging up the bulbs and drying them in a shady place. If frost kills the plants, dig them up at once, cut off all but 6 inches of the tops, and dry the bulbs. True bulbs and corms are then divided, graded and stored. Rhizomes and tubers, on the other hand, are usually left undivided until spring.

All bulbs should be stored in a dark, dry place at about 50°–60°F Corms and true bulbs are usually spread out in a single layer in open boxes or trays. Rhizomes and tubers may be stored in dry sand or slightly dampened peat moss, depending on the genus. All should be examined once or twice during the winter to make sure they are in good condition. Discard at once any which are rotten or mushy. If tubers are badly shriveled, dampen the storage medium a little.

In warm climates these tender bulbs can be grown in the same way or they can remain in the ground the year round if they are not likely to be frozen. They should, however, be lifted and divided in the early spring.

HOW TO GROW TROPICAL BULBS

These bulbs, listed below, can be left outdoors all year in our warmest climates, but they are too tender to be grown in the North except indoors or in greenhouses. The bloom period for each genus is indicated.

Planting times are given in the descriptions that follow. Established bulbs should be dug up, propagated and replanted at the same time. Keep the plants watered well while they are making growth and immediately after flowering. Fertilize twice during the growth period.

Tropical Bulbs

Amaryllis   *spring and summer*
Amazon Lily   *winter, spring and summer*
Babiana   *spring*
Blood Lily   *spring*
Clivia   *spring*
Freesia   *spring*
Ginger lily   *summer and fall*
Ginger, Shell   *spring, summer and fall*
Ginger, Spiral   *summer and fall*
Ginger, Torch   *summer and fall*
Kaffir Lily   *fall*
Morea   *spring, summer and fall*
Nerine   *fall*
Peruvian Lily   *spring and summer*
Scarborough Lily   *summer*
Watsonia   *summer*

Favorite Bulbs

(*The symbol ❃ indicates the very best*)

Achimenes. Zones 3–10. 12–18 inches. Usually grown as a houseplant but suitable for outdoor culture in the summer. Use in hanging baskets or other containers; or plant 9 inches apart in a bed. Plants are usually trailing but may be upright. They have pointed, hairy leaves and tubular flowers resembling gloxinias up to 3 inches across. They bloom in summer in all colors.

Propagate by dividing the little rhizomes in winter or by stem cuttings in summer. Start rhizomes indoors 10 weeks before they are to be moved outdoors. Plant in individual 4-inch pots or in flats filled with equal parts of loam, humus and sand. Lay rhizomes on their side and cover 1 inch deep. Keep moist and in a warm place until growth starts; then move into an east or west window. Keep watered. Fertilize every fortnight. Pinch stems after they are 4 inches tall. Move outdoors after last frost. Plant in a shady bed with good, humusy soil; or transplant to 6-inch or larger containers. Continue regular watering and feeding until flowering stops. Then let the plants die down and cut off the tops. Potted rhizomes can be stored in their pots. Dig up others, clean off soil and store in perforated plastic bags in barely damp peat moss.

Acidanthera. Zones 3–10, but best in the warmest zones. 1–2 feet. Gladiolus relative with similar but smaller leaves. Tubular flowers with six petals are several inches across and borne in loose spikes. Usually white with brown, purple or crimsom blotch. Variety *Murielae* is very fragrant. Blooms in late summer and fall. Use in beds and for cutting. Propagate by division of the corms. From Zone 6 southward, plant outdoors after last frost in a sunny bed with average, well-drained soil. Plant 4 inches deep and 6 inches apart. Water regularly. In colder climates, start bulbs in pots indoors 6–8 weeks before last frost. Store over winter like gladiolus.

Agapanthus. **Lily-of-the-Nile.** Zones 4–10. 18–48 inches. Striking plant with strap-shaped leaves and tall stems supporting a cluster of trumpet-shaped flowers, which are usually blue but may be white or pink. Blooms in summer. On an established plant there are so many flowers per spike that they will keep on opening for a month. Grow from seeds or divide the tubers every 5 years. Divide evergreen varieties after flowering stops; deciduous varieties in early spring, before they start to grow. Don't expect new plants to bloom for several years. In Zones 9–10 agapanthus can be planted directly in the garden, but even there it does best in big tubs which confine the roots. For potting soil use 2 parts loam, 2 parts humus and 1 part sand. Plant tubers in late winter with crowns just below the surface. Keep moist and in a sunny spot. Fertilize every 2 weeks after growth starts. Move tubs outdoors when weather is reliably warm. Grow in sun in all except very dry, hot areas. Store in the tub over the winter in a cool, sunless spot. Water only once a month during that period.

Allium. Zones 5–8. 6 inches–5 feet. Onions, leeks, garlic and shallots are alliums; but don't let that scare you away from the ornamental alliums, because they are handsome flowers with more-or-less ball-shaped clusters of white, pink, red, yellow, blue or violet flowers in late spring or summer. The species called the giant allium is something you won't believe: its flower cluster is 8 inches across, seemingly as dense as a ball, purplish-red and borne almost 5 feet above the leaves on a long, straight stem. Grow large plants in the flower bed; others in the rock garden.

Propagate by the bulblets. Plant in fall or early spring. Sun. Average, very well-drained soil. Plant bulbs to a depth equal to three times their own height. Allow 1-foot space between plants.

Amaryllis. *Hippeastrum.* Zones 9–10. 1–3 feet. Enormous lilylike flowers in white, pink, red, salmon or bicolors, borne in small clusters on stout stems above straplike leaves. Blooms in spring and summer. Purchase bulbs. Plant in autumn in full sun in average, well-drained, humusy soil. The necks of the bulbs should protrude slightly above soil level in Zone 10; but in Zone 9, bulbs are covered slightly. Allow 12–18-inch space between plants. Fertilize after flowering.

Amazon Lily. *Eucharis.* Zones 9b–10. 2 feet. Beautiful bulb with four to six slightly drooping white flowers up to 5 inches across in winter, spring or summer. They resemble giant daffodils and are very fragrant. Divide after flowering stops, but this should not be done often. Plant in fall or early spring in partial shade. Rich, humusy, well-drained soil. Barely cover bulbs. Allow 1-foot space between plants.

Anemone. Windflower. Zones 6–10. 6–18 inches. Two of the tuberous-rooted anemones, *apennina* and *blanda*, are rock-garden plants with daisylike flowers appearing in early spring. Plant in sun or light shade in the fall. Average soil with lots of humus and good drainage. Plant with the stem scar up, 2–3 inches deep; and allow 6 inches between tubers.

Poppy-Flowered Anemone is the large-flowered plant grown by florists. In shades of red, white or blue, it blooms in the spring. Grow in the flower bed and use for cutting. Scarlet Windflower is similar, but in red only. Use it for naturalizing. Both of these tender plants can be grown outdoors the year round only in Zones 8–9. Grow in sun; otherwise handle as above. Don't overwater because this causes flowers and tubers to rot. In Zones 6–7, these two anemones will survive only if you plant them outdoors in the spring after last frost and dig them up in the fall. Soak the tubers in water for 2 hours before planting. In winter, store in vermiculite. Plants are propagated by seeds or by division in spring.

Babiana. Zones 8–10. 1 foot. Has hairy, sword-shaped leaves and loose spikes of blue, lavender, red, pale yellow or white flowers in late spring. Use in edgings, rock garden or containers. Propagate by the cormels. Plant in fall. Sun. Average soil. Plant 3 inches apart and 4 inches deep. Don't overwater.

Begonia, Tuberous. ✻ *Begonia* of various species. Zones 3–10. 6–15 inches. Tuberous begonias are unbelievably beautiful. Every gardener should try them at least once. If you are not fully successful because of your climate, that is unfortunate. But it will not be effort wasted, because even at their poorest, these are lovely flowers. On the other hand, if you succeed, you may never want to grow anything else.

The plants themselves are attractive. They are either upright or pendulous, and have large leaves. The flowers are usually double, up to 6 inches across, and shaped like exquisite carnations, camellias or roses. Colors are white and every possible shade of pink, red, orange and yellow. In some varieties the petals are edged with a second color.

Use these begonias in beds by themselves or with other flowers. They are gorgeous in earthbound containers, hanging baskets and window boxes. And by all means use them for cutting. Once they start blooming in early summer, they will continue until frost.

Although you can grow tuberous begonias anywhere, they are at their best in areas with cool summers. And they thrive on fog.

Grow plants from seeds sown indoors early in the winter or by taking cuttings of succulent stems in early summer. The simplest propagating method, however, is to cut large tubers into two or three pieces, each containing an eye.

Plant tubers outdoors after last spring frost or, for the longest possible season of bloom, start them indoors in flats or better, pots, 6–8 weeks before last frost. The soil can be of average quality but must be mixed with an equal amount of coarse peat moss, leaf mold or finely ground tree bark. Add some dehydrated manure, too. Good drainage is essential. Set the tubers round side down with the buds on the concave side ½ inch below the soil surface. Keep pots in a reasonably cool, bright but not sunny room until you move the plants outdoors. The soil should be moist at all times but not sopping. Apply liquid fertilizer every 3–4 weeks.

Outdoors, tuberous begonias are grown in partial shade. In very cool areas, such as Maine, they will tolerate a considerable amount of sun; but this is not true in warm areas. Border plants should be given 1-foot space between each plant.

Keep plants watered throughout the summer. If you're not in a fog belt, spray the foliage frequently. Continue fertilizing every 3–4 weeks as long as the foliage is a soft green; but if it turns a bluish hue, stop until a good green returns. On the other hand, if the leaves turn pale green, step up feeding to twice a month. Stop feeding 6 weeks before the first fall frost, and stop watering 3 weeks later.

To control mildew, dust the plants with sulfur or spray with zineb or Karathane. Watch out for slugs and snails.

Just before the first frost, dig up plants and move them into a protected spot. Spread them out to dry. Don't remove the tops until they come off with a slight tug. Store in open trays or in vermiculite.

Belladonna Lily. *Amaryllis*, Naked Ladies. Zones 5–10. 2 feet. This is the true amaryllis. It has large straplike leaves and clusters of pink, lilylike, fragrant flowers on stout, bare stems in late summer. Propagate by division after bloom, but not too often. Plant bulbs after blooming in average, humusy soil. Full sun. In warmest climates, bulbs should be barely covered; in colder climates, they should be set 5 inches deep; and in Zone 5, they should be set 10 inches deep. Allow 18-inch space between bulbs. Mark location because leaves appear in the spring and then die down; then flower stems shoot up.

Bletilla. Zones 6–10. 15 inches. Bletilla is an orchid which in early summer produces small lavender flowers shaped like the florist's orchids. Use it in the flower bed or containers. Propagate by spring division of the tuberlike bulbs when a plant forms a big clump—but don't do this too often. Plant in light shade in average, well-drained soil. Plant 1 inch deep and 6 inches apart.

Blood Lily. *Haemanthus.* Zones 9–10. 18 inches. Small, tubular red flowers form a large round cluster at the top of a sturdy, bare stem in the spring. Very showy in beds or containers. Buy bulbs. Don't worry if they are stained or spotted red—this is normal. Plant in late winter in partial shade. Average, well-drained soil. Just cover top of bulbs. Allow 1-foot space between bulbs. Flowers may appear before leaves.

Brodiaea. Zones 6–10. 6–24 inches. There are a great many plants called brodiaea but some belong to other genera. All are slender plants with grassy foliage and clusters of smallish flowers shaped like long tubes with starry faces. They are in just about every color. They bloom in the spring. Use in clusters in the flower bed or rock garden. Propagate by cormels. Plant in the fall in the sun. Average soil with exceptionally good drainage. Cover 3 inches deep and space 6 inches apart. Don't water in the summer.

Bulbocodium. Spring Meadow Saffron. Zones 4–8. 4 inches. Little crocuslike, reddish-purple flowers in very early spring, followed by narrow leaves. Propagate by bulblets. Plant in autumn in a sunny natural setting or the rock garden. Average soil. Set 3 inches deep, 3 inches apart.

Caladium. Zones 8–10. 2 feet. Foliage plant with large, arrow-shaped leaves in variegated colors—green, pink, red, white and silver. Propagate in late winter by cutting tubers into pieces, each containing two eyes. Plant outdoors as soon as weather is reliable, or in pots indoors 4–6 weeks before last frost. Grow in bright shade or where there is a little morning sun. Set tubers 2 inches deep and 9 inches apart. Rich, well-drained, acid soil with plenty of humus. Keep moist and sprinkle with water in dry spells. Fertilize frequently. Watch out for slugs and snails. In Zone 10, tubers can remain in the ground over the winter. Elsewhere store them in dry sand or vermiculite.

Calla Lily. *Zantedeschia.* Zones 7–10. 18–48 inches. The calla has lustrous arrow-shaped leaves in a big clump and upright, lilylike flowers in brilliant white, yellow or pink. Some varieties are bicolors or are spotted. Bloom in spring and summer. Propagate by seeds or spring division of the tubers. Sun in cooler areas but light shade in very hot ones. Soil must be acid, rich and very humusy. Plant tubers 3 inches deep, 12–15 inches apart. Water heavily and feed frequently. In Zone 10 tubers can be left in the ground. Elsewhere, dig them up and dry off completely; then remove all vegetation and store in dry sand or peat moss.

Camassia. **Quamash.** Zones 6–10. 18–36 inches. Star-shaped blue flowers in upright spikes appear in late spring and summer. Use in a natural planting, preferably in a moist situation. Propagate by seeds or bulblets. Sun or light shade. Fertile, well-drained, moist soil. Cover bulbs 3–4 inches deep. Allow 4–6-inch space between plants. Don't disturb.

Canna. Zones 3–10. 30 inches–6 feet. The cannas you see so often in public parks are big and coarse—not at all right for the home. But the new smaller varieties are a huge improvement. They have green or bronze leaves with a tropical look. The flower clusters are in excellent shades of white, pink, red, yellow or orange. Use in the flower bed in small clumps or in beds by themselves—preferably against a wall or other neutral background. Or plant in tubs.

Divide tubers into sections, each containing two buds. Plant outdoors after all danger of frost is past, or start in pots indoors 4–6 weeks earlier. Grow in full sun in rich, humusy, well-drained soil. Plant horizontally 4 inches deep and allow 18-inch space for each plant. Fertilize monthly. In the fall, cut off all but 6 inches of the stem, dry the tubers, and store in peat moss.

Old types of cannas were big and flamboyant, but the newest varieties, like these, are much more mannerly and suited to the home garden.

Clivia. Kaffir Lily. Zones 9b–10. 18 inches. Familiar florist's plant with dense evergreen leaves above which are borne large clusters of funnel-shaped flowers in orange, yellow, red or white. These appear in winter and spring. Grow in shrubbery borders or containers. Propagate by seeds or very occasional division of the tuberous roots after flowering stops. Plant in partial shade in fertile soil with much humus. The tops of the tubers should be just at soil level. Allow 2-foot space between plants. If in pots, don't disturb plants more than once every 3 years.

Crinodonna. Zones 3–10. 30 inches. Crinodonna is a cross between a crinum and an amaryllis. It has big clusters of 4-inch, lilylike, pink summer flowers. Propagate by bulblets; otherwise use and handle like crinum, below.

Crinum. Cape Lily. Zones 3–10. 2–3 feet. Crinum has pretty straplike leaves and in late summer produces, on long stalks, sizable clusters of fragrant lily-shaped flowers in pink, red or white. Grow in the border or in containers. Propagate by seeds or offsets of the big, bottle-shaped bulbs. In Zones 8–10, plant the bulbs in the fall with the neck just above the soil surface. Sun. Fertile soil with much humus and excellent drainage. Allow 3-foot space between plants. Disturb as little as possible. In other zones, plant bulbs outdoors in the spring as soon as frost danger is past. Store in dry peat moss in winter.

Crocosmia. Copper Tip. Zones 3–10. 2–4 feet. Crocosmia is similar to the gladiolus, but its spikes of orange, red or yellow flowers curve downward or at right angles to the slender stalks. They bloom in mid- and late summer. Excellent for arrangements and showy in the flower bed when planted in a group. Try them also in containers. Propagate by cormels. Plant in spring after last frost. Sun. Average, well-drained soil. Plant 3 inches deep, 6 inches apart. In Zones 7–10 the corms can be left in the ground if planted 6 inches deep. Elsewhere, dig them up in the fall and store in open trays.

Crocus. ❄ Zones 3–10, but the plants don't do too well in the warmest areas. 6 inches. Happy little cup-shaped flowers which spear up out of the ground in late winter and early spring. They are purple, blue,

Sprightly little crocuses bring gay color to a border planted solidly with pachysandra.

mauve, yellow, white or bicolored. Grow in a shrubbery border, rock garden or ground cover, or naturalize in grassy areas. They are also nice in containers.

Propagate by division of the corms. Plant in the fall in bright sun and average, well-drained soil. Cover 3 inches deep and space 4 inches apart. If you have trouble with rodents in the garden, enclose the bulbs in wire mesh.

Autumn-flowering crocuses are available. Plant them in the same way in late August.

Cyclamen. Zones 4–10. 4–8 inches. The cyclamens that grow outdoors are like the florist's plant but daintier and much hardier. They are delightful in shrubbery borders and for naturalizing. The leaves are beautifully shaped and marked. The flowers are tidy in shape, and charming in shades of pink, red or white. Depending on the species, they bloom from late winter to late summer.

Grow from seeds sown outdoors after last frost or indoors about 8 weeks before last frost. Or plant tubers in late summer in a partially shaded spot with average, well-drained soil containing much humus. Tubers should be just below the soil surface. Make sure the concave side is facing upward. Allow 9-inch space between plants. In coldest climates, mulch in winter with hay, leaves or evergreen boughs. Don't disturb established plants.

Daffodil ❊ Narcissus. Zones 3–10, but best in the colder zones. 3–24 inches. When the daffodils start blooming, you know spring is really here. A number of the smaller bulbs bloom ahead of them; but there is nothing that lifts the spirit and turns thoughts away from winter to equal a bright-yellow, white or pale-pink daffodil.

All daffodils are alike in having long, narrow leaves, erect flower stalks, and blossoms shaped more or less like trumpets or cups sitting in the center of a saucer. But beyond this, there is considerable variation. Daffodil fanciers, in fact, classify daffodils in ten different divisions. Of these the most spectacular flowers are the trumpet and large-cupped types. These are understandably the most popular—the kind most people plant first. But don't overlook the others. Some have double flowers; some have several small flowers per stem; some have fragrant flowers.

Plant daffodils in clusters or large drifts. They are perfect in flower beds, shrubbery borders, rock gardens and ground covers. And they are superlative in naturalized settings.

Propagate daffodils any time after they die down in the spring, but the sooner the better. They multiply rapidly, especially if they are not planted deep. If you want the largest possible flowers, divide clumps about every 3 to 5 years and bury the bulbs 7 inches deep. Purchased bulbs are usually singles, but are frequently doubles or triples. The latter can be planted as is or broken into single bulbs.

In warmest climates, plant the bulbs in the late fall after the soil has lost some of its warmth. Elsewhere you can plant from late summer on; the longer the bulbs are in the ground before cold weather arrives, the better. Plant where they will get full sun in the spring. The soil can be of average quality but should have good drainage. If you can mix in some extra humus, do so. Plant large bulbs 6–7 inches deep; medium bulbs, 4 inches; and small bulbs, 3 inches. In naturalized areas, all bulbs need to be covered with only a few inches of soil; but if you will take the time to set them at the previously specified depths, you will have bigger flowers. Space the bulbs of large varieties 6 inches apart; tiny varieties, 4 inches. In coldest climates, cover newly planted bulbs with leaves or hay after the ground freezes.

Once planted, daffodils require little attention. They should be watered during very dry springs, however. And they will appreciate a little fertilizer early each spring.

Dahlia. ❀ Zones 3–10. 1–6 feet. If you want to take life easy during the summer but still have a beautiful flower bed supplying lots and lots of flowers for cutting, you might plant it entirely to dahlias. The plants range from low, bushy mounds to sturdy giants—all with attractive leaves. The flowers are in every color except green and blue, and in many delightful formal and informal shapes. Some are less than an inch across but produced in great abundance while others are larger than dinner plates if you don't allow more than 3 or 4 to a plant. All bloom from midsummer till frost. Once planted, all are easy to care for.

Small dahlias are readily grown from seeds sown indoors 8–10 weeks before last frost. Once they are moved outdoors, they soon start to bloom. If you wish, you can treat them as annuals. Or you can dig up the tubers and carry them over to other years.

Most dahlias grown today, however, are hybrids and should be propagated by cutting the large tubers into sections. Each section should have at least one eye and a piece of the old stem.

Dahlias are planted outdoors after last frost in a sunny location with free air circulation but not too much wind. The soil can be of average quality but should be well drained and enriched with some humus. At planting time, dig a hole about the size of a bucket for each tuber and work in a handful of bone meal or dehydrated manure. Then fill the hole to within 6 inches of the ground level; firm the soil, and lay the tuber flat on top. For all but the smallest varieties, drive a stout stake into the ground just behind the bud end of the tuber. Then cover the tuber with 2 inches of soil and water well. Gradually fill in the hole to the top as the plant makes growth.

Allow 12–15-inch space between dwarf varieties. Increase this space in proportion to height to a maximum of 3 feet for huge varieties.

To make small varieties bushy, pinch the stem ends of young plants once or twice. For the largest flowers on big varieties, remove all but one stem. You can also increase flower size by removing all but the central terminal bud on side shoots that develop from the main stem.

Until flowering starts, water the plants only in extreme dry spells; but after flowering starts, water well at least once a week. Fertilize lightly twice before flowering. Tie plants to the stakes as they grow upward.

Keep spent flowers picked off. When cutting flowers for arrangements, plunge the stems as soon as possible into boiling hot water for 1 minute.

As soon as frost kills the plants, cut the tops at ground level, dig up the tubers and dry them in a shady spot. Then store in dry peat moss. During the winter, if tubers shrivel, dampen the peat moss slightly.

Dogtooth Violet. *Erythronium,* Trout Lily, Fawn Lily, Adder's Tongue. Zones 5–9. 6–18 inches. Early spring bloomer used in naturalized settings. It has attractive foliage and little lilylike flowers with pointed, backward-curving petals. These are white, cream, yellow, pink or purple. Propagate by bulblets. Plant in fall in shade. Set 3 inches deep and 3 inches apart. Average soil with humus. Don't disturb.

The popular image of the dahlia is a gargantuan flower of brilliant color. But the best dahlias for the home garden are much smaller. These are about 4 inches across, and shell pink.

Elephant Ear. *Colocasia,* Taro, Dasheen. Zones 5–10. 6 feet. If you're looking for something dramatic, plant elephant ear in a shrubbery border, against a wall or in a large tub. The flowers are insignificant but the heart-shaped leaves are up to 2 feet long. Propagate by division of the tubers, each containing one eye. Plant outdoors after last frost; or, in colder climates, start indoors 6–8 weeks earlier. Grow in partial shade in rich, humusy soil. Plant tubers 2–3 inches deep and 4 feet apart. Give plenty of water and a monthly dose of fertilizer. In Zone 10 plants can be left outdoors all winter. Elsewhere, store the tubers in dry sand, vermiculite or peat moss.

Freesia. Zones 9–10. 8–18 inches. The rich fragrance of freesia blossoms is matched by the beauty of the spikes. The flowers are tube-shaped, about 2 inches long and available in white, cream, yellow, orange, pink or blue. They bloom in the spring. Use in beds and for cutting. Can be grown from seeds sown in midsummer, but for named varieties, propagate by offsets of the corms. Plant the corms pointed ends up and 2 inches deep in the fall. Allow 4-inch space between plants. Sun. Average, well-drained soil.

Fritillaria. Fritillary. Zones 2–10. 6 inches–4 feet. Interesting flowers for the flower or shrubbery border, rock garden or naturalized setting. The blossoms are large, drooping bells in yellow, orange, red or purple and often with unusual markings. Generally each flower is borne on a single slender stem, but in the Crown Imperial species the big flowers are in a cluster under a topknot of leaves. Bloom in early and mid-spring. Propagate by bulblets. Plant in fall in light shade, fertile soil. Small bulbs should be 3 inches deep and 4–6 inches apart. Crown Imperial should be 4 inches deep and 9 inches apart. Don't disturb established plants.

Ginger Lily. *Hedychium.* Zones 9–10. 3–8 feet. Marvelously fragrant flowers like small orchids in dense clusters in late summer and fall. These are white, cream or yellow, and make a splendid show at the back of beds, in large containers or in arrangements. Because of the thick foliage, plants are also effective for screening. Propagate by division of the rhizomes in late winter. Each section must have at least one eye.

Sun or light shade. Rich, very humusy, well-drained soil. Plant 1 inch deep. Allow 2–3-foot space between plants. Cut old flower stems after flowers fade.

Ginger, Shell. *Alpinia.* Zones 9b–10. 8–12 feet. Handsome plant with long, straplike leaves with parallel veins and fragrant white or pink shell-like flowers in hanging clusters from spring through fall. Excellent in borders but not good for cutting. Propagate by division of the rhizomes in late winter. Grow in sun or light shade in a spot protected from wind. Rich, moist soil. Plant 1 inch deep and 3 feet apart. Cut out flower stems after blooming.

Ginger, Spiral. *Costus.* Zone 10. 10 feet. Evergreen plant with leafy stems growing upward in loose spirals and white flowers with yellow centers in a dense spike in summer and fall. Handle like other gingers.

Ginger, Torch. *Phaeomeria.* Zone 10. 20 feet. Flowers shaped something like huge, fiery-red torches. The tip of the torch is pine-cone-shaped and touched with yellow. Spectacular in summer and fall. Grow like other gingers.

Gladiolus. ❋ Zones 2–10. 2–4 feet. Gladiolus is marvelous for planting in groups at the back of flower beds or in front of a wall, because it brings spectacular color (everything except blue and green) and form to the beds throughout the summer and into the fall. And, of course, it is a superb cutting flower. The leaves are sword-shaped. In the common large varieties, the flowers are up to 5 inches across and arranged close together up and down the stalks. In the smaller varieties, which are gaining in popularity because of their delicacy, the flowers are smaller and less closely clustered.

Gladiolus are propagated by the cormels, which are produced in abundance. Plant the corms outdoors about the time of last spring frost or a little before; and for bloom throughout the year, make successive plantings at 2-week intervals. Grow in sun in average, well-drained soil. Set the tallest varieties 6 inches deep; others 4–6 inches. This helps to hold them upright against wind, though staking may be needed for the tallest varieties anyway. Allow 6-inch space between plants.

Keep watered. Fertilize when flower buds begin to appear, once during flowering, and once after flowering. Work a granular systemic poison into the soil to control thrips. When foliage dies in the fall, dig up corms, dry them off, separate the cormels and store in trays.

Gloriosa. **Gloriosa Lily,** Glory Lily, Climbing Lily. Zones 5–10. 2–10 feet. Limp-stemmed plant which climbs by means of the tendrils at the tips of the leaves. Unusual red-and-yellow or red-and-orange flowers resemble lilies with the petals drawn sharply away from the stems. Blooms in summer. Propagate by seeds or division of the tubers. For an early start, plant tubers horizontally in very humusy soil in the house about 6 weeks before last frost; or plant outdoors where flowers are to grow after frost. Sun. Average, well-drained soil with much humus. Allow 1-foot space between plants. Provide a trellis of some sort for vines to climb on. Store in dry vermiculite in winter. In Zone 10, however, you can leave the tubers outside.

Glory-of-the-Snow. *Chionodoxa.* Zones 3–8. 8 inches. Hardy, late winter and early spring bulbs producing open clusters of star-shaped flowers, which are usually blue but may be white or pink. Use in the shrubbery border, foundation planting and natural plantings. Propagate by bulblets. Plant in the fall in sun. Set 3 inches deep and allow 2–3-inch space between plants. Leave plants alone until they become crowded.

Grape Hyacinth. *Muscari.* Zones 3–10. 4–12 inches. Tiny, bell-shaped flowers in erect clusters which have a general resemblance to a bunch of grapes. Usually blue but may be white. They appear in late winter and early spring. Use them for naturalizing, in shrubbery borders and ground covers. Divide and plant bulbs in the fall. Sun. Average soil. Plant 3 inches deep and 3 inches apart.

Hyacinth. *Hyacinthus.* Zones 6–8. 12–15 inches. The large Dutch hyacinths with blunt, fat spikes of very fragrant mid-spring flowers are the most popular kind. They are available in white, pink, red, blue or yellow. Roman hyacinths have smaller, looser flower clusters in white, pink or blue, and they bloom a little earlier in the spring.

Hyacinths are not easy to use in the garden because they are rather stiff and formal in appearance; but try them in masses in naturalized areas, in edgings or in large clusters in shrubbery borders. They are also excellent container plants.

Buy and plant new bulbs whenever flower clusters of established bulbs begin to look thin. Plant in fall in sun. Soil should be average quality, well drained. Set bulbs 6 inches deep and 6 inches apart. Apply a winter mulch for protection during the first year. Fertilize in early spring and again in the fall.

Iris. ❀ Zones 5–10. 6 inches–4 feet. The Iris genus is huge and spectacular, but unfortunately there are enough differences between the many species—not only in appearance but also in habit of growth and climate requirements—to make them rather confusing to anyone except a fancier. So only one type will be discussed here—the bearded iris.

Actually, this is the most popular kind of iris and has been most widely hybridized. As a result, it offers infinite variation. The leaves are crisp, sword-shaped and grow in fanlike clusters. The big flowers have three upright petals forming loose balls. These are called the standards. Below these are three other petals drooping outward and downward, called the falls. Each of the falls has a tuft of hair called a beard. The flowers are wondrously beautiful in shape and come in every color except green. They bloom on upright, branching stems.

In size the bearded irises range from miniature plants under 10 inches to standard talls over 28 inches. The bloom season starts with the miniatures in early spring and ends in late spring with the standard talls. Use all sizes in the flower bed and for cutting.

Like most irises, the bearded group grows from hardy rhizomes (but there are a few irises—not bearded—that grow from true bulbs). The plants are propagated by cutting the rhizomes, after flowering stops, into sections, each with a small fan of leaves. When dividing, cut out rotten spots and examine for borers. If you find borers, borer holes or rotten spots, soak the rhizomes for several hours in a solution of bichloride of mercury.

Bearded iris grows in full sun except in very hot areas, where light shade is needed. Mix average, well-drained soil with a large amount of peat moss and some dehydrated manure, bone meal or balanced fertil-

A *pleasant border of iris and peonies (which have yet to bloom). The reason for the fence is unknown to the author, but it adds charm to the border.*

izer. Acid soil should be limed. Lay the rhizomes flat and cover with ½ inch of soil or a little less. Allow 9-inch space between plants for dwarf varieties; 12 inches for intermediates; and 15 inches for large. Water well.

From then on iris needs to be watered only in dry spells. Fertilize in the spring. Cultivate with care: the rhizomes are easily damaged. Keep dead leaves picked off but don't touch the green leaves except when dividing the rhizomes. Cut off flower stalks after flowering. Spray occasionally with a combination insecticide-fungicide. Divide the clumps every 3–4 years or whenever they get too large or begin to have hollow centers.

Ixia. **African Corn Lily.** Zones 3–10. 12–18 inches. Cup-shaped flowers in loose spikes are white, pink, yellow, red or violet with dark centers. Blooms in mid- and late spring. Grassy foliage. Grow in small beds or the rock garden. Good for cutting. Propagate by the cormels. From Zone 7 southward, plant outdoors in mid-autumn in a protected sunny spot. Average, well-drained soil. Plant 4 inches deep and 4 inches apart. Divide in early fall every year or two. From Zone 6 northward, plant corms outdoors after last spring frost. Grow like gladiolus and store over winter in trays.

Jacobean Lily. *Sprekelia*, Aztec Lily, St. James' Lily, Mexican Fire Lily. Zones 3–10. 1 foot. Unusual scarlet flowers in early summer shaped something like a fleur-de-lis. They grow as large as 5 inches across. Use in the border. Propagate by bulblets. Plant in spring after frost danger is past. Sun. Set bulbs just beneath the surface in fertile, well-drained soil. Allow 9-inch space between plants. Store over winter in vermiculite. In Zones 9–10, plant bulbs outdoors in the fall and leave them there.

Kaffir Lily. *Schizostylis.* Zones 8–10. 18–24 inches. Tuberous plant with evergreen leaves and numerous 2-inch starlike pink or red flowers in the fall. Use in beds. The long-lasting blooms are excellent for cutting. Propagate by division of the tubers in early spring. Leave 3 to 5 eyes per section. Plant at that time in a sunny situation in average soil with lots of humus. Plant 3 inches deep and 1 foot apart. Keep well watered.

Lapeirousia. Zones 3–10. 12–18 inches. Despite its terrible name, this is a nice little plant with grassy leaves and small pink or red flowers like stars in airy clusters. Blooms in summer. Propagate by cormels. In Zones 8–10, these may be planted outdoors permanently in the fall. Elsewhere they are planted outdoors in the spring after last frost and stored in open trays in winter. In all cases, plants need sun and average soil. Cover corms 4 inches deep and allow 3-inch space between plants.

Lily. ✾ *Lilium.* Zones 4–10. 2–6 feet. The word most often used to describe lilies is "aristocratic." It is a proper choice. Even when not in bloom, these are erect, stately plants with leaves arranged in whorls around the stems. And when the big, funnel-shaped flowers appear in clusters at the tops of the stalks, the plants are a sight to behold.

Many, many species of lilies are known; but unhappily, they are not always easy to grow. Today, however, the breeders have produced a vast collection of hybrid varieties that *are* easy and reliable. These are the ones you should grow until you become a lily expert. They will not disappoint you in the slightest. The flowers are available in countless shades of white, pink, red, yellow and orange; many are spotted or striped with a second color. Depending on the variety, they bloom in late spring, early summer, midsummer or late summer.

Lilies are spectacular in the flower border and are sometimes used in shrubbery borders, particularly with azaleas and rhododendrons, which like the same growing conditions.

The flowers grow from bulbs made up of thick overlapping scales. The easiest method of propagating is to divide the clumps of bulbs in the fall. Lilies which produce bulblets on the stems underground or bulbils on the stems aboveground can also be easily reproduced from these. More difficult propagation methods are by seeds and by removing and planting the bulb scales.

Plant bulbs in late summer or fall. Don't keep them out of the ground any longer than necessary. The soil need be of only average quality but must be very well drained; however, for maximum flower production, it pays to dig the soil deeply and mix in a good quantity of peat moss along with a handful of superphosphate. If the soil has a high pH, add sulfur to make it slightly acid. Set the bulbs 4 inches deep. Allow 9–12-

inch space between plants for small varieties; 12–24 inches for large. If you are overrun with mice, enclose the bulbs in wire mesh.

Lilies grow in full sun or light shade. Between the Mississippi River and the eastern borders of the Pacific states they do best in light or dappled shade.

Water newly planted bulbs well; thereafter, see that they get about an inch of water per week. Mulching is advisable. Fertilize in early spring, two months later, and after flowering stops. Keep dead flowers picked off. When no more flowers remain, cut off the top of the stalk just above the lowest bloom. If you cut flowers for the house, leave as many leaves as possible on the plant. In the fall, when the plant is hit by frost, cut the stem at the soil line.

Lycoris. **Spider Lily.** Zones 6–10. 1–2 feet. An attractive plant with leaves appearing and disappearing before the spidery-looking, lilylike flowers shoot up in late summer and fall. Borne in clusters on bare stems, these are yellow, red or white. Grow in sunny borders or containers. Propagate by the bulblets. In late summer plant 3 inches deep in average soil. Allow 6-inch space between plants. Don't disturb too often.

Mariposa Lily. *Calochortus.* Zones 6–10, but does best in the West. 10–24 inches. Large, striking, cup-shaped flowers are yellow, orange, red, white or purple—often with markings of another color. They bloom in spring. Use them in naturalized settings and also in containers. Propagate by division of the corms. Plant in fall in sun or partial shade. Set 2 inches deep and 4 inches apart in a well-drained mixture of loam, humus and sand. Water in winter and spring when making growth, but never in the summer.

Morea. *Moraea,* Fortnight Lily. Zones 9–10. 18–36 inches. Evergreen plant with irislike flowers through spring, summer and fall. The individual bicolored flowers are short-lived, but they keep coming one after the

Hybrid lilies in the front of a tree-and-shrub border. They like the same soil conditions as azaleas, rhododendrons and pines. The feathery plant is an astilbe.

other, mainly in 2-week spurts. Use in beds. Divide and plant the rhizomes any time. Sun or partial shade. Average, well-drained soil. Set 4 inches deep and 9 inches apart. Cut flower stems down only partway after flowers fade.

Nerine. One variety called Guernsey Lily. Zones 7–10 and in sunny, protected locations in Zone 6b. 1–2 feet. Delightful bulbs which are hardy in flower beds in warm climates. Flowers are borne in round clusters above strap-shaped leaves, which in some species are evergreen. The flowers are like small, pink, red, orange or white lilies with narrow turned-back petals. Blooms in the fall. Divide bulbs—but not too often —and plant them in August, 3 inches deep and 5 inches apart. Sun. Average, well-drained soil. Water while plants are growing, but not in the summer.

Oxalis. Sorrel. Zones 3–10. 4–9 inches. Plant with cloverlike leaves and small, five-petaled, yellow, pink or white flowers in late spring or summer, depending on the species. Use for naturalizing. In Zones 7–10, divide tubers and plant them in the fall. Sun or shade. Average soil with humus and good drainage. Set 2 inches deep and 4 inches apart. In colder areas, plant outdoors in the spring after last frost and bring inside for the winter. Store tubers in vermiculite.

Peruvian Daffodil. *Hymenocallis.* Zones 3–10. 2–3 feet. Big, white, fragrant summer flowers resembling rather spidery daffodils. Use in the flower bed or containers. Propagate by offsets of the bulbs. Plant outdoors 3 inches deep after last frost. Full sun. Average, well-drained soil. Allow 6-inch space between plants. Keep well watered during the summer. Store in vermiculite or dry peat moss in winter. In Zones 8–10, however, the bulbs can remain in the garden.

Peruvian Lily. *Alstroemeria.* Zones 8–10. 2–5 feet. These beautiful flowers in loose clusters in spring or summer look like large azaleas. They are usually multicolored. Use in beds or tubs. Grow from seeds or division of the tuberous roots. Plant in the fall in sun or partial shade. Cover with 6–8 inches of rich, humusy, well-drained soil. Allow 1-foot space between plants. Mulch in the winter. Don't disturb any more than necessary.

Pineapple Flower. *Eucomis.* Zones 3–10. 2 feet. Plant with handsome leaves and upright spikes of greenish-white summer flowers which may be tinged with purple. The spikes are surmounted by a small topknot of leaves as on a pineapple. Use in beds and containers. Raise from seeds or bulblets. Plant outdoors after last frost in a sunny spot with average soil. Cover 1 inch deep and space 1 foot apart. Store bulbs in vermiculite or dry peat moss in winter except in Zones 8–10, where they can be left outdoors.

Puschkinia. **Striped Squill.** Zones 3–10, but best in colder zones. 6 inches. Small, early-spring, bell-shaped flowers in clusters surrounded by short linear leaves. The flowers are pale blue striped with dark blue. Use in the shrubbery border, rock garden, ground cover or for naturalizing. Propagate by bulblets. Plant in fall 3 inches deep and 3 inches apart. Average soil. Partial shade or sun.

Ranunculus. Zones 5–10. 15–18 inches. The ranunculus is a gorgeous flower in the garden and for cutting. The blooms, appearing in late spring and early summer, are either like big buttercups with double rows of large, glistening petals or they are completely double and more or less like zinnias. They come in many shades of red, orange, pink, yellow, cream or white. Plant tubers with the claws pointed down, 2 inches deep and 6 inches apart. Sun or light shade. The soil can be of average quality but should be well drained and have considerable humus. In Zones 5–7, plant tubers outdoors after last frost or start indoors 6 weeks earlier. Store tubers over winter in vermiculite or peat moss, except in Zones 8–10, where they can be left outdoors.

Scarborough Lily. *Vallota.* Zones 9b–10. 2 feet. Best grown as a container plant, Scarborough lily has a handsome cluster of brilliant red, lilylike flowers borne in summer above a clump of strap-shaped leaves. Propagate infrequently by division of the bulbs. Plant in late spring. Soil should be a good mixture of loam, humus and sand. Barely cover bulbs.

Space 1 foot apart. Grow in partial shade. Fertilize every 6 weeks while making growth. Don't disturb except when dividing.

Scilla. **Squill,** Bluebell. Zones 3–10. 4–18 inches. The scillas are rather variable spring flowers but all have charming little bell-shaped blossoms, usually in blue but also in white and purple. They are borne in clusters which range from informal and small to rather large and compact. Use all species for naturalizing and in shrubbery borders. Propagate by bulblets. Plant in the fall 3–4 inches deep and the same distance apart. Best in partial shade but do well in sun. Average soil with good drainage.

Snowdrop. *Galanthus.* Zones 3–8. 9–12 inches. This is the earliest-blooming bulb. It may appear in the dead of winter. The nodding, bell-like flowers are white outside, tinged with green inside. Grow in shrubbery borders, rock gardens and naturalized settings. Flowers will bloom earliest if planted at the base of a south-facing cellar wall. Propagate by offsets of the bulbs. Plant in autumn. Can take sun in winter but should have light shade in other seasons. Well-drained, average soil. Cover 3 inches deep. Allow 3-inch space between plants. Don't disturb except when dividing bulbs.

Snowflake. *Leucojum.* Zones 3–10. 9–18 inches. Drooping, white, bell-like flowers tinged with green are much like snowdrops. Use in the same way. The spring snowflake blooms in late winter and is suited only to Zones 3–8. The summer snowflake, blooming in late spring, and the autumn snowflake, blooming in the fall, grow in all zones. Propagate by bulblets. Plant in fall in partial shade. Average soil. Cover 4 inches deep and space that far apart. Don't disturb except when dividing bulbs.

Sparaxis. **Harlequin Flower.** Zones 3–10. 18 inches. Cup-shaped flowers in spikes, which make a good display in beds and rock gardens and are fine for cutting. They are white, red, yellow, blue or purple and usually are blotched with a second color. Bloom in mid- and late spring. Propagate by the cormels. In Zones 7–10, plant in a protected sunny spot in the fall. Average, well-drained coil. Cover 4 inches deep and space 4

Heat from the sun and the furnace behind the foundation wall awakens a clump of snowdrops on a frigid February day.

inches apart. In other zones, plant corms outdoors after last spring frost and store in open trays over winter.

Star-of-Bethlehem. *Ornithogalum.* Zones 7–10, but a few hardy types grow in Zones 5–6. 6 inches–3 feet. Small starlike flowers in clusters in the spring. Usually white or greenish-white but may be yellow. Plant in the rock garden or other natural settings. Good for cutting. Propagate by offsets of the bulbs. Plant in autumn in a sunny location. Average, well-drained soil. In warm climates set bulbs 3 inches deep; in cold climates, up to 6 inches deep. Allow 6-inch space between plants. Divide often.

Sternbergia. **Winter Daffodil,** Yellow Autumn Crocus. Zones 6–10. 8 inches. Sternbergias bear a close resemblance to big, bright-yellow crocuses. They bloom in the fall and make a gay sight in the rock garden and other naturalized settings. Propagate by the bulblets. Plant in midsummer. Sun. Average soil with perfect drainage. Plant 4 inches deep and 4 inches apart. Leaves continue long after the flowers.

Tigridia. **Mexican Shell Flower,** Tiger Flower. Zones 3–10. 18–30 inches. Tigridia has gladiolus-like leaves, but the flowers appearing one after another on upright stalks are unique. They have three outer petals in solid white, pink, yellow, orange or lilac and just above these are 3 smaller petals spotted with a contrasting color. They are effective in the garden in midsummer and for cutting, although they last only a day. Propagate by seeds or cormels. Plant outdoors after last frost. Sun. Average soil. Set 3 inches deep and 6 inches apart. Store over winter in open trays. But corms can be left in the ground from Zone 7 southward.

Tritonia. Often identified as **Montbretia.** Zones 3–10. 1–2 feet. Similar to gladiolus and used in the same way. The spikes of midsummer flowers are in various shades of red, orange or yellow. There are also bicolors. Propagate and grow like tigridia.

Tuberose. *Polianthes.* Zones 5–10. 3 ft. Ever so fragrant flowers in upright clusters are borne above attractive leaf clusters in late summer.

This bed, solid with big white tulips, drew exclamations when the gardener gave a cocktail party on the terrace a few days earlier.

They are waxy white, either single or double. Plant in with other flowers but near the house so you can enjoy the fragrance throughout the day. Propagate by division of the tubers. In warm climates, plant outdoors in the spring after last frost. Elsewhere, start tubers indoors in pots about 6 weeks before last frost. Give sun and rich, humusy soil. Cover tubers 2–3 inches deep. Allow 6-inch space between plants. Store in dry vermiculite over winter.

Tulip. ❋ *Tulipa.* Zones 3–10, but does best in 3–8. 3–36 inches. You need no introduction to the hardy tulip family. The flowers, appearing at various times throughout the spring, depending on the variety, are favorites with everybody. But you may not be familiar with their great range of color—and unless you have been studying catalogs, you probably don't know that they are so variously shaped. There are doubles; parrot tulips with wonderfully fringed or cut petals; lily-shaped, star-shaped and peony-shaped tulips; and big, short-stemmed tulips which look like deep, shiny saucers.

All tulips are excellent for cutting. Grow the larger varieties in clusters in among other flowers or, for maximum effect, in masses by themselves. The low-growing varieties are used in the rock garden, shrubbery border and other informal plantings.

Tulips are propagated by offsets of the bulbs; but they reproduce themselves much less enthusiastically than daffodils. In fact, if you want the biggest possible blooms year after year, it is wise to discourage reproduction by planting bulbs of all except the small, early-blooming species 9–12 inches deep. The small species need to be only 5 inches deep. Allow 6-inch space between plants of all species.

Grow tulips in full sun in average, well-drained soil to which humus has been added. Plant in late summer or fall, except in very warm climates, where the bulbs should be planted in late fall or early winter after you have stored them in the warmest part of your refrigerator for 6 weeks. Water newly planted bulbs well. After that, water is needed in dry spells only. Fertilize lightly every spring. Diseases and insects are rarely problems, but mice like to eat the bulbs, so you may want to enclose them in wire mesh.

After flowers have died, snap them off at the base, but let the stems and leaves go on growing until they die down naturally.

Watsonia. Zones 8–10. 3–6 feet. This is another gladiolus-like plant, but the six-petaled pink or red flowers are smaller and flatter and grow on shoots off the tall stalks. They bloom in late summer. One species is evergreen. Use in the flower bed and for cutting. Propagate by cormels. Plant in late fall. Sun. Average, well-drained soil. Set 4–6 inches deep and allow 6-inch space between plants.

Winter Aconite. *Eranthis.* Zones 3–10. 4–5 inches. Delightful late-winter flowers. These look like large, bright-yellow buttercups, each sitting on a ruff of green leaves. Use in flower and shrubbery borders and rock gardens. Propagate by dividing the tubers. Most species self-seed freely, however. Plant in the fall. Dried-up tubers should be wrapped in damp cloth or peat moss for 24 hours before planting. The plants need sun in winter and spring but light shade in other seasons. Average, humusy soil. Set 2–3 inches deep; allow 3-inch space between plants. Don't disturb too often.

Zephyr Lily. *Zephyranthes,* Fairy Lily. Zones 3–10. 4–12 inches. A pleasant little late summer or autumn plant for the rock garden, the front of the flower bed, or as an edging. Small trumpet flowers look like six-pointed stars when open. White, pink or yellow. Propagate by offsets of the bulbs. From Zone 7 southward, plant in early autumn and leave in the garden the year round. Elsewhere, plant in spring after last frost and store in vermiculite over winter. Sun. Average, humusy soil. Set 2 inches deep. Allow 3-inch space between plants. Watering in dry spells encourages bloom.

·10·

GROWING
ROSES

As I think back now, I am not sure why I resisted growing roses as long as I did. I suppose I thought the plants cost more than I was willing to put into them. I am certain that I thought they required a great deal of care. And probably as justification for my attitude, I tended to downgrade their beauty and usefulness.

At any rate, whenever anyone suggested that I should plant roses, I rejected the idea. But then one of my wife's aunts, who had a marvelous habit of giving us plants of one kind or another for our wedding anniversaries, simply up and sent us a batch of roses. And that, obviously, was that. I dug a bed and became a rose grower.

I have been an enthusiastic one ever since. Everything I previously believed turned out to be wrong. There are no more beautiful flowers. They need not be terribly expensive (as a matter of fact, if you were to amortize their cost over their lifetime, you'd find they actually cost a pittance). And they require no more work than other flowers.

KINDS OF ROSES

Strictly speaking, roses should not be included in this book because, unlike all the other plants discussed, they are shrubs—woody plants. But it's my belief that most gardeners think of them as flowers—as I do myself. So I have reached a dubious compromise. The roses known as "shrub" roses are discussed in my earlier book, *The Gardener's Basic*

Book of Trees and Shrubs. Here I cover the eight other types of roses, which we loosely categorize as flowers.

Hybrid tea roses are the most popular. They form attractive, upright plants 2–6 feet tall, which are in bloom more or less all the time from late spring until frost. Most of the flowers are large doubles with many petals, but semidoubles and singles are available. All are borne singly on long stems or in small loose clusters on shorter stems. Colors are white, pink, red, yellow, orange and lavender. Relatively few varieties are strongly fragrant.

The great majority of hybrid teas grow in Zones 3–10 but they are not so happy in the zones at either end as they might be. For this reason, so-called Sub-Zero varieties have been developed for the coldest areas, but there is nothing comparable for subtropical areas.

Floribundas are smaller than hybrid teas but erect and attractive. They produce moderately large, usually double, sometimes very fragrant flowers in sizable clusters from spring to fall. The color range is the same as for hybrid teas. Zones 3–10.

Grandiflora roses are crosses between hybrid teas and floribundas. As a result, they have double flowers almost as large as hybrid teas, in clusters almost as large as floribundas. Except for the fact that there are no lavenders (which in my opinion is no loss), the colors are the same. Real fragrance is rare. The plants are extremely vigorous and range from 3 to 6 feet tall. Zones 3–10.

Tea roses were the predecessors of hybrid teas and are not too often seen today because the double or semidouble flowers are smaller and less vividly colored than the hybrids. But the plants are particularly well adapted to Zones 8–10; they bloom in all months except the dead of winter; they have excellent resistance to fungus diseases which attack other roses; and they require very little care.

Polyantha roses include sweetheart roses. They are bushy, compact plants 1–2 feet tall and profusely covered with small flowers in white, pink, red, yellow or orange shades. There are doubles, semidoubles and singles; but few are fragrant. They bloom from spring till fall. Zones 3–10.

Miniature roses usually are only a foot high, though a few grow to 18 inches, while others grow to only 6 inches. For the most part they are neat little bushes with dainty blossoms in white, pink, red, yellow, orange or lavender. They bloom constantly in warm weather but are not fragrant. Zones 3–10.

Climbing roses actually climb only if you tie them to, or weave them in and out of, a support. By themselves they just flop. The plants have supple stems 5 to 20 feet long, and in bloom they make a fine big show. The blossoms are variable in size and construction, and come in white, pink, red, yellow or orange; and for the most part their fragrance ranges from slight to only moderate. Some varieties bloom more or less continuously from spring to fall, but most bloom only in the spring, or in spring and again in the fall. Pillar and rambler roses are types of climbing roses.

Climbers grow in Zones 3–10 but generally need very good protection in Zones 3–5. The exceptions are Kordesii climbing roses, which need protection only in Zone 3.

Tree roses are not a distinct kind of rose but are created by grafting a familiar variety of hybrid tea, floribunda or polyantha rose on to a tall, stout stem. The plants range from about 3 to 5 feet high, need to be staked, and are grown as specimen plants in prominent locations. They can be grown in Zones 3–10, but putting them to bed for the winter is such a chore in cold climates that they really should be restricted to Zones 6–10.

USING ROSES

Of all flowers, roses are the most versatile.

The miniatures are excellent in containers and equally good in beds, rock gardens and low edgings.

The polyanthas and small floribundas are used in hedges and as edgings.

Climbers are grown on fences and arbors to provide masses of color.

Climbing roses and pretty fences have a natural affinity for each other.

They are used around porches and terraces to give privacy from neighbors and protection against wind. They conceal ugly walls, frame doorways, and are trained up posts to serve as colorful accents in the landscape. The largest varieties can be used to a limited extent to screen a patio from the sun. You can also plant them to cover rocks and tree stumps.

But the principal use of roses, of course, is to bring beauty to the garden and provide flowers for arrangements. This is where the hybrid teas and teas, floribundas and grandifloras shine.

Many gardeners maintain that roses must be grown in beds by themselves, but I disagree. For one thing, this is tantamount to saying that if you are going to grow roses at all, you must buy at least six or ten or a dozen because anything less than that will not fill a bed. This is nonsense. If you don't know much about gardening, or if you're not sure you should try roses, it's silly to buy more than one or two or three as a starter. And where are you going to put one to three roses unless it is in among your other flowers?

The other reason why I think there is nothing wrong with planting hybrid tea, tea, floribunda and grandiflora roses in with other flowers is that they work together very nicely. This is particularly true when the other flowers are used as edgings around a clump of roses. But there is nothing at all wrong with letting roses on one hand, and annuals and perennials of the same size on the other hand, mingle together side by side. In fact, the effect is very pleasant.

Having issued my protest, however, I'll now back up and say that, if possible, I do think roses are their best when confined in beds by themselves because you can see each plant more or less distinctly and thus enjoy it that much more.

Of equal importance, roses are best in rose beds because they are easier to care for that way. Each plant gets the same treatment at the same time (the only minor exception: not all need pruning at the same time). Furthermore, as you work among them, you are on guard at all times against their thorns and you are less likely to be wounded than when you suddenly come on a rose surrounded, say, by a lot of delphiniums.

How should a rose bed be designed and placed?

1. It must be located so that all parts receive the same maximum

Roses in a sunken garden. The granite walls help to accent the beauty of the blossoms. The potted plants are geraniums.

amount of sunlight per day. Ideally, roses need all the sun that nature provides, but they will do well with as little as six hours. However, even within these limits, if roses in one part of a bed get more sun than those in another part, you will notice a difference in the flowering.

2. The bed should not be within clear view of windows which you look out of frequently. My reason for this is that the garden area you can see from your house should be just as attractive in winter as it is in summer. But unfortunately, rose gardens in winter are not pretty. In cold climates, in fact, they are downright ugly.

3. The bed should take whatever shape and contour are most suitable to your landscape scheme. The fact that so many famous rose gardens are of formal design should not influence you. The bed can be square, rectangular, round, oval, kidney-shaped, ribbonlike, etc.

4. The arrangement of the plants within a bed is controlled by the shape of the bed. In other words, just because you use a straight-line, grid-type planting plan in a square or rectangular bed doesn't mean you should use the same plan in a bed of some other shape. True, the grid-type plan helps a little to simplify maintenance of the bed. But aesthetic considerations are more important. You should arrange the plants so they contribute to the overall beauty of the bed. If the spaces between rosebushes are not uniform in shape or size, it matters naught so long as each plant has at least 4 square feet in which to grow.

5. If the bed is accessible from both sides, it should not be more than 6 feet wide. This permits you to plant three rows of roses in a grid pattern, and enables you to reach the center row with little difficulty.

On the other hand, if the bed is accessible from only one side, it should not be more than 3½ feet wide to permit you to reach the back row. In this case, the plants in the two rows should be staggered so that those in back are centered between those in front.

To be sure, rose beds often exceed these widths. But then maintenance becomes a problem unless the spaces between plants are increased to 30 or 36 inches, thus detracting from the solid, well-filled look of the beds.

BUYING ROSES

If you decide to grow roses, the first thing you must do is to pick out the types you need (hybrid teas, climbers, etc.) and then the varieties you like best. Choosing varieties is fun, but can be difficult because there are so many on the market.

One approach is to pay a visit in June to one of the great public rose gardens scattered around the country or to ask a neighbor to show you his roses. Actually seeing the plants growing gives you a better idea of what they are like than anything else. But unfortunately, in a public garden you will see many varieties that are no longer on the market; and in a neighbor's garden you will see only the varieties he favors.

A second approach is to examine the roses offered for sale in a local nursery or garden center. This is unsatisfactory, however, because the only information available is restricted to the plant labels, and it is very sketchy. Furthermore, nurseries usually stock only a limited number of varieties.

A third way to choose roses is to send for the catalogs put out by the several companies which specialize in growing and selling roses. Any one of these publications offers a wider selection than you are likely to find in a nursery; and two or three together will make your head spin. What's more the pictures and descriptions for each variety are excellent, although sometimes slightly exaggerated. But don't worry too much about this. To the uninitiated, the most misleading information in the catalogs is contained in two innocent-looking phrases: "Plant Patent No." and "AARS Selection."

The fact that a rose is patented and carries a plant patent number doesn't indicate a thing about the quality of the rose. Almost all new roses placed on sale today are patented in order to protect against their sale by unauthorized persons. On the other hand, many old roses which are superior to the new are not patented.

AARS Selection may be written AARS Winner or All-America Winner. The AARS stands for a commercial organization known as the All-America Rose Selections, Inc. After testing roses for several years in different sections of the country, this group annually chooses one or more new varieties as being of outstanding merit; and the varieties are then advertised as AARS Selections for 1972 or 1963 or whatever year they were introduced.

In actual fact, AARS Selections are good roses and you generally won't make a mistake in planting them. On the other hand, it is well to remember that the winner in any one given year may not hold a candle to the winners in other years. Indeed, it may be inferior to roses which the Selections Committee has turned down in other years.

If you are looking for an accurate rating of roses to help in your selection of varieties, send for the leaflet "Guide for Buying Roses," published each year by the American Rose Society, 4048 Roselea Place, Columbus, Ohio 43211. This doesn't contain pretty pictures or complete descriptions; consequently you cannot use it as your sole basis for selecting roses. But it does list all the roses that have been introduced in modern times and assigns to each a national rating arrived at by averaging the ratings given by local rose societies which have tested the plants. A rating of 9 to 10 indicates an outstanding variety; 8 to 9, excellent; 7 to 8, good; 6 to 7, fair; and 5 to 6, doubtful. Beginning rose growers should stick to varieties rated 8 or higher.

Once you have settled on the varieties you want, you're ready to buy plants. Several questions must be answered:

Should you buy locally or from a mail-order firm? It doesn't really make any difference. You will probably get a wider selection from the mail-order firm; but the plants will not be any better than those sold locally and they won't cost any more or less.

Which grade of roses should you buy? Rose plants are graded No. 1, 1½ or 2; and some are not graded at all. The technical differences between the grades are unimportant, but there is no doubt about the differences in quality. Your pocketbook permitting, buy No. 1 roses only. If you're feeling pinched, however, you can settle for No. 1½. But forget No. 2s and all ungraded plants.

Should you buy bare-root plants or canned plants? One is as good as the other. Your decision rests partly on cost but mainly on the time of year you happen to be planting your garden.

Bare-root roses—plants with nothing around the roots except some damp sphagnum moss and wrapping materials—are somewhat less expensive than canned roses and are the only type sold by mail because they are cheaper to ship. They are also sold in local stores. But their main point of distinction is that they are dormant plants and must be planted while they are dormant. In cold and moderate climates the best planting time is in the early spring as soon as the soil begins to warm up and dry out. In Zones 6 and 7, however, planting in late fall is often done. And in Zones 8–10, planting is done at any time from late fall to early spring.

Last spring's shipment of roses arrived in a big plastic bag inside a cardboard carton. The plastic held in moisture, and the plants were in perfect condition.

A canned rosebush can be planted even after it is leafed out and blooming. I bought this one after the old bush at left turned out to be too feeble to keep in the garden for the summer. (Moved into a nursery bed, however, it revived nicely.)

Canned roses—these may actually be in pots or plastic or paper containers, but all have soil around the roots—are sold only in nurseries and other garden-supplies stores. When they are delivered to these outlets by the growers, they are usually dormant. But pretty soon they begin to leaf out and make growth, and after a while they even start to bloom. At these stages, obviously, they are no longer dormant; nevertheless, they are quite safe to plant.

The advantage of canned roses, in other words, is that you can plant them at any time the ground can be dug—in spring, summer or fall.

PREPARING THE SOIL

Unlike most other flowers, roses are permanent residents of the garden. Once you plant them, you probably will never move them. It's essential, therefore, that you prepare the soil with great care because the roses will be dependent on it for nourishment for many years.

Soil preparation is the same whether you are planting individual roses by themselves or a group of roses in one large bed. The only difference is that if you dig a single hole, it need be only 18 to 24 inches in diameter whereas if you are preparing a bed, the entire area must be dug. In either case, the depth to which you dig should be no less than 18 inches. If you feel up to digging down 24 inches, so much the better.

Roses do not require soil of exceptional fertility but they do want it to have very good drainage, to contain a lot of humus in order to provide nutrients and retain moisture, and to have a pH of 6 to 7. The soil should also be free of large stones and other rubble and roots of nearby trees and shrubs which would compete for nourishment. The roots should be cut out ruthlessly. Then, to keep them from growing back in, put a barrier of aluminum flashing across the side of the rose bed down to a depth of 2 feet. The alternative is to plant the roses in some other location far from trees and shrubs.

Further directions for preparing a planting bed are given in Chapter 2.

PLANTING ROSES

There is no rush about planting canned roses when you bring them home. As long as you keep them watered and in the sun, they will grow on happily in their containers until you're ready to put them in the ground.

But bare-root roses are another matter. If possible, you should plant them as soon as they arrive. But I don't think I have ever been able to do this; and I doubt if your chances are any better. In this case, the first thing you should do is to open the bundle and check whether the roots are surrounded with damp packing material. If the material is dry and if you intend to plant the bushes within 24 hours, dampen the material with water and wrap the package up tightly again. Put it in a cool place but not where it will freeze. Exposing rosebushes to low temperatures is as fatal as letting them dry out.

If you will not be able to plant the bushes for several days, remove them from the package and heel them into the ground. Dig a rough, shallow, slanting hole about as long as the bushes and high in a shady place protected from cold and wind. Then lay the plants on a slant in the hole without untying them and cover them with soil. Water thoroughly. If you don't let them dry out, they can be kept heeled in for about a week.

To heel in roses, simply dig a shallow trench, lay the plants in at an angle and cover them with moist soil. Keep watered.

Planting holes must be large enough to accommodate the roots of each rose plant easily.

When you're ready to plant a bare-root rosebush permanently, fill a pail of water and soak the roots in it for 2 to 12 hours. Meanwhile, dig a planting hole large enough to accommodate the roots, and then some. Build up the soil in the center of the hole in a wide cone, and firm it well. Remove the strings from around the plant and check it quickly for broken or mangled roots or branches. Cut these off with pruning shears. Then spread the roots down over the soil cone and start filling in around them.

The planting depth for a rosebush is determined by the knoblike swelling on the stem between the roots and the branches. This is the bud union—the point at which the top has been grafted on the roots. In Zones 3–5, the bud union should be 1–2 inches below the soil level when the planting hole is completely filled. In Zones 6–7, it should be just at the soil level—partly under, partly above. In Zones 8–10, it should be 1–2 inches above the soil level.

When planting, hold the bush with the bud union at the proper height and work soil in around, under and over the roots. Firm it well as you fill in. When the hole is filled within 1 or 2 inches of the top, tramp the soil down. You don't want it to be hard as a rock, but it must be firm so that the bush doesn't wobble. Now if you find the bud union is too low, don't try to correct matters by pulling the plant upward because that might damage the roots. Scoop out the filled-in soil instead and start over again. Similarly, if the bud union is too high, don't try to shove the plant deeper. Remove the soil instead.

After tramping down the soil, fill the hole to the top with water and let it soak in completely. Then fill the hole all the way with soil and keep on adding soil until you have built up a mound about 8 inches high over

LEFT *After a planting hole is partially filled with soil, which is then firmed around the roots of a rosebush, it is filled the rest of the way with water.* RIGHT *Final step in planting a dormant rose is to mound soil up high around it.*

the bud union and lower portions of the branches. The purpose of the mound is to protect the plant against cold and keep it moist.

Remove the mound when the new buds on the branches have attained a length of about ¼ inch. This will take a week or longer in the spring (autumn-planted roses should not be uncovered till the following spring). Use a trowel or hand cultivator to pull off the outer part of the mound. Use your fingers on the inner part so you don't damage the buds. Hose off whatever soil remains. Finally smooth the surface to the proper level around the bud union.

Canned roses are easier to plant. Just cut away the can with a knife or tin snips, being careful not to slice into the root ball. (You will do less damage to the root ball this way than if you try to pull the plant out of the can.) Set the plant in the planting hole so that the top of the root ball will be level with the ground when the hole is filled in. Fill the hole and firm the soil well. Then build a collar of soil 1 or 2 inches high around the outer edges of the hole and fill the saucer thus formed with water. Do not mound soil up over the plant.

ROUTINE CARE

Plenty of water is the main key to successful rose growing. From the time plants begin to show signs of life in the spring until they start losing their leaves in the fall, they need roughly 1 inch of water per week over their entire root system (not just around the stem, in other words).

Even if you live in an area which has more than enough rainfall to supply this requirement, it is highly advisable to mulch the soil around each plant. My favorite mulching material for roses (as well as other shrubs and trees) is chopped tree bark. But you can use any other attractive organic material such as buckwheat hulls, cocoa-bean hulls or coarse peat moss. Apply a continuous 2–4-inch thickness over an entire rose bed. Use the same thickness for individual plants and spread it out to cover the ground well beyond the ends of the branches.

Special inorganic fertilizers are sold for roses but they are no better than ordinary 5–10–5 or 5–10–10. Apply ½ cupful per plant in early spring as growth starts; ¼ cupful about when flowering starts; and another ¼ cupful during the first two weeks of July. From Zone 7 northward, no additional feedings should be made after this because they would encourage succulent growth, which would probably be killed by the first frost. In Zone 8, however, an additional feeding should be made about the end of August. And in Zones 9–10, yet another feeding can be made in October.

If you prefer organic fertilizers such as bone meal, cottonseed meal or dried blood, double the quantity given at each feeding.

Cultivation of the soil is unnecessary if your roses are mulched. Otherwise, you must do the job regularly to eliminate weeds and keep the soil surface crumbly. Just be careful not to dig or scratch so deeply that you damage the roots.

Pest control is the most demanding part of rose growing because roses have more than their share of insect and disease enemies. The job is not laborious or particularly time-consuming, however. It's just frequent. You should start spraying or dusting when the leaves appear in the spring and continue until they begin to drop in the fall. In humid climates or humid weather, application should be made once a week. In dry climates or dry weather, an every-other-week feeding is enough.

Use a combination insecticide-fungicide made specifically for roses or, if you have fruit trees, use an all-purpose fruit-tree spray. This should control almost all pests. But you may occasionally have to apply malathion to put down an infestation of aphids, or Sevin to control Japanese beetles or thrips.

When cutting flowers, don't take more than 12–15-inch stems if you can help it. The more leaves that are left on the plants, the more flowers you will eventually get. Cut the stems with sharp shears ¼ inch above a leaf with five or seven leaflets. Slant the cut upward and parallel with the leaf. A new flower stem should then develop from the tiny bud in the elbow at the base of the leaf.

PRUNING ROSES

Pruning roses is easy and takes little time. The burden of the work comes in early spring. Two methods are used for bush roses.

In the high-pruning method, you simply go over the plants carefully and cut all branches back to a little below the dead wood (or if you live in a warm climate, to a manageable height of 18 to 24 inches). Some branches are simply shortened to ¼ inch above a side branch or bud; others which are completely dead are removed entirely. If there is an excess number of live branches, some of the smaller ones should be cut out also. This type of pruning yields the maximum number of flowers during the growing season. By the end of the season, however, the bushes will have grown so large that they may crowd the bed and make care and cutting difficult.

The other pruning method, called moderate pruning, is designed to produce the largest possible flowers but somewhat fewer of them. Completely dead branches are removed; all others are cut back severely. In the North, hybrid teas should be reduced to a height of 6–8 inches; floribundas and grandifloras, to a height of 12–15 inches. The corresponding figures for warm climates are 10–12 inches and 10–15 inches.

Once thorough spring pruning is done, bush roses need little attention. Just cut out dead and broken branches as you see them. If suckers sprout up from below the bud union, pull back the soil and cut them off close to the main stem.

Climbing roses should be allowed to grow for a couple of years before you do anything more than cut out the dead wood in early spring. Thereafter you should remove about a quarter of the canes at the base. Take off the old canes; save the new. On old varieties that bloom only in the spring, this pruning is done after the flowers fade. On other

This rose grower believes in moderate pruning of his plants. Here he is cutting a floribunda back to about 12 inches. Hybrid teas are cut back even lower. All cuts are made just above buds. Garden is mulched with buckwheat hulls.

varieties that bloom continuously or a couple of times during the year, prune in early spring.

On all climbers, after the flowers fade, cut off the spent blossoms and shorten the branches on which they grew to two or three buds.

Tree roses are pruned much like bush roses. Shape the head carefully in early spring and reduce the canes to a length of 8–12 inches.

WINTER CARE

In the fall, when roses begin to lose their leaves and cold weather sets in, it is time to put the plants to bed. In the case of bush varieties from

Zone 7 southward, all you have to do is shorten any unusually long branches which might be whipped around by the wind. But from Zone 6 northward, you must also take steps to protect the base of the plants from low temperatures and drying winds. This is done by mounding soil up over each plant to a height of 8 inches in the warmer areas to as much as 15 inches in the coldest areas.

If the plants are mulched, rake this material to one side. Then shovel soil carefully over the plants. Don't take the soil from the spaces between plants unless these are 30 inches wide or more; bring it in from elsewhere in the garden.

Climbing roses are mounded up in the same way in Zones 3–6. In addition, in Zones 5 and in exposed parts of Zone 6, you should take the canes down from the trellis; bundle them together and tie them with twine; and then wrap them in a thick layer of hay or evergreen branches. In Zones 3 and 4, after taking down the canes and tying them together, lay them on the ground and cover them from end to end with about 6 inches of soil.

Winter protection for climbers is not required in Zones 7–10. But make sure the canes are securely anchored to the trellis so they don't get whipped around in the wind.

In Zones 9 and 10, tree roses need no protection; but in 7 and 8 you should wrap the heads in straw or hay and burlap. North of Zone 7, dig under the roots on one side of the plant until you can pull the plants down to the ground. Take care not to break all root connections. Then cover the entire plant with 6 inches or more of soil.

TRANSPLANTING ROSES

Moving roses from one location to another involves only a little more work than setting out new roses. The job is done in early spring while the plants are dormant. After pruning, dig all the way around each plant with a spade. Make the cuts 9–12 inches from the stem. Then dig down under the plant and lift it out of the ground. The more soil that clings to the roots, the better; but don't worry if it all falls off.

Trim any broken roots you find with your shears. Then plant the bush in its new hole in the way described earlier. It will never know it has been touched.

PROPAGATING ROSES

Roses which are covered by plant patents should not be propagated without the authoriy of the patent holder—and it is unlikely that he will grant this. There is nothing illegal about propagating unpatented roses, however.

The best method is by making cuttings of vigorous young flowering stems in June or early July. As soon as the petals on the flowers start to fall, cut off and discard the upper part of the stem ¼ inch above the highest leaf with five leaflets. Then cut the stem just below the third or fourth five-leaflet leaf farther down. Remove all but the two top leaves and follow the directions on page 148. Root the cuttings in vermiculite or sand in a 6-inch flowerpot covered completely with plastic.

When the cutting is rooted, transplant it to a bed outdoors. In the autumn, from Zone 8 northward, cover it completely with a big mound of soil.

Another way to propagate climbing roses is to make a lengthwise 1- or 2-inch knife cut in the bottom of a young, vigorous cane growing close to the ground. Make the cut 12–18 inches from the end of the cane and slip a toothpick into it to hold it open. Then dig a hole several inches deep in the ground, lay the cut part of the cane in this and cover it with soil and a rock to hold it down.

The following spring, dig up the cane, which should then be rooted, and cut it in two just below the roots. Plant the end portion upright where you want it to grow.

Some Very Special Favorite Roses

Baby Betsy McCall. *Miniature.* Only 10 inches high but well covered with light-pink double flowers no more than 1 inch across.

Blaze. *Climber.* Grows to 15 feet. There are probably more Blaze roses growing on fences and trellises in the United States than all other climbers put together. The 2-inch semi-double flowers are scarlet and borne in sizable clusters that sometimes almost conceal the plant. Improved

Hybrid teas bear flowers singly or in small, loose clusters.

X <u>Blaze</u>—the kind to buy—blooms in spring and fall and sporadically in between.

Charlotte Armstrong. *Hybrid tea.* A prize rose for over 30 years. It's a tall, free-flowering plant with moderately fragrant 6-inch blossoms ranging from dark pink to light red.

✱**Chrysler Imperial. *Hybrid tea.*** Chrysler Imperial is rare among modern roses because of its intense fragrance. The flowers are large and dark red; the foliage, deep green.

Crimson Glory. *Hybrid tea.* An old-timer with dark-red, deliciously sweet-smelling flowers of perfect shape. Unlike many red roses, these do not turn bluish as they age. Give plenty of space.

Dr. W. Van Fleet. *Climber.* Grows to 20 feet. An extremely vigorous old rose with wicker thorns and charming flesh-pink flowers in the spring. These are borne on long stems and are as fine for cutting as any hybrid tea.

Eclipse. *Hybrid tea.* One of the outstanding yellow roses. The long pointed buds open to large deep-yellow flowers up to 5 inches across. They have some fragrance.

Electron. *Hybrid tea.* A new rose with lovely deep rose-pink flowers standing out above the dark-green foliage. The blooms appear singly and in small clusters.

Else Poulsen. *Floribunda.* A charming small plant, excellent in hedges as well as gardens, with bright-pink, semi-double—almost single—flowers in big clusters. The foliage is bronze-colored and susceptible to mildew.

Fashion. *Floribunda.* One of the best floribundas, Fashion has distinctive coral-peach-pink flowers suffused with a hint of gold. The plant measures about 4 by 4 feet.

Frau Karl Druschki. *Hybrid perpetual.* Hybrid perpetuals make up an old class of roses that I didn't mention earlier because they are now quite rare. But Frau Karl is still readily available and cannot be by-passed because she has the most perfect white blossoms I have seen on a rose. Unfortunately, although blossoms are plentiful, they appear only in the spring. The plant needs frequent pruning to keep it from out-growing the garden.

By contrast, floribundas bear smaller flowers in large clusters. These are semi-doubles.

A large-flowered climber.

Garden Party. *Hybrid tea.* Beautiful flowers to match a creamy-white satin wedding gown. The petals are lightly brushed around the edges with pink. The plant is strong and vigorous but subject to mildew.

Gene Boerner. *Floribunda.* Profuse flowers are a clear medium pink and about 3 inches across. The erect, bushy plant can be used in hedges.

Golden Showers. *Climber.* Grows to 12 feet. It is an almost continuous producer of 3- to 4-inch yellow flowers with prettily pointed buds.

Gruss an Aachen. *Floribunda.* Introduced almost 70 years ago, this is still one of the best floribundas. The pale-pink flowers are more than 3 inches across, and are borne in profusion.

Helen Traubel. *Hybrid tea.* A tall, prolific plant with long pointed buds opening to big, high-centered, exquisitely pink blooms.

John F. Kennedy. *Hybrid tea.* Among the few truly great white roses. The blooms are 5 inches across, with a noticeable fragrance.

John S. Armstrong. *Grandiflora.* This is one of the tiptop-rated roses, and it more than deserves the praise. The plant is large, sturdy and covered with dark-green leaves. The 4½-inch flowers start out as almost black-red buds and open into gorgeous dark-red blossoms suggesting the softest, most velvety camellias.

A beautifully shaped hybrid-tea blossom.

Margo Koster. *Polyantha.* The flowers are globe-shaped—like ranunculus—and salmon-colored. They appear continuously on tidy plants not over 1 foot high. Use for edgings as well as in beds.

Memoriam. *Hybrid tea.* This is a fairly new rose, which unhappily is not widely available. I thought it superior to all but one of the All-America selections introduced in the same year. The beautifully shaped flowers are pale pink. Although there are not many of them, each is a gem.

Mr. Lincoln. *Hybrid tea.* Mr. Lincoln has velvety deep-red flowers as large as 6 inches across and perfectly formed. They have better-than-average fragrance. The plant is dark green and sturdy.

Gruss an Aachen—a very old floribunda and still tops.

Montezuma. *Grandiflora.* The flowers of Montezuma will stand out in any rose bed. In early season they are salmon-pink; later, they are a mixture of pink, salmon and orange with touches of yellow at the center. They are borne singly and in small clusters.

Paul's Scarlet. *Climber.* Grows to 15 feet. This old rose has lost its top place in climber popularity but is still excellent. The flowers are large, semi-double, vivid scarlet. They appear in profusion in the spring.

Peace. *Hybrid tea.* Peace is the superrose. Ever since it was introduced in 1945, it has been called the best rose ever. Once you've seen it—especially once you've grown it—you will concur with this accolade. The big yellow bud has a deep pink edging on the petals. This opens into an enormous high-crowned flower ranging from pale gold to ivory. Pink edgings on the petals gradually suffuse the entire petal. The plants are large and vigorous, with dark, tough, glossy foliage and stout stems capable of holding the flowers erect.

Queen Elizabeth *Grandiflora.* A magnificent rose by all standards. The plant is vigorous, upright, as tall as 6 feet, and clothed with glossy dark-green leaves. The large flowers, which appear singly and in clusters, are a medium-deep pink and have a modest perfume. They are superb for cutting.

Spartan. *Floribunda.* Spartan is a spectacular, continuous bloomer. The 3½-inch flowers are a deep coral or orange-red and look like small hybrid teas. They are carried singly and in clusters.

Sutter's Gold. *Hybrid tea.* Another top yellow, this strong rose has yellow buds brushed with red; the pure golden flowers with veins of faint bronze are strongly fragrant.

Vogue. *Floribunda.* Vogue's blossoms—as much as 4 inches wide—are unusually big for a floribunda. A lovely pink, they start out as much darker pink buds. The plant is tall and glossy.

Rain or heavy dew adds extra beauty to rose blossoms.

A tiny polyantha named Mrs. R. M. Finch.

APPENDIX

STATE AGRICULTURAL EXTENSION SERVICES

ALABAMA	Auburn University, Auburn 36830
ALASKA	University of Alaska, College 99701
ARIZONA	University of Arizona, Tucson 85721
ARKANSAS	Division of Agriculture, University of Arkansas, Fayetteville 72701
CALIFORNIA	College of Agriculture, University of California, Berkeley 94720
COLORADO	Colorado State University, Fort Collins 80521
CONNECTICUT	College of Agriculture, University of Connecticut, Storrs 06268
	Connecticut Agricultural Experiment Station, New Haven 06504
DELAWARE	School of Agriculture, University of Delaware, Newark 19711
FLORIDA	University of Florida, Gainesville 32601
GEORGIA	College of Agriculture, University of Georgia, Athens 30601
HAWAII	University of Hawaii, Honolulu 96822
IDAHO	College of Agriculture, University of Idaho, Boise 83701
ILLINOIS	College of Agriculture, University of Illinois, Urbana 61801
INDIANA	Purdue University, Lafayette 47907
IOWA	Iowa State University of Science and Technology, Ames 50010
KANSAS	College of Agriculture, Kansas State University, Manhattan 66502
KENTUCKY	College of Agriculture, University of Kentucky, Lexington 40506
LOUISIANA	Agricultural College, Louisiana State University, Baton Rouge 70800
MAINE	College of Agriculture, University of Maine, Orono 04473
MARYLAND	University of Maryland, College Park 20740
MASSACHUSETTS	College of Agriculture, University of Massachusetts, Amherst 01002
MICHIGAN	College of Agriculture, Michigan State University, East Lansing 48823
MINNESOTA	College of Agriculture, University of Minnesota, St. Paul 55101
MISSISSIPPI	Mississippi State University, State College 39762
MISSOURI	College of Agriculture, University of Missouri, Columbia 65201
MONTANA	Montana State University, Bozeman 59715

NEBRASKA	College of Agriculture, University of Nebraska, Lincoln 68503
NEVADA	College of Agriculture, University of Nevada, Reno 89507
NEW HAMPSHIRE	University of New Hampshire, Durham 03824
NEW JERSEY	Rutgers—The State University, New Brunswick 08903
NEW MEXICO	College of Agriculture, New Mexico State University, University Park 88070
NEW YORK	College of Agriculture, Cornell University, Ithaca 14850
NORTH CAROLINA	College of Agriculture, North Carolina State University at Raleigh, Raleigh 27600
NORTH DAKOTA	North Dakota State University of Agriculture and Applied Science, Fargo 58102
OHIO	College of Agriculture, Ohio State University, Columbus 43210
OKLAHOMA	Oklahoma State University, Stillwater 74074
OREGON	Oregon State University, Corvallis 97331
PENNSYLVANIA	Pennsylvania State University, University Park 16802
PUERTO RICO	University of Puerto Rico, Box 607, Rio Piedras 00928
RHODE ISLAND	University of Rhode Island, Kingston 02881
SOUTH CAROLINA	Clemson University, Clemson 29631
SOUTH DAKOTA	South Dakota State University, Brookings 57006
TENNESSEE	College of Agriculture, University of Tennessee, Knoxville 37900
TEXAS	Texas A. & M. University, College Station 77843
UTAH	College of Agriculture, Utah State University, Logan 84321
VERMONT	State Agricultural College, University of Vermont, Burlington 05401
VIRGINIA	Virginia Polytechnic Institute, Blacksburg 24061
WASHINGTON	Washington State University, Pullman 99163
WEST VIRGINIA	West Virginia University, Morgantown 26506
WISCONSIN	College of Agriculture, University of Wisconsin, Madison 53706
WYOMING	College of Agriculture, University of Wyoming, Laramie 82070

INDEX